Desire for Race

D0927286

What do people mean when they talk about race? Are they acknowledging a biological fact, a social reality, or a cultural identity? Is race real, or is it merely an illusion? This book brings analytical clarity to one of the most vexed topics in the social sciences today, arguing that race is no more than a social construction, unsupported in biological terms and upheld for the simple reason that we continue to believe in its reality. Deploying concepts from the sociology of knowledge, religion, social memory, and psychoanalysis, the authors consider the conditions that contribute to this persistence of belief and suggest ways in which the idea of race can free itself from outdated nineteenth-century notions of biological essentialism. By conceiving of race as something that is simultaneously real and unreal, this study generates a new conceptualization that will be required reading for scholars in this field.

SARAH DAYNES is an Assistant Professor of Sociology at the New School for Social Research in New York.

ORVILLE LEE is an Assistant Professor of Sociology at the New School for Social Research in New York.

Desire for Race

Sarah Daynes and Orville Lee

CAMBRIDGE
UNIVERSITY PRESS

CAMBRIDGE UNIVERSITY PRESS
Cambridge, New York, Melbourne, Madrid, Cape Town, Singapore,
São Paulo, Delhi

Cambridge University Press
The Edinburgh Building, Cambridge CB2 8RU, UK

Published in the United States of America by Cambridge University Press,
New York

www.cambridge.org
Information on this title: www.cambridge.org/9780521680479

First published 2008

Printed in the United Kingdom at the University Press, Cambridge

A catalogue record for this publication is available from the British Library

Library of Congress Cataloguing in Publication data
Daynes, Sarah.
    Desire for race / Sarah Daynes, Orville Lee.
        p. cm.
    Includes bibliographical references and index.
    ISBN 978-0-521-86210-3 (hardback) – ISBN 978-0-521-68047-9 (pbk.)
    1. Race–Philosophy.   2. Race relations–Philosophy.   3. Racism.
    I. Lee, Orville.   II. Title.
    HT1523.D39 2008
    305.8001–dc22
    2008025500

ISBN 978-0-521-86210-3 hardback
ISBN 978-0-521-68047-9 paperback

For, dear Crito, you may be sure that such wrong words are not only undesirable in themselves, but they infect the soul with evil.

(Plato, *Phaedo*, 115e)

Contents

Acknowledgements

We want to thank our colleagues and friends Alexander Riley and Terry Williams for reading and discussing early drafts of the manuscript. We are grateful to Marisol López-Menéndez and Catherine Bliss for their work on the index. At Cambridge University Press, we had the pleasure to work with John Haslam, Carrie Cheek, Rosina Di Marzo, and Caroline Howlett; we warmly thank them, as well as the anonymous reviewers, whose comments were most helpful. Finally, we also thank our students at the New School for Social Research, whose support sustained our faith in intellectual life during difficult times.

Introduction

Situating race and the question of reality

> ... and was it not truly interesting the way man uses words and how he
> makes thoughts of them!   (Thomas Mann, *Doctor Faustus*, 1999: 112)

This book is not about race; it is about the belief in the existence of
something called race. This distinction – between "race" and "belief in
race" – forms the cornerstone of this book, and from it spring both our
questions and our analyses. As a point of departure and basic hypothesis
of our work, we argue that race exists only because people believe it exists.
And while this distinction might seem pointless, we will show that, on the
contrary, the confusion between the object and the belief in the object lies
at the very heart of the difficulties encountered in the scholarly attempts
to conceptualize race in the past century, and consequently in their failure
to account for its persistence. The modalities of this double failure vary;
however, we will try to read its deep consequences as one and the same: a
resurgence, often hidden and sometimes unconscious, of the very racial
essentialism that social science has sought to overcome. By keeping this
distinction between race and the belief in race as the guiding line of our
work, we will conduct a double project: a sociology of knowledge and a
sociology of meaning. These projects lead us to pose two critical questions
that we use to guide our own thinking about race: what are the conditions
of possibility for our knowledge of the social world? And what are the
conditions of possibility for social meaning? The former question pertains
to the scholarly apprehension of race, while the second articulates the
ways in which race becomes meaningful in society.

But before we further elaborate on this double project, we have to
inquire more deeply into the modalities and consequences of the
distinction that grounds our work. In a small book devoted to one of the
most studied phenomena in social anthropology, totemism, Lévi-Strauss
raised a problem that could also be applied to another well-studied
phenomenon, race. He asserts,

To accept as a theme for discussion a category that one believes to be false always entails the risk, simply by the attention that is paid to it, of entertaining some illusions about its reality ... The phantom which is imprudently summoned up, in the hope of exorcising it for good, vanishes only to reappear, and closer than one imagines to the place where it was at first. (Lévi-Strauss 1963 [1962]: 15)

Since the beginning of the twentieth century, indeed, one of the major projects in the social sciences has been to refute the racial science of the nineteenth century. Quite paradoxically, this project has led, in particular since the 1960s, to a proliferation of scholarly discourses on race, whether in the form of books, articles, conferences, or courses. The paradox lies in the fact that this proliferation of discourses on race accompanies the general scholarly consensus that race is a fundamentally false category; and it raises the question, already posed by Lévi-Strauss, of the role such a proliferation might play in maintaining, or even creating, the illusion of the reality of race.[1]

That is not all. In their effort to both free themselves from racial science and show its negative consequences, scholars have unwittingly let the phantom of essentialism reappear. Despite the genuine intention of these scholars to either de-essentialize the concept of race or get rid of it altogether, we pose the hypothesis that essentialism has persisted, if only by taking a different form. In fact, this displacement has been made on the level of *reality*. No longer conceived as an innate reality or natural essence, race has become understood as a social construction. In other words, against the nineteenth-century belief that race was a *natural reality* was opposed the assertion that race is a *social reality*. This distinction is not problematic per se; but, in the form it has taken and in the way it has been conducted, it raises heavily consequential difficulties, which range from conceptual problems to the inability to renounce the category in the social world. We will argue that the two pivotal reasons for the scholarly failure to de-essentialize race are the confusion made between race and the belief in race on the one hand, and an almost pathological relationship between thought about race and the natural world on the other hand. The persistence, and even exponential increase, of academic discourses on race – although they disqualify it as a natural reality in their content – constitute race as an essential and incontestable social reality, by their simple overwhelming presence. In other words, if so many scholars study and write about race, and if so

---

[1] A question that, for instance, has been raised concerning the 2000 US census as well: how much does the use of racial categories in the census actually perpetuate these same racial categories? See, for example, Nobles (2000).

many university courses take it as their main focus, then how would it not exist? As Lévi-Strauss suggests, the simple fact that scholars continue to use the category, even while believing it to be false, might actually act to legitimate it as an empirical phenomenon in the social world – a strong paradox, since their goal is to bring about the demise of racial essentialism.

We believe that the issue of reality is crucial. Without confronting the paradoxical relationship of the simultaneous reality and unreality of race, contemporary discourses on race risk producing a new essentialism, which we will argue is a 'displaced phantom' that reappears at a different level: once living on the ground of nature, essentialism now haunts the realm of the social. In other words, discourses *on* race have unwittingly become discourses *of* race.

So far, we have ascribed race to a spatial binary of nature or society; and we have implied that race was situated either on the side of nature – as in nineteenth-century racial science, which took race as an innate quality of human beings – or on the side of the social – as in, for instance, social constructionism, which holds that race has no existence per se, and is an ideational construct. Both nature and society can be considered a reality. The proponents of a social conception of race do not claim that race is unreal, but rather that race is not natural. In other words, the social world is taken as a reality, different than the reality of the natural world but, nonetheless, real.

Racial science treats the social world as a reflection of the natural world. While there are consequences of race in society – such as natural hierarchies existing between different "races" – racial science understands them as the product of biology. This view clearly denies the *sui generis* quality of society; it also emphasizes a strictly biological quality of race. On the other hand, in the second half of the twentieth century, most of the social science research on race has situated race exclusively within the social world, and erected a clear distinction between nature and society (see Wade 2002: 112). Therefore, while in the case of racial science race was unproblematically real (it is a natural fact, with possible social consequences), in the case of social science a problematic paradox arose: on one hand, it denies the natural reality of race and, on the other, it has to assert the social reality of race. As long as this paradox is held in place, racial essentialism is unavoidable: race is fixed on the social body and on the bodies of individuals who comprise racial groups.

The sociological object of this book is precisely this paradoxical insistence that race is not real and that race *is* real in the social sense. We approach this paradox from a sociological point of view that recognizes that race is neither real in nature nor in society, but that it does exist as the (fantasized) object of a belief. However, the social sciences have made race real through the binary opposition of nature and society that is employed to analyze the reality of race. This view, which invokes the paradox with greater insistency, makes race real only in the form of this paradox. Our goal is to make sense of this paradox in the social scientific study of race and to break with the structure of such paradoxical thinking about race.

It would be too simple to stop here. While social scientists have come to focus on the social reality of race and to simultaneously deny its natural or biological reality, they also seem unable to formulate a definition of race, even when it is construed as a discourse, which would not imply phenotypical diversity. Peter Wade is right to point out this constant reference to phenotype (2002: 4–6). So we have here a second paradox: race becomes an exclusively social fact that nonetheless remains linked to nature. It is at this very level that Wade's agenda is situated: his criticism of most social theories of race concerns this vague but continuous presence of the reference to phenotype in the very midst of the denial of any biological reality of race. We agree with Wade: not only are racial classifications, often made on the basis of phenotype, a social construction, but our very perception of the phenotype is a social construction as well. In other words, the existence of a racial system of representation, through which meaning is assigned to physical differences, has an influence not only on how we classify and interpret, but also on the very way we perceive others.[2]

However, we believe that Wade does not go far enough. There is something more to say, which pertains to the way in which the scholars he criticizes – and maybe Wade himself – are confounding the perception of the object and the object itself. We assert that race is not, *in the first instance*, based on phenotype, but rather it is based on social representations that are attached to physical differences. Our position is that phenotype is not the primary characteristic of social constructions of race. Distinctions in phenotype and the recognition of phenotype itself form a second-order mental/discursive operation that occurs on the side of the social, but it is an operation that takes place *on something*, on physical bodies whose diversity is not predicated on the perception of phenotype. The first-order mental/discursive operation, therefore, entails the recognition of physical diversity, while the

---

[2] In contrast to Wade, Lawrence Hirschfeld (1986: xii) argues that human beings are "susceptible" to race because it is rooted in human cognitive endowment: "arguing that we have an inborn susceptibility to race does not mean that race (or racism) is innate. Rather, like smallpox or tuberculosis, race emerges out of the interaction of prepared inborn potentialities and a particular environment."

second-order operation entails a recognition of phenotypical differences as essential characteristics of this underlying physical diversity. This is an absolutely crucial point, because only the distinction between the object and the perception of the object, that is to say between physical differences and the perception of these differences, can allow for a non-paradoxical conceptualization of race. We need to acknowledge the existence of physical differences that are independent of the collective representation of race. Race is a social reality that *coincides* with a natural reality – physical difference. In other words, race is not produced by nature. However, there cannot be an efficient system of representation without a referent. What is repressed by the insistent social constructionist vision of race, the reality of physical differences among human beings, returns in the form of the paradox that perceptions of phenotype and the system(s) of collective representation of race seem to refer only to themselves and not to any reality that stands apart from them. In our view, the acknowledgement of the independent reality of physical difference does not lead back to scientific racism but, on the contrary, liberates social construction from this fatal paradox; however, it does indicate the limits of social construction: ideas are limited by bodies. In other words, there is a reality of physical difference, but this reality is not equivalent to race in either the biological or social sense. Social and biological constructions of race coincide with, but are not causally dependent upon, these physical differences.[3] Once liberated from the obsessive need to repress "nature," the study of race can focus on a fundamental question: why do people remain ascribed in a system of racial representations that have no reality apart from the social constructions? To foreshadow the second part of the book, we will show that race is pure meaning, that physical differences become racially meaningful through processes of belief, memory, and desire.

Our discussion of reality, illusion, and belief might leave the impression that we are writing in the spirit of Freud's classic critique of religion (1927). While Freud hoped that religious illusions might give way to scientific reason just as each individual is compelled to give up infantile wishes in the course of acquiring psychological maturity, he recognized the practical difficulties involved for the believer and for the mature individual. We proceed from a slightly different premise. Unlike

---

[3] The absence of a causal link but presence of a coincidental tie will prove to be absolutely crucial in order to explain the persistence of race in the social world; we will return to this point later. Our conceptual frame is constituted by the hypotheses developed by Marcel Mauss in his essay *Seasonal Variations of the Eskimo* (1979 [1906]).

Freud, we find it unnecessary to take a clinical or prescriptive position on the fact that people believe in things that are not real. This belief itself is the positive fact that orients our inquiry. Moreover, because we hold that the only reality of race is the belief in race, unlike Freud's account of religion, we do not need to define race. "Race" is whatever people take to be race at a given time and in a particular place. Therefore we shall discuss what different fields of inquiry have taken race to be at different points in the twentieth century in order to illustrate the logic of social thought on race and to propose an alternative logic by which to account for the reality of race as the belief in race. However, our initial position requires further justification.

What justifies our assertion that the phenomenon that is called race is nothing else than the belief in race that varies in time and space? If, as we have just argued, collective representations of race have a referent that is not "race" as a sort of primordial essence but rather physical difference, is it not still possible to define race with respect to social experience? Do not instances of racial subjection in the form of slavery, segregation, lynching, and forms of symbolic violence constitute the reality of race? Are these instances not a matter of belief but rather a matter of experience? Again, Lévi-Strauss's small book on totemism is good to think with; he begins with the following observation:

Totemism is like hysteria, in that once we are persuaded to doubt that it is possible arbitrarily to isolate certain phenomena and to group them together as diagnostic signs of an illness, or of an objective institution, the symptoms themselves vanish or appear refractory to any unifying interpretation. (Lévi-Strauss 1963: 1)[4]

The point of departure of Lévi-Strauss, indeed, is the conceptual fragmentation, multiplication, and atomization found in the definitional attempts of both hysteria by psychoanalysts and totemism by anthropologists. This fragmentation, which he demonstrates throughout the book, is linked to epistemological errors, in particular the bending of empirical reality for the sake of theory (Lévi-Strauss 1963: 77).[5] This level of criticism leads Lévi-Strauss, at the very beginning of his text, to

---

[4] "Il en est du totémisme comme de l'hystérie. Quand on s'est avisé de douter qu'on pût arbitrairement isoler certains phénomènes et les grouper entre eux, pour en faire les signes diagnostiques d'une maladie ou d'une institution objective, les symptômes même ont disparu, ou se sont montrés rebelles aux interprétations unifiantes" (Lévi-Strauss 1962: 5).

[5] "We shall never get to the bottom of the alleged problem of totemism by thinking up a solution having only a limited field of application and then manipulating recalcitrant cases until the facts give way, but by reaching directly a level so general that all observed cases may figure in it as particular modes." Lévi-Strauss speaks here mainly in reference to Firth and Fortes.

question the reality of totemism; he quotes Robert Lowie's general analytical premise: "We must first inquire whether ... we are comparing cultural realities, or merely figments of our logical modes of classification" (Lévi-Strauss 1963: 10).[6] The language used in the original version of Lévi-Strauss's text, in which Lowie is quoted in French, is significant, in that it refers explicitly to psychoanalysis: instead of "figments," Lévi-Strauss uses "fantasies" (*fantasmes*), a term that has, in French, an explicit psychoanalytic nuance. He then boldly asserts that "totemism is an artificial unity, existing solely in the mind of the anthropologist, to which nothing specifically corresponds in reality" (Lévi-Strauss 1963: 10).[7] The foundation of his book is therefore a double pillar: first, he parallels the conceptualization and definition of totemism in the field of anthropology with that of hysteria in psychoanalysis; second, "so-called totemism" (1962: 26) is viewed as, or at least suspected to be, the product of the ethnologist's thought and nothing else.

Can an analogy be drawn from this characterization of totemism studies to the field of race studies? We will do so not in the form of analogy but as a schematic frame, using Lévi-Strauss as a point of departure to question the reality of race, and its articulation with both practice and the ideal. Could it be that race is in fact a concrete experience simply represented in diverse ways in popular and scholarly thought? Or could the social knowledge of race be the product of fantasy, of ideational processes – in a manner similar to totemism? Or finally, could we go as far as to ask whether it could be that ideational processes create the feeling of concrete experience?

These three questions form the backbone of our inquiry into race, in particular the third one, which bears witness to the unavoidable answer made to ideal or discursive theories of race: the reality of race has to do with the reality of its consequences *in practice*. One goal of this book is to address the relentless use of experience to prove the reality of race; scholars as different as Eduardo Bonilla-Silva and Howard Winant assume that the very existence of *racial experiences* implies a correspondent *racial object* that can be treated as a theoretical concept.

And hence, the concreteness of experience overshadows the ideal or ideational character of race, which becomes insignificant in the sense that it is not considered modifiable. We shall address the internal

---

[6] "Il faut savoir si nous comparons des réalités culturelles, ou seulement des fantasmes, issus de nos modes logiques de classification" (Lowie in Lévi-Strauss 1962: 18).

[7] "De même, le totémisme est une unité artificielle, qui existe seulement dans la pensée de l'ethnologue, et à quoi rien de spécifique ne correspond au dehors" (Lévi-Strauss 1962: 18).

contradictions found in theories of race in Chapter 5. It suffices for now to address the broader problem of articulation between the concrete and the ideal, the tangible and the intangible, which forms a very complex theoretical problem in the case of race.

It might indeed be suspected that beneath the level of fantasy lies the tissue of reality. After all, if one could trace the emergence of race back to an epoch, to an event of culture contact, the subsequent profusion of racial discourses and imagery would indeed be shown to have a basis in concrete experience. Although race might not have a biological reality, it surely has a historical reality that runs from the discovery of the New World for Europe, the conquest of African lands, the importation and incorporation of indigenous peoples within the modern world system. This reality led to the generation of different forms of knowledge of the Other (from the European perspective), some classificatory of observed differences, others justificatory of domination. However, did the diverse versions of this event of culture contact bring about a social experience that can be called race? Does the experience of culture contact directly call into being a racial experience? The claims for experience become questionable when one considers that everyday sociability bears the mark of culture contact; every encounter with an Other brings with it multiple forms of difference. Ordinarily, these conditions of sociability do not generate racial experiences. If this is the case, then an explanatory conundrum arises: how are representations of race related to experience if a direct causal link between culture contact, experience, and representations of experience does not exist?

Again, the question calls for an account of processes that generate the *fantasy* of race, *apparently* in connection to experience. Freud's study of hysteria provides the schematic frame that shows the links between fantasy and experience. In the first report on hysteria of Freud and Breuer (1895), the onset of hysterical symptoms was bound up with seduction theory: a real experienced sexual event in childhood was held to produce symptoms of hysteria in adults which were viewed, originally, as "direct derivations of repressed memories of sexual experiences in childhood" (Freud 1905b: 5); in other words, when confronted by the reality of the historical experience (i.e., the hysterical symptom), Freud assumed that there must be a necessary correspondence between this symptomatic experience and some real event in the past. A few years later, Freud not only revised his theory, he completely reversed it; the implications of this reversal are of tremendous importance for the study of race. Freud ceased to assume that a real experience (i.e., the hysterical symptom) must be produced by a real event. It is not a seduction event that produces, almost mechanically, the real experience of the symptom; it is the ideation of that seduction event – whether the latter actually existed or not. Hence, Freud is arguing that one concrete experience does not have to be produced by another concrete experience; it can also be the product of ideational processes. As a result, the structural relationship of symptoms and reality is other than what it appears in the self-report of patients: "Hysterical symptoms are not attached to actual memories" of events, but rather "to phantasies erected on the basis of memories" (Freud 1900: 529–530). It is the form taken by the relationship between symptoms, fantasies, and "screen memories" (Freud 1899: 4) that is of interest with respect to understanding the relationship between representations of race and experience. In the case of hysteria, traumatic events of seduction in childhood are not held to be the necessary causal factor that generates symptoms of hysteria in adolescents and adults. In fact, these events might not have existed at all. In a similar way, we would argue that the existence of racial experiences does not presuppose that a racial reality exists. Consequently, the process by which historical and contemporary social interactions are perceived as racial experiences is what matters and what needs to be explained. To reformulate the psychoanalytic frame in terms of the race problematic: fantasies (i.e., social beliefs) about race, which coincide (and *only* coincide) with physical differences between individuals, are attached to experiences that are perceived as racial.[8] A concrete, lived experience that one feels as a racial experience can actually be produced by ideational processes and not only by concrete reality. In other words, it is not because we experience race that race is real; it is because we hold beliefs about race, and because these beliefs coincide with real physical differences, that we perceive racial experiences as being caused by race – and therefore as proving the existence of race as an object.

Our purpose here is not to provide a psychoanalytical account of race. However, there lies in Freud's account of the work of the unconscious the discovery of a mechanism that will prove very precious to us, and to the conceptualization of race: if there is an ideational process that links

[8] We are not positing an exact analogy between race as a system of collective representations and hysteria for the following reason: while it is tempting to describe systems of racial representation as symptoms of collective hysteria, it would appear risky to attribute to societies a form of psychic abnormality (related to the repression of libidinal energies) solely on the level of the psychical. On the other hand, the obverse course of explanation that seeks a causal relationship between social structures and social-psychological phenomena as the source of racial representations again places undue emphasis on actual experience. Here, we maintain that there is no direct experience of race. Rather, representations of racial experiences arise from fantasies (or beliefs) about social experiences that are made available to individuals and groups.

the symptom – the epitome of reality, felt not only in daily life but also in the very flesh of the individual – with an event that might not have existed in reality, then it means that *there can be no assumption that a concrete experience necessarily implies the existence of a foundation in reality.* We can locate this mechanism at the level of the social through a consideration of the sociology of Émile Durkheim and Marcel Mauss. We want to repeat here that we do not make a correspondence between the individual and the social, which operate in different, although related, spheres. But the structural process that links representations and reality at the social level is enlightened by the structural process that links the symptom and the event in hysteria. For example, building on Hubert's work on calendars (1905), Mauss asserts that while representations of time and calendars may *seem* to originate in climatic, seasonal changes, there is in fact no direct causal relationship between the latter and the former:

Instead of being the necessary and determining cause of an entire system, true seasonal factors may merely mark the most opportune occasions in the year for these two phases to occur. (Mauss 1979: 79)

Mauss's hypothesis, hence, is of a *coincidence* found between seasonal change and the year calendar in the Eskimo society, that is, a coincidence between the physical world and a system of representation, as opposed to a causal relationship that would consider the calendar as being *produced* by seasonal change. The coincidence amounts to a sort of fortuitous convenience that legitimizes a system of representation that, nonetheless, would still be able to survive without it. While systems of representation are not produced by the natural world, they remain linked to it, and one could argue that they cannot last (and be efficient) without some sort of adequation with the natural world.

This hypothesis has several fundamental ramifications for the conceptualization of collective representations, to which we shall return in due time; but at this stage the most interesting of these ramifications concerns the reversal, similar to Freud's, that Mauss operates in his understanding of the relationship between "material reality" and "ideal representation." If we formalize the elements of this reversal, we find a highly complex system of understanding the natural and social spheres, and the relationship between them; and we also find a system that provides a new way to look at representations and thought that is useful for the study of race.

First, *the representation is independent from the natural object, and belongs to a sphere that lies outside of, and distinct from, the sphere of the natural world.* The representation of time, and the modalities of the time calendar therewith, are fundamentally social, and are distinct from the constraints posed by the climate or environment of a given society. Second, *there is no relationship of causality between natural reality and the social representation*. Climatic conditions and seasonal changes do not *produce* the representation of time, nor do they produce the rhythm found in the calendar. Third, *causality is found in the social sphere, not in the relationship between natural reality and the social representation*. Following Durkheim, the rhythm found in the representation of time and calendars is a structural element of the social: there needs to be rhythm not because man is confronted with a rhythmic succession of seasonal changes, but because it is the way in which any society is structurally organized. This rhythm (which we shall come back to later in this book) is caused by the necessary cycle between high peaks and low peaks in social life, between the sacred and the profane, between excitement and exhaustion. Fourth, *the relationship between natural reality and the social representation is one of convenience, coincidence, and efficiency, not one of causality*; this implies that the natural world plays a role in the construction of representations, albeit not a causal role. Again this has to be situated within Durkheim's general sociology, which takes the natural world into account and does not conceive of representations as being free-standing in the ideal; in the case of time, the closer the adequation between seasonal changes and the calendar, the more efficient and long-lasting the representation will be.

Therefore, the reversal operated by Mauss concerns the fact that instead of considering representation as being mechanically and causally linked to a necessary fact or event in the natural world, that is, to some reality, he argues that representation – which is a concrete experience for the individuals who compose society and which, above all, *feels natural* to them – is in fact only *related to reality* but not *caused by it*. As a matter of fact, similar to Freud's revised account of hysteria, Mauss asserts that the calendar could very well exist even if seasonal changes did not. The discovery of both Freud and Mauss, in very different cases and fields, is that there should be no assumption of *causality* in reality, even when there happens to be a *correspondence* with reality.

This structural process, we argue, provides an extremely helpful theoretical frame for thinking about race. Race, indeed, is a representation; just like time, it definitely has to be placed on the side of what *men think*. In a Durkheimian vein – and in a Mannheimian vein as well – we argue for the fundamentally social character of thought, of representations. Representations are situated within the sphere of the social; they belong to what not only men, but also society, elaborate in relationship with the natural world. Can we solve the puzzle, then, by using Mauss

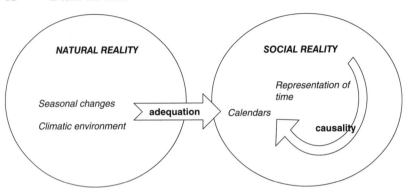

Figure 1 Time, calendars, and the natural world

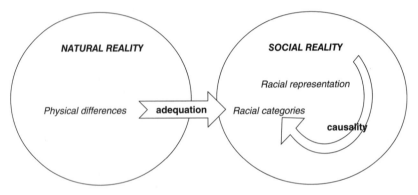

Figure 2 Race, racial categories, and the natural world

and Durkheim alongside Freud? At the least, the former helps to situate race in a clear way, to position the different elements of a complex representation. Figures 1 and 2 facilitate the visualization of the different pieces of the "representation puzzle."

Natural reality and social reality are two distinct, independent spheres; and yet they are related. Following Mauss and Durkheim, we must recognize this relationship – if only at the level of the efficiency of social representations. Just as representations of time and the elaboration of a calendar have to coincide to a certain degree with seasonal changes and climatic characteristics in order to be efficient in society, we argue that representations of race and racial classifications have to use existing physical differences in order to be socially efficient and lasting. This, we argue, might be one way to explain the success of an entirely arbitrary focus on the distinction between "blacks" and "whites" in American history, for instance: there is no biological foundation to this specific classification, and yet it works in society. The obviousness and, we could almost say, the ease in perceiving the physical difference between "blacks" and "whites," generally and in most cases, helps racial categories to become felt as "natural", as objectively grounded, by individuals. Marginal cases – at the margins of the two categories – can hence be felt as unproblematic, and do not endanger the general (and overwhelming) distinction between two groups: black and white. Let us imagine that the racial categorization would have focused on aquiline noses versus flat noses instead; it could perfectly work. But would it be as efficient as the black versus white classification? Probably not; and not because of the lack of differentiation in the natural world – there *are* people with flat noses and others with aquiline noses – but because the physical difference is less marked, less easy to spot immediately, and hence less efficient *socially*.

As Figure 2 indicates, we make a distinction between racial classifications and the representation of race, which correspond in Figure 1 with calendars and the representation of time. This distinction indicates that there is a superseding category of thought, broad and generally detached from experience, which frames individual experiences and collective representations. This category of thought is "time" or "race." Distinct from it exist social constructions that have a material, practical side to them: a calendar or a way to distinguish different racial groups. Society elaborates these systems in a very practical way. Moreover, these practical systems both shape and are shaped by experience: that is, they are concrete, although they are also ideational. Here, we are still in the domain of the ideal, of the mind; but classifications are also experienced by individuals in their daily life, whether it is through identification or through discrimination, or through the concrete consequences of these classifications (what is more concrete, indeed, than lynching, slavery, or genocide?). Hence, a very concrete experience of race still is grounded neither in nature nor in reality, but rather in ideation. A thing (e.g., a social fact) that does not exist other than in its social significance can still be felt as natural, as real.

Hence, we argue that there are two distinct spheres of reality – natural reality and social reality. But these two spheres interact in such a way as to pose limits to a post-modern view of the social: while the social, society, can *invent* anything, it has to *deal with* the natural world if these inventions are to operate with efficiency. With Mauss and Durkheim, we therefore propose to theorize representations within a complex web of interactions not only within the social sphere (where causality is located)

Table 1 *Representations*

Representation of the normal	Representation of time	Representation of race
Hysterical symptomatology	Calendar	Racial classifications
Experience of the symptoms ("being an hysteric")	Experience of time ("being in time")	Racial experience ("being black" or "being white")

but also between the natural and social spheres (where efficiency, and limits to the symbolic construction, are to be found).

However, there still remains the complexity found in the multidirectional making of representations (Table 1). Indeed, we are still left with a system of thought (the representation of race) and a system of practice (racial classifications), but also with a set of consequences at both levels, which may be political, economic, cultural, psychological, legal, or crudely practical, for instance lynching.

It appears obvious that the system of thought does not simply shape or "produce" a system of practice; indeed, there is a bi-directional relationship between these two systems, wherein practice also exists as a producer of thought, or at least as a reinforcement of it. When a calendar is in place for a long period of time, it not only accompanies the wider representation of time, it also makes it impossible for any other representation of time to arise. And the same condition arises with race: racial practice indubitably reinforces racial thought, in a crucial way since it solidifies it as something that feels natural; in other words, *it is with practice that thought becomes naturalized*, and hence successful socially.

But that is not all. The consequences that derive from the conjunction between a system of thought and a system of practice also play a role in shaping them; and again we are not facing a simple situation here. It could be said that these consequences, nonetheless produced by representations, also shape them in return.

Let's take the example of racial lynching in the United States. Lynching is a "hyper practice" in the sense that it is both highly physical (such as beating, whipping, killing) and highly emotional (some might argue that much of what happens in lynching is related to the emotions of individuals and of the crowd, for instance). This hyper practice could therefore be considered, to some extent, as contingent to "emotional eruptions" and hence dependent on circumstances, on a crowd "gone crazy," on uncontrolled feelings and impulses. And yet it is also a "hyper idea," which does not leave much to emotions and impulses: it is ascribed within a system of thought that views the "black group" in a specific way and provides a justification for lynching its members, within a system of racial classifications that designates who is "lynchable." It is also ascribed within a tradition (or habit) that makes it imaginable, possible, and practicable. The phenomenon of lynching did not happen in an isolated manner; it is surrounded first by a tradition of lynching individuals for legal reasons, and second by a tradition of lynching individuals who belong to one specific group. Racial lynching, hence, is both produced by, and situated within, a system of racial representation specific to the United States. In other words, the practice is produced, made possible, and allowed by a system of representations. It becomes a ritual, practiced by individuals who share the same language and representations – the same beliefs. One need only look at the faces in the crowd to realize that lynching, far from being a mere act of savagery, of uncontrolled impulse on the spur of the moment, is also an act of cohesion, a ritualized practice that reinforces the bonds between the individuals of the crowd in the lynching of another individual.[9] The binding character of the practice – through the participation in and/or witnessing of the act – is also binding on the level of thought: racial lynching also implies that the individuals in the crowd share the same belief in race and the same adherence to a specific racial classification.[10] However, racial lynching as a located act, as a concrete event occurring in a specific place and at a specific time, can also be seen as legitimating not only individual experiences of race, but also the larger representa-tions of race: the act itself functions as a concrete justification of the thought; the repetition of the act banalizes the practice, and reinforces its normality – and the system of representation behind it. In other words, practice validates and reinforces the system of representation; because we are acting, the representations behind the act become real – if they were not real, we would not act upon them. And through repetition a point is reached where both the ritual (lynching) and the belief (race) become natural. One could wonder if this is not the specific reason why lynchings were photographed and then distributed as postcards, which people would actually buy, stamp, and mail. Through postcards, the heavily localized act – which happened between human beings, in one specific place on one specific day – becomes *dis*located or translocal: it becomes part of one body of multiple acts, all related, and ultimately all interchangeable. "Lynching" becomes a collective practice, instead of an

[9] See for instance the photographic documentation of lynching in James Allen *et al.*, *Without Sanctuary* (2000).
[10] An emphasis on the ritual – and religious – aspect of lynching can be found in Patterson (1998).

aggregate of isolated acts: it becomes familiar, normal, and accepted on the part of those who participate in lynching.

Hence practical experience, while produced in the first place by an ideational system of representation, in turn makes the system of representation real. *Thought justifies the act, but then in turn the act justifies the thought.* It is no wonder that the idea of race has become so pervasive. In studying race we are confronted by an idea that produced a practice and thereby reinforced itself. The efficiency of the contemporary representation of race – through the use of a hardly contestable and highly visible physical difference – also means that it has had time to reinforce itself in a circular process of legitimacy. How could anyone oppose an idea that has become so well entrenched in virtually all the social mechanisms of American society – which thereby function as some sort of permanent reinforcement of the idea?

Durkheim and Mauss, therefore, provide one helpful manner to think clearly about race without confusing different objects, elements, and spheres that all come into play in the construction and conceptualization of race. First, we can avoid the confusion between "physical differences" and "racial categories"; they are different objects, which belong to different spheres. Second, we avoid the confusion between "racial categories" and "race"; both are representations, but as in the case of time, they are distinct although closely related. Third, we can avoid the eviction of natural reality, accompanied by the overwhelming focus on social reality, which is characteristic of post-modern theories of race as well as the conception of race that is prevalent in the political sphere. With Mauss, we can acknowledge the importance of the natural world – here translated mostly in terms of physical differences among human beings – while keeping it outside of any causality. Finally, we can also avoid the eviction of social reality, accompanied by the overwhelming focus on natural reality, which is characteristic of racial science.[11] Representations are distinct from and not subjected to the natural world; and yet they are still related to it.

Our detour through Lévi-Strauss, Freud, Durkheim, and Mauss, each of whom posed the question of the relationship between reality, representations, and knowledge in fruitful ways, demonstrates a way out of the confusion in the study of race we introduced earlier, and which is the launching point of this book: the confusion between the

---

[11] Here of course we could also argue for an analysis of science as a discourse. "Science" is a representation as well; hence, when we speak of "natural reality," we refer not to "science" but to the object of science. In other words: "racial science" is a discourse that evicts the social sphere from the conceptualization of race, and yet its very discursive nature places it on the side of the social.

object "race" and the belief in the object.[12] Consequently, we shall address both the "object" as it has been understood and the conditions of the belief in race in the chapters that follow. We have divided the book into two movements. The first addresses the paradox in which the social scientific study of race maintains the illusion of the reality of race in spite of the insistence that race is a category of knowledge. Specifically, we reconstruct the development of knowledge of race in the twentieth century as different "styles of thought."[13] The reconstruction of several main currents of racial thought, American sociology (Chapter 1), Marxism (Chapter 2), British social anthropology (Chapter 3), and British cultural studies (Chapter 4), will show that different styles of racial thought developed in reaction to nineteenth-century scientific racism. However, while each of these styles of thought makes a claim to depart from scientific racism and to de-essentialize "race," they can be in fact seen as different, largely unconscious modulations of the same essentialist (i.e., biological) view of race.

American sociology has given a central importance to the social reality of race, which is conceptualized in opposition to biological accounts. Two main, distinct positions have developed over time: the cultural and structural accounts of race's social reality. We will show that because proponents of both these accounts substitute the social reality for the biological reality of race advanced by nineteenth-century racial science, American sociology of race, as a style of thought, puts forward an unrecognized, essentialist view of race, while believing this view has been surmounted.

The tradition of Marxist thought mostly argues for the primacy of class over race. In other words, race is seen as an ideology that is used in capitalist societies as a screen for class; racial situations are viewed as a concealed class situation, and race is discovered to be a tool for diverting the dominated class from class struggle. This view accounts for the unreality of race by treating it as ideology; however, it is unable to explain the efficacy and reproduction of race outside of class relations.

[12] The use of Lévi-Strauss, Freud, Durkheim, and Mauss to frame the question of the relationship of race to reality is necessitated by the inadequacy of existing theories of race that specifically address this question. Circumstances have led us to draw upon a range of heterogeneous theories in order to locate the tools with which we can reconceptualize race as an object of analysis that, from the very start, acknowledges its paradoxical constitution.

[13] We appropriate the concept of styles of thought from Karl Mannheim (1985: 3): "Thus, it is not men in general who think, or even isolated individuals who do the thinking, but men in certain groups who have developed a particular style of thought in an endless series of responses to certain typical situations characterizing their common position."

In the 1960s, British social anthropology, from the impulse of Edmund Leach and then Fredrik Barth, reintroduced the long-forgotten Weberian conceptualization of ethnicity. The result of this important turn was a very pertinent apprehension of ethnicity as being a dynamic social process situated in interaction. However, the problem raised by this style of thought has been durable and serious: it is mostly expressed by a substitution of ethnicity for race, as well as by the boundless extension of "ethnicity" to "social identity." Race becomes one of the modalities taken by social identity, along with religion, class, or nation.

Another attempt at "de-essentializing" race is found in British cultural studies. In Chapter 4, we focus on the work of Stuart Hall and Paul Gilroy, who articulate concepts of culture and diaspora in order to account for the fluid character of race, and to actually bypass the conceptualization of race altogether. While cultural studies stand as one of the most successful attempts at "de-essentialization," they nevertheless face a major problem: culture and diaspora prove not to be a fully adequate means to achieve a post-biological understanding of race. British cultural studies will be presented as a case that illuminates the real difficulty of apprehending race in non-racialist terms.

At the end of this first movement, we will pause and use the material found for each of these currents to build an ideal-typology of the conceptualization of race in the twentieth century. In the comparison of the four cases, American sociology is a paradigmatic case for the paradox of racial thought discussed above, since it has been most insistent about the social reality of race. Yet, the *reality* of race, the empirical basis of the social concept, has been displaced by culture and racism, which stand in as proxies for race itself. The other cases also present a typology of displacement: in Marxism, race is displaced by the concept of class; in British social anthropology, race is displaced by the concept of ethnicity; and in cultural studies, race is displaced by the concept of diaspora. What the four cases share in common is that essentialism is reproduced, albeit to a varying degree and in different ways and notwithstanding efforts to avoid it; and we shall argue that this is so because of a lingering confusion between race (conceived as an object) and the belief in race. Although there is a change in terms, there is no decisive departure from the discursive ensemble and epistemological paradox instituted by nineteenth-century racial science.

The first movement in our analysis can be seen as a classic sociology of knowledge as Mannheim defined it in the 1930s. In a second movement, we address the social processes behind the pursuit of race as a social reality. We argue that grasping race in terms of belief, memory, and desire allows for a sociological understanding of race that explains its social persistence while departing from the illusion of the reality of race. Moreover, these new terms also avoid the tendency in cultural studies towards a post-modern or relativist dilution of knowledge on race.

Chapter 6 ("Belief and social action") initiates this second movement in the book. Whereas the first part of the book analyzes the cul-de-sac in which various styles of racialist knowledge are now trapped, this chapter reorients the study of race to two essential questions: first, we pose the question of the *object of inquiry*, e.g. race; second, we pose the question of the *belief* that sustains the existence of race in the social sphere. What exactly is the object we are looking at? What explains the persistence of the social commitment to race, and what are the primary conditions of this commitment? To address these questions, we take up the approach to the study of society developed by Max Weber; our approach focuses on the relationship between belief and social action and, therefore, holds that the persistence of race can be explained by a process of believing. In Chapter 6 we elaborate upon this conceptual framework, from which three questions then arise: (1) How is this belief validated and reproduced? (2) What is the role played by this belief in the actual "reality" of race as a social fact? (3) To what degree is this belief socially pertinent? These questions will be addressed in Chapters 7 ("Theorizing the racial ensemble"), 8 ("The politics of memory and race"), and 9 ("Desire").

If there is a belief in race, then there are conditions of validation and reproduction of this belief. Every religious movement implements some process of validation, without which believing does not last and transmission founders. In Chapter 7, we take a close look at the processes of validation and legitimacy that allow the belief in race to solidify and to last. We analyze in detail the different elements of what we propose to call the *racial ensemble*, a system of thought and practice which contains different elements, in interrelation with each other, which together form the object of inquiry and also allow for an understanding of the persistence of the belief in race in the social sphere.

The reproduction of race and the persistence of a belief in race then lead us to the question of its pertinence. As Durkheim pointed out, no social fact can persist over time if it does not have some sort of social relevance. Notwithstanding Durkheim's trust in the social system and its ability to auto-regulate, it remains that indeed there must be a social interest in the belief in race for it to persist so powerfully over time – especially when the "fact" of the biological unreality of race has come to be taken for granted, and when the history of the twentieth century has shown the dangerous consequences of the racialization of society. Still, the belief in race persists, and racialism resurfaces in different forms, as we have seen in the first part of this book. Therefore, we will look at the conditions of social interest and social pertinence of the belief in race. In Chapter 8, we analyze the reproduction of the belief in race that occurs in various efforts to *remember* race, to place the experience of race within a framework of social memory, and the way in which politics intersects with the work of remembrance.

Finally, we want to look at the deeper aspects of the persistence of race beyond "social pertinence." In Chapter 9, we investigate the modalities of "attachment" to race by inquiring into the neglected question of the unconscious dimension of social life; we use psychoanalysis to move from an analysis of the "belief in race" (based on a rational reconstruction of its conditions of existence) to an analysis of a "desire for race." This affective dimension of identity is not well articulated, especially when affect is tied to collective categories that are unreal. We analyze different ways in which pleasure is related to belief: in the form of thought, fantasy, and the body, as well as the sense of danger that pervades negative feelings toward racial Otherness.

1　American sociology

> We want to look at the thinkers of a given period as representatives of different styles of thought. We want to describe their different ways of looking at things as if they were reflecting the changing outlook of their groups; and by this method we hope to show both the inner unity of a style of thought and the slight variations and modifications which the conceptual apparatus of the whole group must undergo as the group itself shifts its position in society. (Mannheim 1971: 262–263)

The development of the sociology of race in America did not occur in a vacuum. It was shaped from the beginning by the pre-existing racial science of the nineteenth century, which is frequently referred to as "scientific racism." Opposition to scientific racism and its emphasis on biology and nature has set the fundamental terms on which "race" has been queried over the last one hundred years in American sociology. In epistemological terms, this opposition is simple enough: it involves an exchange of objects, biology (or nature) for society. Yet, as an example that confirms the psychoanalytic law of the return of the repressed, biological (i.e., essentialist) notions have invariably found their way back into putatively sociological conceptions of race. This chapter traces both the exchange of objects in the study of race and the return of a repressed racial nature in sociological arguments about race that form a distinctive style of thought. Following Paul Ricœur (1970: 18), our task is not only to illuminate "the relation of meaning to the thing," but also the "architecture of meaning, in a relation of meaning to meaning." In other words, both the epistemological shift from biology to society *and* the structure of thought producing this shift must be analyzed. To do this, a methodological innovation is required that brings the sociology of knowledge into an intimate relationship with the sociology of meaning. In his classical sociology of knowledge, Mannheim (1985: 3, 4) stresses the "inherited situation with patterns of thought" which influences the thinking of individuals and that individuals do not merely contemplate the world but "act with and against one another in diversely organized groups, and while doing so they think with and against each other."

In this regard, sociologists of race thought with and against inherited patterns of racial thought from the nineteenth century. Hence, they will be treated as a *group* with an evolving style of thought on race.[1] However, we add a further element to the classical framework: the structure of discourse that defines a style of thought. In this respect, we extend Mannheim's collective action-centered sociology of knowledge to include the constitutive rules of knowledge itself (what Foucault termed *connaissance*[2]) and the process of making and disclosing meaning that gives rises to a style of thought about race in American sociology.[3] These rules and processes have brought forth a concept of race that, by the late twentieth century, is "plurivocal." The plurivocality and duality of symbols is described by Ricœur (1970: 16) as follows:

In order to give consistency and unity to these scattered manifestations of symbol, I define it by a semantic structure that these manifestations have in common, the structure of multiple meaning. Symbols occur when language produces signs of composite degree in which the meaning, not satisfied with designating some one thing, designates another meaning attainable only in and through the first intentionality.

The analysis undertaken in this chapter will demonstrate that the race concept in American sociology bears a double meaning, one manifest (social), and one latent (biology or phenotype). And it is this characteristic duality that marks a style of thought about race. Over time, two variants of this style of thought have emerged that emphasize culture or social structure respectively. Although these variants have been set in opposition by their proponents, they share a common basis: the double meaning of the race concept. What matters here is that natural and

---

[1] Michael Omi and Howard Winant theorize paradigms of racial theory in their book *Racial Formation in the United States*. Their approach, however, is more materialist than the one we pursue; they relate the different paradigms (ethnicity, class, and nation) directly to "existing race relations." Moreover, they posit that one paradigm is dominant during specific conditions: "Within any given historical period, a particular racial theory is dominant – despite often high levels of contestation … Challenges to the dominant racial theory emerge when it fails adequately to explain the changing nature of race relations, or when the racial policies it prescribes are challenged by political movements seeking a different arrangement" (Omi and Winant 1994: 11). In contrast to this approach, we focus on the internal logic of each style of thought in keeping with our view that race is a matter of knowledge and meaning (belief).

[2] "By *connaissance* I mean the relation of the subject to the object and the formal rules that govern it. *Savoir* refers to the conditions that are necessary in a particular period for this or that type of object to be given to *connaissance* and for this or that enunciation to be formulated" (Foucault 1972: 15 n2). The focus in this book is on *connaissance* rather than *savoir*.

[3] Failure to account for the structure of discourse undermines efforts to destroy the concept of race by putting it to what could be called a "reality test."

social concepts of race continue to hang together: social constructionist knowledge of race reaches back to phenotype because the problem of the reality of race is not adequately confronted. As a consequence, a curious situation has emerged: American sociology, which rejected nineteenth-century racial science, now rejects the contemporary biological sciences' view of race not because it is essentialist or racist but because it undermines the sociological conception of race (which is, paradoxically, more essentialist than contemporary science).[4]

To recapitulate the main thesis: to understand race, a definition and three conditions for analysis are essential; race is a belief that is conditioned by (1) the structure of thought that seeks to know the truth of race, (2) social conditions that reproduce the structure of belief, and (3) the forms of affect and attachment that bring the belief to life. Here, we are concerned primarily with the first condition, which immediately presents a methodological problem. It is difficult to isolate a single description of the study of race in American sociology that fits all scholars and their approaches. Moreover, unlike Marxism or British social anthropology, the sociology of race in America is a diffuse field, lacking a fixed axiomatic basis (Marxism) and a stable set of relatively coherent "schools" (aside from the "Chicago School"). However, it is possible to articulate a series of common structural features that reproduce, and are reproduced in, the sociology of race in the United States. Given the plethora of works dealing with race within the sociological discipline, we shall restrict our analysis to several leading figures and paradigmatic approaches to race that portend a break with nineteenth-century racial science: the nascent race theory of W. E. B. Du Bois, the cycle of racial assimilation of the early Chicago School (represented by Robert Park), the pluralist model of cultural groups (Horace Kallen), and more recent studies that put forward a structural (William J. Wilson, Eduardo Bonilla-Silva) or cultural (Michael Omi and Howard Winant) concept of race. One difficulty in accounting for the concept of race in American sociology in general is the striking imprecision that arises regarding the distinction between *race* and *racism*. This phenomenon will be addressed at the end of the chapter.

Nascent race theory: Du Bois

We are concerned here with the paradigmatic ways in which American sociology has understood and produced knowledge about race, races, and race relations. Unlike Marxism, for example, sociological studies of race have tended not to treat race as an epiphenomenon but rather have

---

[4] See Lewontin (1993, 1995).

sought to understand it as a primary phenomenon. The second half of the nineteenth century created a specific knowledge on the ground about race, both on the social and political levels and in the dominant currents of social thought. Jim Crow, "lynch law," and polygenism worked together to re-enforce the idea that biological differences lay at the root of cultural and political differences in the life experience of white and black Americans. The first steps toward a sociological conception of race confronted this knowledge on the ground: the self-evident natural differences between the races. What did not persist from this era, remarkably, is the dispute over the quantity and quality of racial groups, which ceased to exist within the American sociology of race relations. Whereas nineteenth-century natural scientists struggled to name and define races, to fix the point where one race ended and another began, and to articulate the specific experience of racial hybrids (e.g., mulattos, quadroons, octoroons, etc.), American sociology no longer engages the problem of classification itself.

One seminal figure in turn-of-the-century sociology was W. E. B. Du Bois, who took up the question of race and developed a nascent theory of race in a stream of speeches and publications over the course of seven decades. For the purpose of tracing the main paradigms of racial knowledge in sociology, his essay "The conservation of races" stands as an important document of the early period. While the main argument of the essay is directed toward the promotion of a specific orientation of blacks in relation to their social circumstances in *fin de siècle* nineteenth-century America (and is not exclusively intended as an exercise in race theory), it does present an effort to shift the terrain of racial knowledge from biological disposition to social and historical conditions.

Toward the beginning of the essay, Du Bois poses a series of questions: "What is the real meaning of Race; what has, in the past, been the law of race development, and what lessons has the past history of race developments to teach the rising Negro people?" The answer he proposes relates race to the twin poles of early racial theory: physical characteristics and social practices. While refusing to define the "meaning of race" exclusively by physical differences, Du Bois also does not disengage his discussion of race from physical differences, and, in fact, articulates the relation between physicality and the socio-historical manifestation of groups. He argues, on the one hand, that the "grosser physical differences of color, hair and bone" do not explain in themselves the "different roles which groups of men have played in Human Progress"; on the other hand, he holds that there "are differences – subtle, delicate and elusive, though they may be – which have silently but definitely separated men into groups" (Du Bois 1986a: 816). In other words, while the value of differences conceived only on biological lines is not sufficient to distinguish social groups, nonetheless these groups do exhibit differences which can be characterized as racial differences. Historically, a law-like development can be observed in the persistence of distinct – albeit elusive – racial differences: "While these subtle forces have generally followed the natural cleavage of common blood, descent and physical peculiarities, they have at other times swept across and ignored these. At all times, however, they have divided human beings into races, which, while they perhaps transcend scientific definition, nevertheless, are clearly defined to the eye of the Historian and Sociologist" (Du Bois 1986a: 816–817). What is significant in this claim is that races thus conceived, while lacking a strictly scientific – namely, biological – definition, can be defined by sociology and history, and their existence does not depend on whether they can be mapped onto "natural cleavages" without contradiction.

Based on this premise, Du Bois describes human history as the history of groups and races, rather than individuals and nations, and asserts that race is the "central thought of all history." Again, Du Bois elaborates the meaning of a race: "It is a vast family of human beings, generally of common blood and language, always of common history, traditions and impulses, who are both voluntarily and involuntarily striving together for the accomplishment of certain more or less vividly conceived ideals of life" (Du Bois 1986a: 817). A race, as a vast family, arises from both biological and social sources: blood, language, history, and ideals.

As clear as these conceptualizations are, Du Bois continues to return to the basic question of race in the essay, adding new refinements at each progressive stage. After identifying eight distinct races, which correspond to specific nations, he asks,

What is the real distinction between these nations? Is it the physical differences of blood, color, and cranial measurements? Certainly we must all acknowledge that physical differences play a great part, and that, with wide exceptions and qualifications, these eight great races of to-day follow the cleavage of physical race distinctions ... But while race differences have followed mainly physical race lines, yet no mere physical distinctions would really define or explain the deeper differences – the cohesiveness and continuity of these groups. The deeper differences are spiritual, psychical, differences – undoubtedly based on the physical, but infinitely transcending them. The forces that bind together the Teuton nations are, then, first, their race identity and common blood; secondly, and more importantly, a common history, common laws and religion, similar habits of thought and a conscious striving together for certain ideals of life. The whole process which has brought about these race differentiations has been a growth, and the great characteristic of this growth has been the differentiation of spiritual and mental differences between great races of mankind and the integration of physical differences. (Du Bois 1986a: 818)

These compact statements by the pre-eminent sociologist of race relations in the 1890s indicate that, in fact, Du Bois did not seek to overthrow racial science's biological conception of race entirely. He repeatedly insists that physical differences matter for the constitution of racial groups, and includes them with the psychical and spiritual differences that mark the boundaries of these groups. However, he draws a limit on physical differences insofar as they cannot *explain* spiritual and psychical differences, and the "ideals of life" that correspond to the various races. Contrary to the critical reading of Du Bois by Anthony Appiah (1992), whose penetrating analysis seeks to demonstrate the ultimate frustration of Du Bois's effort to define race based on common blood, language, and history, it would be more plausible to find in "The conservation of races" a conceptualization of race that sets physical and socio-historical difference in a relation of continuity rather than opposition. A presentist reading of this essay either over-emphasizes Du Bois's restricted view of the efficacy of physical difference to account for the socio-historical existence of racial groups as a rejection of biology or finds only ineluctable contradictions in the social and psychical conception he proffers. Both interpretations fail, ultimately, to take Du Bois on his own terms, as neither dismissing biology nor offering a purely "social" conception of race. In this regard, Du Bois stands at the precipice of a new race concept that, over the course of the next one hundred years, would explicitly reject the relationship between "grosser physical differences of color, hair and bone" in favor of a purely social concept of race. The problem that arises from Appiah's otherwise brilliant deconstruction of Du Bois's race concept is that he denounces the concept from the standpoint of objective truth rather than treating it as a problem in the sociology of knowledge: such a denunciation cannot destroy the object that Du Bois's theory aimed to capture. In this case, a better interpretive methodology is to uncover the logic that holds race as a *contradictory object* in place in the mind. In "The conservation of races," there is not yet a contradiction – or full-blown opposition – between biology and society. Consequently, Du Bois's race concept is not yet plurivocal, because biology is not a latent meaning.

Race, ethnicity, and biological inheritance: Kallen and Park

Du Bois stands at the forefront of what Appiah terms "anti-racist racism" and the reversal or re-valuation of the moral terms of racial hierarchy. There is no effort in Du Bois to subtract race from the social equation. Rather he adds it in a way that turns vertical relationships of hierarchy between racial groups into horizontal ones of equality and difference, and that turns purported racial differences that are marked as inferior into unique qualities that conjoin to enrich humanity at large. Racial assimilation is, on this account, not conceived as a real possibility or as a desired end. Races are immutable: again, immutability is a product of both gross physical and finer cultural constitutions. The question of assimilation is, however, part of the theorization of ethnic and racial groups by two other influential, early twentieth-century scholars, Horace Kallen and Robert Park. Kallen is best known as an advocate of the notion of cultural pluralism; Park was a founding member of the Chicago School of sociology and proponent of an eco-logical view of social relations. Like Du Bois, both retain biological inheritance as part of the constitution of ethnic groups and races. However, they disagree on the nature of the impact of ethnic and race relations on the groups themselves.

Horace Kallen's writings responded to two historical currents: the Progressive Era's faith in the "melting-pot" as the future of American democracy and the anti-immigrant backlash of the 1910s and 1920s that culminated in the Immigration Act of 1924 (effectively closing down the stream of European immigrants). On the one hand, Kallen wished to debunk Zangwill's (1914) metaphor of the melting-pot as a description of social life in the United States and, on the other hand, to resist the strong current of anti-assimilationist nativism. In a series of essays published in 1924 with the title *Culture and Democracy in the United States*, he affirmed the view, articulated by his contemporary Edward Bok, that "the foreign-born [makes] a better American." Unlike other Progressives, who thought that immigrant cultures required American-ization, and the nativist view, which held that American democracy required the purification of native values, Kallen defined the problem of democracy in an age of immigration otherwise:

The problem of Democracy is to perfect the organization of society that every man and every group may have the freest possible opportunity to realize and perfect their natures, and to attain the excellence appropriate to their kind. In essence, therefore, Democracy involves, not the elimination of differences, but the perfection and conservation of differences ... It involves a give and take between radically different types, and a mutual respect and mutual cooperation based on mutual understanding. (Kallen 1924: 61)

Not the elimination of cultural differences, but the creation of condi-tions for mutual respect, cooperation, and understanding, is the proper task of American democracy. Whereas the Great War in Europe demonstrated the possibility that the "natural hyphenation of the American citizen" might lead to social disruption, Kallen argued, on the contrary, that "it is absurd to lose sight of the truth that the hyphen unites very much more than it separates, and that in point of fact, the greater the hyphenation, the greater the unanimity ... There is ethnic hyphenation in the differences of race, origin, and character among the various peoples who constitute the American citizenry" (Kallen 1924: 63). To the extent that Americanization occurs at all, it only touches the "external differences" between old and new Americans:

All immigrants and their offspring are by the way of undergoing "Americanization" if they remain in one place in the country long enough – say six or seven years. The general notion of "Americanization" appears to signify the adoption of the American variety of English speech, American clothes and manners, the American attitude in politics. "Americanization" signifies, in short, the disappearance of the external differences upon which so much race-prejudice often feeds. (Kallen 1924: 79)

What is not assimilable through Americanization is, according to Kallen, the immigrant's *natio*, her ancestral nativity, which is borne within each individual and reinforced through daily interactions with others sharing the same *natio*. This cultural inheritance remains a permanent feature of the life of the immigrant.

Behind him in time and tremendously in him in quality, are his ancestors; around him in space are his relatives and kin, carrying in common with him the inherited organic set from a remoter common ancestry. In all these he lives and moves and has his being. They constitute his, literally, *natio*, the inwardness of his nativity, and in Europe every inch of his non-human environment wears the effects of their action upon it and breathes their spirit. The America he comes to, besides Europe, is Nature virgin and inviolate: it does not guide him with ancestral blazings: externally he is cut off from the past. Not so internally: whatever else he changes, he cannot change his grandfather. Moreover, he comes rarely alone; he comes companioned with his fellow nationals; and he comes to no strangers, but to kin and friends who have gone before. (Kallen 1924: 94)

The second generation of immigrants explicitly promote their similarity as an ethnic group. Each individual immigrant "remains still the Slav, the Jew, the German or the Irish citizen of the American state. Again, in the mass, neither he nor his children's children lose their ethnic individuality" (Kallen 1924: 96). Moreover, once they are freed from the stigma attached to foreignness, they "learn, or they recall, the spiritual heritage of their nationality" (Kallen 1924: 106). Consequently, Kallen argues: "What is the cultural outcome likely to be, under these conditions? Surely not the melting-pot" (Kallen 1924: 108). Rather than rooting out all evidence of ethnic difference, the proper social policy towards ethnic groups "would seek to provide conditions under which each might attain the cultural perfection that is *proper to its kind*" (Kallen 1924: 121).

Deploying the term race, Kallen rejects the idea that *natio*, the inherent quality that makes it impossible for the individual to change his grandfather, is weakened by cultural assimilation or intermarriage.

From the negation or neutralization of heredity to the acknowledgement of its persistence and influence is no inconsiderable step. Yet Mr. Bryce has taken it and it is a wise step. It is a step supported by such anthropological evidence as exists to-day. Intermarriage or no intermarriage, racial quality persists, and is identifiable, as Mr. Bryce recognizes, to the end of the generations ... different races responding to the same stimuli are still different, and no environmental influence subtle as thought and overwhelming as a tank can ever remold them into an indifferent sameness. It may scatter them. It may neutralize and repress their traits. But it cannot identify their traits ... Intermarriage, consequently, is not racial assimilation ... The older types persist, and there is nothing to keep them from so continuing on any principle of the relation of heredity to environment that may be applied to them. (Kallen 1924: 176–177)

Kallen can be seen, like Du Bois, to conceptualize group identity (either ethnic or racial) on the basis of cultural heredity that is organized along national lines (the *natio*) and cultural practices that are specific to heredity. Like Du Bois, Kallen does not conceive of these hereditary, cultural differences as negative but rather as a necessary and positive feature of American democracy and an inevitable consequence of immigration. Thus, as it was for Du Bois, assimilation is not the end goal (and is impossible in any case); a state of mutuality of difference is held by Kallen to be a singular achievement of American democracy.

Similar to Du Bois and Kallen, Robert Park did not reject the biological constitution of racial groups in his otherwise ecological analysis of race relations. In his work on race (published in a cumulative volume entitled *Race and Culture* [1950]) can be found the following claims: races exist; blood lines define the boundary of races; and the mentalities and degree of assimilation of blacks depend on spatial social relations, on their proximity to whites. For example, in a discussion of culture, Park argues that

Every individual is the inheritor of a double inheritance, physical and moral, racial and cultural. It is, however, by association, by education and, fundamentally, by communication, that these individuals come into possession and become the bearers of their cultural heritage. All this indicates what culture is. It is not an artifact merely, not something that can be bought, sold, and "distributed" ... cultural traits cannot be exported or transported. They can be transmitted or diffused. A cultural trait is transmitted from one generation to another, or diffused from one culture to another. (Park 1950: 4)

Individuals inherit a culture from multiple sources, one of which is racial. However, the social component is required: only through education and communication does a cultural heritage become recognized. If an individual's racially related cultural heritage only becomes recognizable through social practices, the same holds true for race relations. These relations depend on a race consciousness.

> Race relations ... are the relations existing between peoples distinguished by marks of racial descent, particularly when these racial differences enter into the consciousness of the individuals and the groups so distinguished, and by doing so determine in each case the individual's conception of himself as well as his status in the community. Thus anything that intensifies race consciousness; anything, particularly if it is a permanent physical trait, that increases an individual's visibility and by so doing makes more obvious his identity with a particular ethnic or genetic group, tends to create and maintain the conditions under which race relations, as defined here, may be said to exist. Race consciousness; therefore, is to be regarded as a phenomenon, like class or caste consciousness, that enforces social distances. Race relations, in this sense, are not so much the relations that exist between individuals of different races as between individuals conscious of these differences. (Park 1950: 81)

Race consciousness enforces social distances, but on the basis of what? Anything might intensify this consciousness; however, Park emphasizes the existence of a "permanent physical trait" which increases the visibility of individuals and makes them more identifiable with a group. It is worth pointing out here that Park, like Du Bois and Kallen, does not raise the question of the reality of race; it is assumed to be real and is one of the real bases of groups (physical traits plus consciousness).

However, while there is largely agreement among these early race theorists on the race concept, Park diverges on the matter of assimilation. Racial group boundaries, while constituted in part by racial (i.e., physical) inheritance, are not immutable in Park's view. His concept of the race relations cycle is illustrative of his view of the lack of fixity of racial boundaries.

> It is obvious that race relations and all that they imply are generally, and on the whole, the products of migration and conquest. This was true of the ancient world and it is equally true of the modern. The interracial adjustments that follow such migration and conquest are more complex than is ordinarily thought. They involve racial competition, conflict, accommodation, and eventually assimilation, but all of these diverse processes are to be regarded as merely the efforts of a new social and cultural organism to achieve a new biotic and social equilibrium. (Park 1950: 104)

Against Kallen's pluralist model, Park argues that the United States and the world are a melting-pot. Moreover, the race relations cycle of contact, competition, accommodation, and assimilation is inevitable and irreversible: "Customs regulations, immigrant restrictions and racial barriers may slacken the tempo of the movement; may perhaps halt it altogether for a time; but cannot change its direction; cannot at any rate, reverse it" (Park 1950: 150).

To be sure, Park is referring to cultural assimilation, not physical assimilation (although racial hybridity matters).[5] Here, however, he also exhibits caution regarding the extent to which what he called "racial temperament" can be "disposed of" by policies that promote "naturalization, assimilation, Americanization, Christianization, and acculturation more generally" (Park 1950: 281). Thus, he writes:

The question remains still to what extent so-called racial characteristics are actually racial, i.e., biological, and to what extent they are the effect of environmental conditions. The thesis of this paper, to state it again, is (1) that fundamental temperamental qualities, which are the basis of interest and attention, act as selective agencies and as such determine what elements in the cultural environment each race will select; in what region it will seek and find its vocation in the larger social organization. (Park 1950: 281)

In other words, Park proposes that "fundamental temperamental qualities" are a baseline condition for all races, which act as a mechanism for selecting different elements from the cultural environment. These elements then become the social aspect of racial groups. Du Bois also found that the different races had special vocations and here Park seems to affirm his perspective.

The confluence of racial temperament and cultural environment produces a "racial will." In discussing this racial will, Park articulates his view of the relationship between race as inherited characteristics and the social manifestation of the qualities of races.

This racial will is, to be sure, largely social, that is, modified by social experience, but it rests ultimately upon a complex of inherited characteristics, which are racial. It follows from what has been said that the individual is the bearer of a double inheritance. As a member of a race, he transmits by interbreeding a biological inheritance. As a member of society or a social group, on the other hand, he transmits by communication a social inheritance. The particular

[5] "What I have called the mentality of the racial hybrid – that is to say, his peculiar mental bias, the character of the intelligence which he displays, and the general level of the intellectual life he has achieved – is very largely due to the social situation in which his mixed origin inevitably puts him. He is biologically the product of divergent racial stocks, but just because of that fact he is, at the same time, the cultural product of two distinct traditions. He is, so to speak, a cultural as well as a racial hybrid" (Park 1931: 540). In this article, Park identifies W. E. B. Du Bois as a racial hybrid: "The two most eminent figures among Negroes in the United States, Booker T. Washington and W. E. B. Du Bois, were both mixed bloods" (Park 1931: 539).

complex of inheritable characters which characterizes the individuals of a racial group constitutes the racial temperament. The particular group of habits, accommodations, sentiments, attitudes, and ideals transmitted by communication and education constitute a social tradition. Between this temperament and this tradition there is, as has been generally recognized, a very intimate relationship. My assumption is that temperament is the basis of the interests ... That is to say, temperament determines what things the individual and group will be interested in; what elements of the general culture, to which they have access, they will assimilate; what, to state it pedagogically, they will learn. (Park 1950: 282)

Park's argument can be summarized in three points. First, he posits the existence of a biological racial inheritance that is transmitted by individuals. Second, he identifies a second inheritance that is social, and that is also transmitted, not by breeding but rather through education and communication. Third, the biological and social inheritance stand in a close relationship to each other. Again, the connective link is supplied by temperament, which, in the final analysis, is biologically grounded. As racial groups consolidate customs and values that are suited to their temperaments, these "racial qualities become the basis for nationalities, a nationalistic group being merely a cultural and, eventually, a political society founded on the basis of racial inheritances" (Park 1950: 282).

The early theories of race and ethnicity in the United States share a common structure. While Du Bois, Kallen, and Park engage the concept of race from different positions, and with different purposes, all three take race to be, in the first instance, a matter of biological constitution, and, in the second instance, to be more significant at the level of culture. Each sees limits in strictly biological accounts of race but, at the same time, the biological basis for racial classification is recognized as valid. Indeed, for all three thinkers, the biological constitution of racial groups is a necessary, if not sufficient, condition for the existence of racial groups. Biological differences are real, even if Du Bois, Kallen, and Park circumscribe the efficacy of purely biological accounts of race; these accounts are affirmed, rather than refuted. Over the course of the twentieth century, biology became problematic for sociological accounts of race, in part because the natural sciences increasingly (although not entirely) grew suspicious of a biological basis of race, and in part because political events and social movements problematized and stigmatized any emphasis on a link between biology and race. In the second half of the twentieth century, sociologists came to prefer exclusively social concepts of race that either remain silent on the question of biology or explicitly refuse any role for biology aside from the function of phenotypical differences as markers of race.

Between structure and culture: race and social essentialism

During the civil rights struggle of the 1950s and 1960s, race became closely linked with the analysis of social inequality in American social science. The study of "race relations" tended to take two different but often converging paths: on the one hand, social-psychological studies of racial prejudice and, on the other hand, the search for the causes of economic inequality between whites and blacks, and, in particular, the problem of poverty. One impetus for the latter path emerged from outside sociology. In the early 1960s, Oscar Lewis published two ethnographic studies, *The Children of Sanchez* (1961) and *La Vida* (1966b), as well as a summary article in *Scientific American* (1966a) that introduced the social scientific concept of a "culture of poverty." In his work, Lewis claimed that cultures of poverty eventually become self-perpetuating, thus implying that policymakers' attempts to change poor people's material conditions would do little to lift them out of poverty. "By the time slum children are six or seven," wrote Lewis, "they have usually absorbed the basic attitudes and values of their subculture. Thereafter they are psychologically unready to take full advantage of changing conditions or improving opportunities that may develop in their lifetime" (Lewis 1966a: 21). Because of this emphasis on the cultural hard-wiring of dysfunctional behavior, the cultural explanation of social inequality came to symbolize a conservative approach to remedying inequality in an era of increasing government intervention into social problems in the United States that was stimulated in part by a decade-old Civil Rights movement. Consequently, structural explanations were invoked against cultural ones: the impact on the study of race was the emergence of structural accounts of racism and inequality.

One of the most influential structural explanations of race in the last thirty years has been developed by William Julius Wilson. In the wake of the controversy surrounding the culture-of-poverty thesis that was employed to account for persistent, intergenerational experiences of poverty among blacks, Wilson emphasized "social structural" conditions (related to the economy and polity) rather than cultural factors (ideologies and beliefs about race) as the defining feature of social reality that made race significant in varying ways during different historical eras. In two books, *Power, Racism, and Privilege* (1973) and *The Declining Significance of Race* (1980), Wilson offered compelling historical accounts of the place of power in race relations and of how race relations are shaped by the changing structure of the labor market and urban politics. In the 1970s Wilson posited a "declining significance of race" (or racism) for middle-class blacks, whereas the life chances of poor blacks were influenced primarily by the shifting economic landscape and growing scarcity of low-skilled jobs in American cities: "Race relations in America have undergone fundamental changes in recent years, so much so that now the life chances of individual blacks have more to do with their economic class position than their day-to-day encounters with whites" (Wilson 1980: 1). Conversely, race *mattered* primarily between 1865 and 1950: in particular, the late nineteenth and early twentieth centuries were marked by virulent racist ideologies that directly impacted blacks' access to the labor market.

In this respect Wilson departed from a social constructionist theory of race, which contributed to a rejection of the biological definitions of race that were prevalent in the late nineteenth and early twentieth centuries. This analytical break with biological conceptions accomplished the following: it freed the study of race from explicitly hierarchical understandings of the social relationships between racial groups. Moreover, it shifted the focus of study from physical characteristics to social relationships between racially defined groups and set the terms for distinguishing ethnicity (defined in positive terms of a national-ethnic culture) and race (defined in negative terms of subordination, discrimination, and subjection). Two characteristic ways of studying race developed from the early social construction paradigm: the race relations approach (ranging from social-psychological studies of racial attitudes to empirical studies of racial conflict) and the study of patterns of assimilation of ethnic groups. In relation to these approaches, Wilson substituted a social-structural explanation of racial attitudes and racial conflict for the cultural and psychological approaches.

A striking feature of Wilson's work is that in neither of his books is a definition of race offered. In *Power, Racism, and Privilege*, but not in *The Declining Significance of Race*, there is a definition of racial groups. However, what is primarily discussed in both books is racism. So, whereas Wilson argues that "racial groups are distinguished by socially selected physical traits" (Wilson 1973: 6), what is primarily the object of conceptualization and analysis is racism. It would be fair to argue that conceptualization of race is subsumed – or subordinated – to the conceptualization of racism. According to Wilson,

The position taken in this study is that there is an essential difference between ethnocentrism and racism and that it is indeed misleading to treat the latter as a special instance of the former. Let me be more specific. The fundamental distinction between these two concepts is that ethnocentrism is a principle of invidious group distinction, whereas racism is a philosophy or ideology of racial exploitation ... racism is defined as an *ideology of racial domination or exploitation*

that (1) incorporates beliefs in a particular race's cultural and/or inherent biological
inferiority and (2) uses such beliefs to justify and prescribe inferior or unequal treatment
for that group. The crucial distinction in this definition is that racism has two
major dimensions – biological and cultural. (Wilson 1973: 31–33)

On this account, racism (but not race?) has a biological and cultural
dimension. However, biology matters only insofar as it is associated with
inherent inferiority of subordinate racial groups as perceived by the
dominant racial group. Why is there no specific definition of race in books
that concern race and use the term with great frequency? Two complementary interpretations are possible: (1) the definition of race is taken for
granted because racial groups are viewed as self-evident; (2) racism is
manifested only under the condition of competition (i.e., conflict). So, for
example, Wilson argues that only under conditions of direct competition
for jobs did a virulent ideology of racial supremacy flourish in the post-
Civil War era. Yet beneath this explicit articulation of racism lies an
unstated assumption that race (or racial groups) have a reality that stands
independent of competition; after all, racial groups could not have
emerged suddenly during the Reconstruction and modern industrial eras.
For Wilson, then, the conceptualization of race is both manifest (in racist
ideology) and latent (in pre-existing racial groups).

In addition to Wilson, a strong structural approach to conceptualizing
race has been developed by Eduardo Bonilla-Silva. Although his focus is
primarily on a "structural interpretation of racism," Bonilla-Silva's
approach has implications for understanding race. His main foils are
what he identifies as psychological and economic explanations of racism,
and he identifies several problems in these explanations. On the one
hand, (1) if psychological explanations treat racism as an idea, it is not
viewed as a foundation or structure of social systems; (2) if racial attitudes determine the level of racism in society, then racism operates at
the individual level rather than at the level of social structure; (3) if
racism (and racist individuals) are viewed as irrational, then racism has
no social basis. On the other hand, if racism is treated as a function of
economic domination (i.e., in neo-Marxist thought), (1) racist actions
that are not overt are difficult to conceptualize; (2) contemporary racism
is necessarily tied to a previously existing *racial* situation; and (3) racism
tends to be analyzed in a circular manner. Both psychological and economic approaches fail to ground racism in social relations among races.
Consequently, Bonilla-Silva argues that racism (and race) are fundamental
aspects of racial systems: "*racialized social systems* ... [refer] to societies in
which economic, political, social, and ideological levels are partially
structured by the placement of actors in racial categories or races." Races,
he argues, are typically "identified by their phenotype, but ... the

selection of certain human traits to designate a racial group is always socially rather than biologically based" (Bonilla-Silva 1997: 469). Social systems are always already racialized rather than being dependent on the ebb and flow of measurable racist beliefs. From this perspective, he argues that racism only describes "the racial ideology of a racialized social system" (Bonilla-Silva 1997: 467). For Bonilla-Silva, only a social-structuralist conception provides an "adequate theoretical foundation" that can resist the reduction of race (and racism) to either a reflection of class structure or the product of an irrational ideology.

One implication of this view is that races are conceived as "truly social collectivities" (Bonilla-Silva 1997: 466). But what is race itself? It is easier to understand what racism is for Bonilla-Silva than it is to find a specific statement on race. After posing the question "what is the nature of races, or, more properly, of racialized social groups?" he turns to Omi and Winant (see below) for a conceptualization: "Omi and Winant state that races are the outcome of the racialization process, which they define as 'the extension of racial meaning to a previously racially unclassified relationship, social practice or group.'" He goes on to claim "historically the classification of a people in racial terms has been a highly political act," that the "invention of such categories entails a dialectical process of construction" of the categories of "other" and "same," and that "the racialization of peoples was socially invented." However, Bonilla-Silva provides no indication of the referent of "racial meaning" or what entity is put in play during the process of racialization. If, as he argues, "races ... are not biologically but socially determined categories of identity and group association" (Bonilla-Silva 1997: 472), the basis of these socially determined categories is never articulated: racialization produces race(s). On the one hand, Bonilla-Silva affirms the persistence of racialization by insisting on its extra-individual basis and, on the other hand, by accounting for its persistence on the basis of the objective (and collective) racial interests that are produced by practical struggles within racialized societies.[6] In this case, race or racialization is the result of a felicitous combination of a racialized social order (which produces race[s]) and power-laden race relations (which produce racial interests). This conceptualization effectively moves race from being a matter of knowledge and meaning to a matter of racial conflict: "What or who is

---

[6] "Insofar as the races receive different social rewards at all levels, they develop dissimilar objective interests, which can be detected in their struggles to either transform or maintain a particular racial order. These interests are collective rather than individual, are based on relations between races rather than on particular group needs, and are not structural but practical; that is, they are related to concrete struggles rather than derived from the location of the races in the racial structure" (Bonilla-Silva 1997: 470).

Black or White or Indian reflects and affects the social, political, ideological, and economic struggles between the races" (Bonilla-Silva 1997: 472).

In contrast to the structural accounts of race in Wilson and Bonilla-Silva, a robust cultural concept of race has been put forward by Michael Omi and Howard Winant. Their influential book *Racial Formation in the United States* was intended to resuscitate the concept of race, which had, in their view, been smothered under concepts of ethnicity, class, and nation. Race should not be understood as the outcome of class relations; nor should it be placed under the rubric of an ethnic identity that would eventually disappear in a process of assimilation; race is also wrongly construed as a matter of national oppression. Instead, they propose a politicized cultural concept of race. Their definition is situated in relation to two other ways of handling race, as an unchanging essence or as a grand illusion.

There is a continuous temptation to think of race as an *essence*, as something fixed, concrete, and objective. And there is also an opposite temptation to imagine race as a mere *illusion*, a purely ideological construct which some ideal non-racist social order would eliminate. It is necessary to challenge both these positions, to disrupt and reframe the rigid and bipolar manner in which they are posed and debated, and to transcend the presumably irreconcilable relationship between them. (Omi and Winant 1994: 54)

In order to avoid these oppositions, Omi and Winant propose a non-essentialist, social concept of race (what Walter Benn Michaels [1995] has called the "no drop rule"): "*race is a concept which signifies and symbolizes social conflicts and interests by referring to different types of human bodies.* Although the concept of race invokes biologically based human characteristics (so-called 'phenotypes'), selection of these particular human features for purposes of racial signification is always and necessarily a social and historical process" (Omi and Winant 1994: 55). The race concept figures centrally in the analysis of "racial formations," which they define as "the sociohistorical process by which racial categories are created, inhabited, transformed, and destroyed." These categories are deployed in "racial projects" which are "*an interpretation, representation, or explanation of racial dynamics, and an effort to reorganize and redistribute resources along particular racial lines*" (Omi and Winant 1994: 56). Omi and Winant use the concept of racial formation to describe various cultural and ideological movements that have sought to impose their own racial projects on the American state and society. These projects involve both social structural claims made on the State and cultural struggles over identity.

Unlike the race structuralists, Omi and Winant begin with the race concept rather than racism. By starting with race, they confront directly the paradox of the reality and unreality of race as an object. However, rather than treating the dilemma this paradox presents for concept construction as a matter of knowledge, they construe the dilemma as a matter of politics, as arising from the contemporary political situation (circa the 1980s). The claim that race is an "illusion" is characterized by Omi and Winant as a strategy of a neo-conservative racial project that would, through a roll-back of social policy aimed at the amelioration of the effects of racial discrimination, establish a "color-blind" society; a society which, in any case, they describe as "utopian" (Omi and Winant 1994: 57). Posing the dilemma of conceptualization as an aspect of political struggle rather than as a problem of reality (and, therefore, as a problem of knowledge), their race concept aligns with an anti-racist – but not anti-race – racial project. Hence, their theory falls on the side of the reality of race (and affirms it), which is, however, not biological but social. But the meaning of race in society – or rather a society shaped by racial formations – is not immutable but changes according to the ebb and flow of racial formations. It is reasonable to assume that an anti-race project that is not bound up with a neo-conservative political project is a possibility within the racial formations framework. However, Omi and Winant head off this possibility, which would bring an end to racial formations, with the argument that "it is rather difficult to jettison widely held beliefs, beliefs which moreover are central to everyone's identity and understanding of the social world" (Omi and Winant 1994: 55). Thus the paradox of the simultaneous reality and unreality of race returns or, rather, persists: the meaning of race is mutable (it is not real in any essential way) but the social reality of race is immutable (i.e., race is essential for understanding society).

In subsequent writings, Winant further elaborates this claim concerning the permanency of race in modern society. In *Racial Conditions*, he argues that

> Rather than suggesting that race is a problem to be solved, I argue in this book that race is a condition of individual and collective identity, a permanent, though tremendously flexible, element of social structure. Race is a means of knowing and organizing the social world; it is subject to continual contestation and reinterpretation, but it is no more likely to disappear than other forms of human inequality and difference ... Race is an epochal phenomenon that took on most of its importance as a result of the creation of the modern world ... The five-hundred-year domination of the globe by Europe and its inheritors is the historical context in which racial concepts of difference have attained their present status as fundamental components of human identity and inequality. To imagine the end of race is thus to contemplate the liquidation of Western civilization. (Winant 1994: xii–xiii)

It is plausible to interpret these claims, in particular the one linking the end of race to the liquidation of Western civilization, as hyperbolic. To be sure, the claim that race is unlikely to disappear as a condition of identity at some point in the future can only be properly described as speculative. Indeed, the assertion that "the social fact – in the Durkheimian sense – of racial difference persists" (Winant 1994: 3) could be seen as drawing an undefended analogy between social facts like the sacred, the family, law, and race. Nonetheless, what makes these claims plausible within the cultural framework is the treatment of the question of race as a political rather than epistemological issue. Winant's concern is to maintain the race concept in the face of perceived efforts to impose a "color-blind" worldview on society; to be color-blind is not simply to refuse to see race, it is also to reject affirmative efforts to attenuate and eradicate the persistence of racism.

The styles of thought of Bonilla-Silva and Omi and Winant, despite their manifest differences over the conceptualization of race/racism, share a similar inner logic: their arguments submerge the question of race beneath the problem of racism (see Bonilla-Silva 1999). Contemporary race analysts have become predisposed to subordinate the critical questioning of the concept of race to social policy considerations that are deemed vital for anti-racist politics. In 2002, the American Sociological Association published an official statement on race, *The Importance of Collecting Data and Doing Social Scientific Research on Race*, which posed the issue as a choice between two ethical-political views, that racial classification is in itself harmful and that counting people by race is necessary to ameliorate racial inequality. As the executive summary states:

Some scientists and policymakers now contend that research using the concept of race perpetuates the negative consequences of thinking in racial terms. Others argue that measuring differential experiences, treatment, and outcomes across racial categories is necessary to track disparities and to inform policymaking to achieve greater social justice. The American Sociological Association (ASA), an association of some 13,000 US and international sociologists, finds greater merit in the latter point of view.[7] (American Sociological Association 2002)

---

[7] The American Anthropological Association (AAA) has taken a diametrically opposed position in its statement related to the census: "The American Anthropological Association recommends the elimination of the term 'race' from OMB Directive 15 during the planning for the 2010 Census. During the past 50 years, 'race' has been scientifically proven to not be a real, natural phenomenon. More specific, social categories such as 'ethnicity' or 'ethnic group' are more salient for scientific purposes and have fewer of the negative, racist connotations for which the concept of race was developed. Yet the concept of race has become thoroughly – and perniciously – woven into the cultural and political fabric of the United States. It has become an essential element of both individual identity and government policy. Because so much harm has been based on 'racial' distinctions over the years, correctives for such harm must also acknowledge the impact of 'racial' consciousness among the US populace, regardless of the fact that 'race' has no scientific justification in human biology. Eventually, these classifications must be transcended and replaced by more non-racist and accurate ways of representing the diversity of the US population" (American Anthropological Association 1998).

Hence, the question of the reality of race is over-determined by the politics of race, or, rather, the question of reality is posed in exclusively political terms, because the anti-racist struggle is presupposed to necessitate a claim that race is a permanent feature of social life, even if race is viewed to have come into existence *historically*. Race is simultaneously – and without apparent logical contradiction – held to be historical (it is a feature of Western modernity [Bonilla-Silva and Winant]) and transcendental: once called into existence, race can neither be transcended nor fall into disuse. Consequently, by the end of the last century, a socially essentialist concept of race has become a prevalent means by which to replace the lingering biological essentialism of the early social scientific race theorists.

Conclusion

In this chapter, we have illustrated a paradigmatic style of thought among several key figures in the sociology of race in the United States. Whereas the early social scientific theorists of race and ethnicity (Du Bois, Kallen, and Park) did not detach their concepts of race and the formation of racial groups from biological and physical traits, by the end of the twentieth century physical differences only figure as "signs" of difference and references to biology are typically rejected as essentialist (for scholars as different as Wilson, Omi, Winant, and Bonilla-Silva). Nonetheless, even in the explicitly non-biological concepts of race one finds in the work of contemporary race scholars, some notion of a biological order of racial groups is implied if not necessitated. It is a logical impossibility to characterize racial groups without an *a priori* notion of biological difference (based on phenotype). It is our view that these overtly non-essentialist concepts are covertly essentialist; in other words, because they do not rethink the concept of race adequately, a biological understanding of race, instantiated under the guise of a "social fact," is the unacknowledged elephant in the room. Thus, the race concept that predominates in contemporary American sociology is a plurivocal symbol: phenotype persists as a latent meaning (and referent) in the manifestly non-biological social concept of race. This structure of racial thought is enabled by the lack of a direct engagement with the reality problematic. The early theorists did not question the reality of race because the reality of biologically constituted races was self-evident; contemporary theorists do not question the reality of race because their first inclination is to give a political answer to what is a problem of knowledge (epistemology) and meaning (belief). As a result, the concept of race in American sociology is engaged in a recurrent *pas de deux* with biology, even when biology has been ostensibly rejected as a meaningful way to define race and racial groups.

2   Marxism

> Where speculation ends – in real life – there real positive science begins: the representation of the practical activity, of the practical process of development of men. Empty talk about consciousness ceases, and real knowledge has to take its place. When reality is depicted, philosophy as an independent branch of knowledge loses its medium of existence.
>
> (Marx 1978: 155)

> It is probable that without capitalism, a cultural chance occurrence among whites, the world might never have experienced race prejudice.
>
> (Cox 2000: 31)

A second style of thought that has contributed to existing theories of race is Marxism. Whereas American sociology's style of thought on race has consistently found race to exist *in reality*, the style of thought associated with historical materialism has refused to conceptualize race as a thing of reality. Moreover, unlike sociological race relations theory, the Marxist tradition has bequeathed to sociology (and social thought in general) a robust and parsimonious, if not controversial, theory of social knowledge. Insofar as Marxism has contributed to a theory of race, the account it presents is, on the surface, straightforward. Based on a radical rejection of biological explanations of race, Marxists of various stripes have treated race as a form of ideology.[1] Thus Marxist thought offers a direct answer to the paradox of race, its simultaneous reality and unreality: *race is not real*. In a single *coup de main*, it clears the field of all the conceptual dilemmas that have plagued other styles of thought with which it competes for the most definitive statement of knowledge on race. However, in the end, this victory is by no means complete; Marxism has neither vanquished its foes in the "bourgeois" sociology of race relations, social anthropology, and cultural studies for the monopoly on truth about race, nor has it ultimately removed the paradox of race from reality (see Chapter 5). Nonetheless, Marxist thought provides a refreshingly reflexive theory of knowledge with

---

[1] Even scholars who are not "Marxist" in other respects have borrowed (explicitly or implicitly) from Marxism to analyze race relations (for example, see Wilson 1980).

which to interrogate the race concept. In this chapter, we reconstruct this theory and its implications in a nutshell, in particular Marx's approach to the relation of ideas and material reality in general, and an application of Marxist theory to race relations in the work of Oliver Cromwell Cox and Robert Miles.

Marx on ideology

The German Ideology (Marx 1978: 147–200) represents Marx's historical materialist approach to the analysis of social and historical phenomena. In this work, Marx answers several questions that also pertain to the central concerns of this study of race, the questions of knowledge, social reality, and truth. What is knowledge? What is true or correct knowledge? What are the conditions of possibility for knowledge, true and false, correct and incorrect? And, finally, what is the relationship of Marx (or a historical materialist observer of social life) to this knowledge and the conditions of possible knowledge? These questions pertain to all types of expert knowledge. However, we should locate these questions within a specific domain: knowledge of the social, of society. Marx wrote *The German Ideology* in an era in which sociology – as an intellectual discipline – did not yet exist. While Marx's interests do not rest in building sociology as a field of knowledge, his claims about knowledge in general provide one basis for this sociological field. This basis can be described as materialism, or historical materialism, and it involves a distinct definition of the social and a method of knowing the social. Our intention is not to offer a definitive reading of Marx but rather to develop one reading that draws out themes that interconnect with our interest in knowledge of race. In *The German Ideology* we emphasize the materialist theory of knowledge as Marx developed it in relation to philosophical or religious forms of knowledge.

Marx's thought aims at concreteness, at the real, at reality. His intent is not to develop a theory of knowledge for its own sake, but rather to comprehend and to advance the movement of historical class struggle. Nonetheless, Marx can be situated initially within a tradition of thinking about thought or knowledge itself, within a tradition of properly philosophical attempts to articulate the conditions of knowledge in relation to thinking. It is appropriate, therefore, to link Marx to René Descartes and, of course, to the "idealist" tradition in philosophy against which *The German Ideology* mounts a formidable rebellion. Ever since Descartes took it upon himself, in his *Meditations on First Philosophy* (1641), to "apply myself earnestly and openly to the general destruction of my former opinions," in order to uncover "those things that can be called into doubt"

(Descartes 1979: 13), the theory of knowledge or epistemology has been an integral part of all the sciences, but especially the human sciences. The result of Descartes's meditations is summarized in his famous statement "cogito ergo sum": I am thinking, therefore I exist. This statement first appeared in Descartes's *Discourse on Method* (1637).[2] In the *Meditations* published four years later, Descartes expresses this view as follows:

> I judge that nothing else clearly belongs to my nature or essence except that I am a thing that thinks, I rightly conclude that my essence consists in this alone: that I am only a thing that thinks. Although perhaps (or rather, as I shall soon say, to be sure) I have a body that is very closely joined to me, nevertheless, because on the one hand I have a clear and distinct idea of myself – insofar as I am a thing that thinks and not an extended thing – and because on the other hand I have a distinct idea of a body – insofar as it is merely an extended thing, and not a thing that thinks – it is therefore certain that I am truly distinct from my body, and that I can exist without it. (Descartes 1979: 49)

In this formulation, the essence of a human being is that it is a "thing that thinks"; it knows itself only as *thinking* and not as *being*; it knows itself as mind, not as a body, since the body is not a thing that thinks. Thus, Descartes sets up a dualistic account of knowledge. At the level of individual knower, subjectivity stands over against objectivity; thought stands over against physical reality.

In addition to defining the knower as an existence that thinks, in the *Rules for Guiding One's Intelligence in Searching for the Truth*, Descartes stipulates that intuition and deduction are the only "actions of our intellect, by which we can arrive at knowledge of things without any fear of error."[3] Intuition, for Descartes, is understood as "the conception of a pure and attentive mind that is so easy and so distinct that no doubt remains subsequently about what we understand ... the undoubting conception of a pure and attentive mind which arises from the light of reason alone, and which is more certain than deduction because it is simpler" (Descartes 1999: 123). Deduction is defined as a "form of knowing ... by which we understand everything that follows necessarily from other things that are known with certainty" (Descartes 1999: 124).

Ex. All the marbles from this bag are blue.
     These marbles are all from this bag.
     Therefore, these marbles are blue.

---

[2] *Discourse on the Method for Guiding One's Reason and Searching for Truth in the Sciences.* See Descartes (1999: 5–54).

[3] *Rules for Guiding One's Intelligence in Searching for the Truth* (1628, published 1701). See Descartes (1999: 123).

Starting from things that are known with certainty, the marbles from the bag are blue and all the marbles are from the bag, the knowledge that the marbles are blue follows from the logical necessity of the things known with certainty. Intuition and deduction comprise a method for knowing "the truth about things":

By a "method," however, I understand easy and certain rules such that, if anyone were to use them carefully, they would never accept what is false as true and, without wasting their mental efforts but always increasing their scientific knowledge gradually, they would arrive at a true knowledge of all the things that they are capable of knowing. (Descartes 1999: 125)

Leaving little doubt about this proposition, Descartes asserts "the only way to acquire scientific knowledge is by intuition and deduction" (Descartes 1999: 126). We can observe here that both intuition and deduction involve mental operations and not an observation of material reality that is accessed by the senses.

At this point, we can pause to consider what this Cartesian perspective might mean for a theory of race. Based on the notion of the *cogito*, the thought of race cannot be said to reside in the body or to be a matter of physicality. Race is, therefore, an idea whose efficacy rests in the realm of thought. As a form of knowing that takes the method of deduction at its basis, we can rework the example of the marbles.

Ex.   All the people in this group are blue.
       These people are all from this group.
       Therefore, these people are blue.

While at first glance this deductive sequence seems inappropriate to the analysis of race, it is, in fact, the form of logical deduction implied by the "one-drop rule" of racial identification that has become prevalent since the early twentieth century. Race relations are blood relations; and these blood relations are construed as logical relations between individuals and groups defined by blood.

Like Descartes's *Meditations*, Marx's *The German Ideology* begins with an effort to uncover doubt. However, Marx's critical questioning is aimed primarily at religion and philosophy, both of which he condenses under the term "ideology." In the preface to *A Contribution to the Critique of Political Economy*, Marx lays out the basic elements of his theory. In what can be seen as a reply to Descartes's *cogito ergo sum*, Marx argues

In the social production of their life, men enter into definite relations that are indispensable and independent of their will, relations of production which correspond to a definite stage of development of their material productive forces.

The sum total of these relations of production constitutes the economic structure of society, the real foundation, on which rises a legal and political superstructure and to which corresponds definite forms of social consciousness. The mode of production of material life conditions the social, political and intellectual life process in general. It is not the consciousness of men that determines their being, but, on the contrary, their social being that determines their consciousness. (Marx 1978: 4)

For Marx, social being and social existence have priority over thought and ideas. What social being *is* becomes the thing that needs to be conceptualized, because the nature of social being will determine *how* we know social life and *what* we can know about social life.

Marx's theory of knowledge can be summarized briefly. Knowledge of social life requires inquiry into the material conditions that shape social life. Society's structure is defined by the sum total of the material conditions shaping social life: for Marx this means the economic means of production and the social relations of production that correspond to the means of production; particular forms of the economic means of production and the social relations of production comprise the *division of labor*. *Society*, that is civil society, is identified with *economic society*; society is shaped by the division of labor. *Historical change* can be understood on the basis of the development of material forces of production on the one hand, and a theory of class action and struggle on the other hand. Finally, the *problem of knowledge* for Marx involves the subjection of human consciousness to, or the overcoming of, ideology. Ideology takes several forms including religion, philosophy, political ideas, and non-materialist economic theories. Our access to the truth of material reality is masked and distorted by ideological representations of that material reality. However, the *real forces* that move society and history can be revealed by a proper form of *materialist thought* or, rather, *consciousness*. Marx's critique of religion (which is indebted to Ludwig Feuerbach) is the model for the critique of philosophy and ideology more generally. Thought is alienated from material reality; this gap or dualism must be overcome. Philosophical and religious thought on the one hand, and the theories of political economy on the other, are alienated forms of thought: neither philosophers, theologians, nor bourgeois economic theorists bring reality, the real activity of human beings, into their thinking about the world. Consequently, at the time Marx wrote *The German Ideology*, he held that the existing knowledge of theologians, philosophers, and political economists distorted the understanding of reality, rather than providing enlightenment about the real conditions of social life.

In *The German Ideology*, Marx pursues a rigorous and insistent argument for the historical materialist point of view – or rather, knowledge – in opposition to "ideology." What is specifically German about this ideology is that other would-be critical thinkers of Marx's generation (the Young Hegelians) did not quit, as he says, "the realm of philosophy." Marx makes a set of associations, between ideology and philosophy, and between religion, philosophy, and ideology, and, ultimately, between ideology and false consciousness. The primarily negative association of ideology, philosophy, and religion with "illusion," the "mystical," and the "theological" is contrasted with materialism, which is oriented to the empirical or reality or actual facts. Indeed, the strong emphasis in *The German Ideology* on the primacy of material economic relations, social being, and sensuous activity is intended to set German thought on its feet. But this righting comes at the cost of the denigration of philosophy as a form of knowledge about knowledge and as a form of knowledge about the social world.

For the purpose of construing Marxism as a style of thought in relation to race, we can pose to Marx and historical materialism the following question: according to historical materialism, what is the sociological basis of knowledge? The answer is fairly straightforward: material life conditions give rise to specific forms of knowledge of these material life conditions. Social classes possess their own forms of knowledge that reflect the different material basis of classes *and* their antagonistic relation to each other. Reality, or social being, is identified with material conditions: the means and relations of production. Consciousness should correspond to these material conditions; however, the natural relationship between consciousness and life is interrupted by the power of the ruling class, which produces ideas that mystify or distort reality. The ideas of this class are held to be the ruling ideas of an epoch and are imposed upon the subordinate class. Hence, the problem of knowledge arises from this distortion. The subordinate, working class misunderstands its social situation, because its *thought* is held under the sway of the ideology of the ruling class. Hence the proletariat's ideas stand in contradiction to reality, their consciousness is not determined by social being but rather by fantasies such as religion; and the philosophers who write about reality but fail to cut through to the actual material relations that determine reality are also locked in the domain of fantasy – philosophy – which is cut off from reality.

This historical materialist style of thought, which opposes two types of knowledge – materialism against philosophy (thinking *qua* thought), and empirical truth against distortion – has been taken up with respect to the issue of racism in the working classes. In Marxist analyses, racism is treated as one type of ideology the ruling (capitalist) class uses to maintain its class power over the working class; racism is used to divide the working class or, conversely, it is employed by the upper tier of the white working class, which seeks to maintain its marginal economic advantage over black workers. In either variant of the application of historical materialism to race relations, the classical statement of Marx's theory of knowledge is invoked: between the social being of the working class and their consciousness of this being has been imposed a set of false ideas (race and racism) that distorts the view of the workers' social being. Because of racist ideology, the workers from different "races" are unable to see their reality as an *economic* reality (comprised of opposed economic classes). Instead, they view their social reality as a *racial* reality (comprised of opposed races). Consequently racism and race are criticized within Marxism as false, as a distorted picture of empirical reality, and as impediments to true *class* consciousness. In other words, racism mystifies the actual social relations between capitalists and workers, which depend on the economic exploitation of the latter by the former.

Before turning to examples of a Marxist theory of race in the writings of Cox and Miles, one relevant difficulty with Marx's opposition of truth (i.e., historical materialist thought) and ideology can be discussed. Paul Ricœur offers a rather trenchant insight into this problem, the simultaneous reality and unreality of ideology: "In his early works, Marx's task is to determine what is the real. This determination will affect the concept of ideology, since ideology is all that is not this reality ... the difficulty of the Marxist concept of ideology: on the one hand ideology is excluded from the concrete basis of existence, but on the other hand it is somehow ineluctably generated from this basis at the same time" (Ricœur 1986: 21, 22). From Ricœur's framing of this difficulty, a direct parallel can be drawn to the problem of conceptualizing race: how can something that is unreal and untrue, something that is a distortion and a mystification, arise from "concrete existence"? According to Ricœur, Marx's theory overcomes this difficulty with class theory, which bridges the gap between false ideas and a true empirical reality. Ideologies are the ruling ideas of the ruling class, which possess the power to impose their false vision on the rest of society. We will return to this "solution" below, after considering the materialist analysis of race in Cox and Miles. For now, however, it can be said that the problem of the relationship between race and reality that confronts race scholars has a precursor in Marx's formulation of the relation between ideology and reality.

Cox: political-economic power as the determinant of race relations

In 1948, Oliver Cromwell Cox published his seminal work *Caste, Class, and Race*.[4] Cox endeavors to break from a dominant trend in the study of race in America – which understood race relations as a matter of caste – and employs a Marxist framework with which he situates race relations within a class-analytical perspective. Distancing himself from biological conceptions of race, he first defines race as one variant of ethnicity based on "physical distinguishability" (the other variant is culture). "When, on the other hand, the ethnics recognize each other physically and use their physical distinction as a basis for the rationale of their interrelationships, their process of adjustment is usually termed race relations or race problems" (Cox 2000: 1). In the absence of a "universally accepted definition of race" Cox argues for a sociological definition of race relations, claiming

The biologist and the physical anthropologist may indeed have considerable difficulty with this, but for the sociologist a race may be thought of as simply any group of people that is generally believed to be, and generally accepted as, a race in any given area of ethnic competition. Here is detail enough, since the sociologist is interested in social interaction. Thus, if a man looks white, although, say in America, he is everywhere called a Negro, he is, then, a Negro American. (Cox 2000: 3)

This commonsense definition of race suffices for Cox, both because he believes sociologists are primarily interested in social interaction and also because he does not believe the definition of race per se is the crucial factor in the constitution of race relations. Cox also rules out three other ways of understanding race relations, as a function of ethnocentrism, racism, and intolerance. The manner in which he rejects "racism" offers the first inkling of the materialist direction of his analysis of race.

Finally, the term "racism" as it has been recently employed in the literature seems to refer to a philosophy of racial antipathy. Studies on the origin of racism involve the study of the development of an ideology, an approach which usually results in the substitution of the history of a system of rationalization for that of a material social fact. (Cox 2000: 5)

Racism, as an ideology or "system of rationalization," is, for Cox, the consequence of "the capitalist exploitation of peoples and its complementary social attitude" (Cox 2000: 5).

---

[4] An abbreviated version of this book (the section on "race") is consulted here (Cox 2000).

The origin of racial antagonism between physically distinct groups is found in the "rise of capitalism and nationalism": "all racial antagonisms can be traced to the policies and attitudes of the leading capitalist people, the white people of Europe and North America" (Cox 2000: 6). Cox describes the slave trade as primarily a matter of beneficial economic relations for European capitalists rather than a matter of racist discourse or the fact of physical difference itself. "This trade did not develop because Indians and Negroes were red and black, or because their cranial capacity averaged a certain number of cubic centimeters; but simply because they were the best workers to be found for the heavy labor in the mines and plantations across the Atlantic." Against the trans-historical view of racial antagonism that was asserted by Robert Park, Cox argues "it was not an abstract, natural, immemorial feeling of mutual antipathy between the groups, but rather a practical exploitative relationship with its socio-attitudinal facilitation" (Cox 2000: 17). Hence, Cox finds that racial ideology and prejudicial attitudes are the products of the ideological imposition of the ruling capitalist class in its effort to "proletarianize" the working classes.

But the fact of crucial significance is that racial exploitation is merely one aspect of the problem of the proletarianization of labor, regardless of the color of the laborer. Hence racial antagonism is essentially political-class conflict. The capitalist exploiter, being opportunistic and practical, will utilize any convenience to keep his labor and other resources freely exploitable. He will devise and employ race prejudice when that becomes convenient. As a matter of fact, the white proletariat of early capitalism had to endure burdens of exploitation quite similar to those which many colored people must bear today. (Cox 2000: 18)

Imperialism is not a sin or "problem of morals," but rather "a problem of production and of competition for markets"; thus relations between imperialists and natives are "race relations: they are definitely not caste relations. They are labor-capital-profits relationships: therefore race relations are proletarian bourgeois relations and hence political-class relations" (Cox 2000: 21). Not only is imperialism and slave labor a political class relation, the controversy over Japanese and Chinese labor in late nineteenth-century America is less a matter of race than a matter of class.

This apparently racial conflict, then, is in fact an extension of the modern political-class conflict. The employer needs labor, cheap labor; he finds this in Asiatic workers and displaces white, more expensive labor with them. White workers then react violently against the Asiatics. (Cox 2000: 103)

When Cox discusses contemporary race relations and race prejudice (circa the 1950s), he again finds a class basis rather than a strictly racial basis for conflict: "Race prejudice in the United States is the socio-attitudinal matrix supporting a calculated and determined effort of a white ruling class to keep some people or peoples of color and their resources exploitable" (Cox 2000: 171).

Thus we see *en nuce* the logic of the materialist analysis of race in Cox's work. Race is a product of the imperialist and capitalist conquest. Racial ideologies and the attendant racial prejudice reflect efforts by "white" Europeans to exploit labor, regardless of ethnicity. Racism is, therefore, a product of class relations, not biologically inherent racial antipathy, a primordial prejudice against the "Other," or "ethnocentrism." Concerning the inadequacy of the concept of ethnocentrism to elucidate the meaning of racism, Cox engages in a critique of Ruth Benedict: "'Racism,' asserted Dr. Benedict, 'is essentially a pretentious way of saying that "I" belong to the Best People ... the formula "I belong to the Elect" has a far longer history than has modern racism'" (Cox 2000: 173). Against this view, Cox argues that all groups exhibit ethnocentrism as a positive aspect of association. The reason ethnocentrism is not a precursor to racism is that it does not involve conflict. The ethnocentrism of racially conscious groups, he writes, "is immediately a function of its solidarity rather than of its racial antagonism. Indeed, the essential fact of ethnocentrism is not so much antagonism as it is a propensity in members of a cultural group to judge and estimate, in terms of their own culture, the cultural traits of persons in other cultures" (Cox 2000: 173). Because ethnocentrism is not a function of class relations, ethnocentrism does not give rise to racism; on the contrary, racial antagonism "includes ethnocentrism." Cox describes a cycle of racial antagonism involving "first, a capitalist need to exploit some people and their resources; then the more or less purposeful development among the masses, the public, of derogatory social attitudes toward that particular group or groups whose exploitation is desired – here the strategy of the capitalist will depend upon the nature of the ethnic situation" (Cox 2000: 175). Racism has a material basis: the opposition of different economic classes and the rationalization (by which Cox means an explanatory justification) of exploitative relations of power by the super-ordinate class. Hence race and racism originate from early capitalist social relations and this origin continues to determine race relations at the time of Cox's writing.

Miles: race, racism, and ideology

Writing in the context of discussions of race in the United Kingdom, Robert Miles has been a fervent critic of the field of "race relations" and the concept of race. One of the clearest statements of his critique is found in an article that lays out his differences with otherwise similar positions taken by scholars working with the Marxist tradition and the Centre for Contemporary Cultural Studies (CCCS). Miles develops his view of a properly Marxist treatment of race that does not fall into the trap of reification. In particular, Miles has honed in on the problem of the "liberal sociology of 'race relations,'" which he identifies as the "reification of 'race' and 'race relations'" (Miles 1984: 218). For Miles such reification arises when race and race relations are attributed an independent (or quasi-independent) empirical status from the relations of production (i.e., economic class relations) and when independent causal consequences are derived from their existence. Hence, he distinguishes between what he calls the "theorists of the radical sociology of 'race relations'" (i.e., putatively Marxist scholars working on race relations and scholarship associated with the CCCS) and Marxism. For example, the radical sociology of race relations, which retains aspects of the reification problematic of the liberal sociology of race relations, is criticized for retaining notions like "the existence of a 'black community' or 'the black masses' which are either conceptually or empirically presented as being 'apart from' or 'outside' the working class" (Miles 1984: 219). The isolation of the explanation of racism from political class relations is a problem from Miles's point of view, and he uses it to illustrate what a more rigorous Marxist perspective would bring to the study of race.[5] Taking the CCCS position that "racism is the primary determinant of the experience and material position of all 'black people' in Britain" as an example, Miles argues

What is actually being claimed here is that the political consciousness and practice of the 'black masses' in Britain is determined, if not solely, then primarily in the political and ideological sphere. No mention is made of their position in production relations. (Miles 1984: 222)

This silence presents difficulties for the radical sociology of race relations, since it does not account for actual divergences between the alleged unity of consciousness and antagonistic practices among "blacks": "My claim against the radical theorists of the sociology of 'race relations', then, is that the class struggle has a greater complexity than they allow,

---

[5] "Rex and Tomlinson, Sivanandan and the CCCS group either pass over or explicitly deny the significance of production relations on the political practice of a capitalist system. In so doing, one finds a silence on the question of the class divisions within the 'black masses' and on the ideological and political continuities, as well as divergences, in the consciousness and practice of various 'fractions' of the British working class" (Miles 1984: 221).

partly because of the differential location of 'black' agents to different sites in production relations and the determinate effects that this has upon political practices" (Miles 1984: 225–226). Miles notes a tendency, in the mid-1980s, for the "'black' petite-bourgeoisie" to "act as an agent of social control over the 'black' revolt" and for "sections of the 'black' working class'" to "engage in common struggle with other fractions of the working class" (Miles 1984: 226).

The missing discussion of production relations also poses a problem for the critique of "ethnic relations" by the radical theorists. According to Miles, although CCCS criticizes "ethnic relations" scholars, both CCCS and ethnic relations attribute autonomy to cultural factors; consequently, the only difference between the two orientations is that ethnic relations fails to acknowledge the impact of "the cultural tradition of resistance to colonialism" (Miles 1984: 227). Otherwise, Miles finds that CCCS is open to the same criticism it aims at ethnic relations, precisely because both emphasize cultural autonomy and overlook production relations.

Miles, accordingly, finds fault with the radical sociology of race's understanding of racism. By missing the class roots of racism, Miles finds a reification of racism in these putatively Marxist critiques. "In order to avoid the reification involved in such a project, racism (as a central component in the process of racialisation) is better grasped in terms of its effects by first establishing the structure of class relations and then examining the means by which persons are allocated to specific positions within these relations" (Miles 1984: 229). Unless racism is conceived against such a class structure, it becomes an independent, that is, reified, phenomenon, analogous to a concept of race that is detached from the relations of production. Thus, Miles articulates the correct perspective on race, race relations, and racism:

The "black masses" are not a "race" which has to be related to class but, rather, are persons whose forms of political struggle can be understood in terms of racialisation within a particular set of production (class) relations. What they become conscious of is an historical question and depends upon both the effects of those economic relations (because they provide the raw materials) and upon political and ideological relations. (Miles 1984: 230)

As with Cox, Miles's Marxist framework puts into question the very idea of race and race relations. His criticism is typical for this framework: (1) it criticizes a liberal (i.e., "bourgeois") form of knowledge of race relations because it detaches "race" from class relations, and (2) it criticizes other putatively radical forms of knowledge of race for also failing to fully relate race (conceived as ideology) to class relations. Miles, however, goes further regarding British critical race theory by asserting that it *legitimates* the idea of race. He advances this argument in various writings, including the 1984 article.

Sivanandan and the CCCS authors retain the ideological notion of "race" in order to endorse a particular form of political action. In so doing, they legitimate the common sense understanding of "race". Although they divest the notion of its negative ascriptions which are part of the hallmark of racism, they nevertheless confirm the racial categorization which is the product of practices by the state and political parties, and within the working class ... Thus, they struggle against racism, but retain and legitimate the idea of "race" for ideological and political reasons. (Miles 1984: 232)[6]

Rather then keeping in place categories which "have no scientific credibility" or creating an opposition between "race" and class, Miles argues "the reproduction of class relations involves the determination of internal and external class boundaries by economic, political and ideological processes" (Miles 1984: 232, 233). The reproduction of class relations is the space in which the ideology of race operates. It follows, therefore, that "the totality of 'black people' in Britain cannot be adequately analysed as a 'race' outside or in opposition to class relations" (Miles 1984: 233).

So far, we have considered the Marxist perspective on race in the example of Miles's internal critique of radical theories of race and race relations. How does Miles's Marxist framework deal with the race as an "object" that is encountered ordinarily within "liberal race relations" theory or in commonsense understandings? In other writings, Miles articulates a perspective on race and racism that defines both as ideological. For instance, in an essay which discusses nationalism in relation to racism, Miles emphasizes both biological (i.e., phenotype)[7] and cultural (i.e., imagined) factors as contributing to the existence of race. However, biology remains an unreal foundation:

Like "nations", "races" too are *imagined*, in the dual sense that they have no real biological foundation and that all those included by the signification can never know each other, and are imagined as *communities* in the sense of a common feeling of fellowship. Moreover, they are also imagined as *limited* in the sense that a boundary is perceived, beyond which lie other "races." (Miles 1987: 26–27)

---

[6] "Thus 'race relations' sociology takes for granted and legitimates commonsense definitions ... In other words, it assumes something that needs to be explained" (Miles 1988: 9).

[7] "Concerning the idea of 'race', the criterion is biological, usually phenotypical (e.g., skin colour) but occasionally genetic" (Miles 1987: 26).

When situated within a Marxist framework, the imagined biological basis of race is linked to "an ideological appeal to create a sense of community which overrides the conflicting interests arising from the social relations of production" (Miles 1987: 27). However, he notes that race is not itself an ideology, but rather is an "ideological construct, to which additional assertions have to be appended in order to refer to the existence of racism and nationalism" (Miles 1987: 31).

   This understanding of the ideological nature of race as it arises from class relations puts into question the standpoint of what he terms liberal race relations theory. Miles defines the problematic as a situation in which phenotypical variation is taken as an explanatory factor.

Historically, and in the contemporary world, people attribute meaning to particular patterns of phenotypical variation and act in accordance with that process of signification. The occurrence of this complex process of cognition and action is not contested. What is contested is the analytical method and concepts employed to understand and explain it. The conventional sociological method is to claim that, as a result of this process, "races" are constituted and thereby come to relate to one another, and that the means and consequences of this fall into regular patterns which can be theorized. Thereafter, and crucially, "race" is transformed into a real phenomenon which has identifiable effects in the social world. "Race" becomes a variable with measurable consequences ... That is, sociologists employ the idea of "race" as an explanans, as an analytical concept identifying a phenomenon with determinant effects. (Miles 1988: 8)

To employ race as an analytical category in this way, Miles argues, is to reify race: "There is no identifiable phenomenon of 'race' which can have such effects on social relations and processes. There is only a process of signification in the course of which the idea of 'race' is employed to interpret the presence and behavior of others" (Miles 1988: 9). Miles acknowledges the reality of phenotypical differences. However, they cannot be the basis of a race concept: "reality of phenotypical variation is usually regarded as an adequate explanation of signification. But not all phenotypical differences are interpreted as evidence for the supposed existence of 'race' ... Therefore, there is an ongoing process of ideological construction and re-construction which required explanation" (Miles 1988: 9). "Race" and "race relations" are, therefore, "an ideological process which occurs in particular circumstances" (Miles 1988: 10). This is not to argue that race relations theory is meaningless, for, as Miles indicates, it arose historically to analyze the problem of racism. However, it is important to understand the "essential relations that underlie the origin of 'race relations' sociology," for, on this basis, "it is possible to employ a more adequate analytical framework within which to locate the process of racialisation" (Miles 1988: 12).

Based on this criticism of the sociology of race relations, the one important concept Miles retains is racism (rather than race or race relations). He justifies this position in the introduction to a book (co-authored with Malcolm Brown) intended to derive a rigorous analytical concept of racism: "We therefore retain tenaciously the conception of racism as an ideology because it represents human beings, and social relations, in a distorted manner while never denying that, qua ideology, racism can be simultaneously deeply embedded in the contemporary *Weltanschauung* and the focus of struggle on the part of those who challenge its hegemony ... Racism distorts human beings and social relations" (Miles and Brown 2003: 9, 10).

In the passages dealing with race and racism, Miles and Brown take what could be called a cognitive position on the inadequacy of the biologically derived race concept and its commonsense, socially derived ideology of racism. Like Marx, they employ the term ideology to indicate distortion and falsity. However, unlike Marx (and Cox), they do not delimit racist ideology exclusively to the dynamics of class conflict. In other words, race and racism are distortions of reality *independent* of their relationship with economic relations. (However, this distortion takes on a particular function and meaning within capitalist relations of production.) This allows Miles and Brown to set racism within different situations and exigencies. Concerning biology, they distinguish between the non-existence of race in scientific terms, the everyday recognition of race, and the association of race with culture. While, from the perspective of the biological and genetic sciences, "'races' do not exist ... in the everyday world, the facts of biological difference are secondary to the meanings that are attributed to them and, indeed, to imagined biological difference" (Miles and Brown 2003: 88). However, in addition to this imagined biological difference, "People differentiated on the basis of the signification of phenotypical features are usually also represented as possessing certain cultural characteristics (such as diet, religious belief, mode of dress, language, etc.)" (Miles and Brown 2003: 89). Hence, Miles and Brown argue that "race" combines "phenotypical and cultural attributes," and this combination is "one moment in the ongoing social construction of reality: 'races' are socially imagined rather than biological realities" (Miles and Brown 2003: 89).

The authors go further, however, by arguing against social scientists who use the concept of race, even within quotation marks ("race"): "Thus, perversely, social scientists have prolonged the life of an idea that should be consigned to the dustbin of analytically useless terms" (Miles and Brown 2003: 90). They prefer, for "reasons of analytical clarity" (Miles and Brown 2003: 100), the concept of racialization to race.

In sum, we use the concept of racialisation to denote a dialectical process by which meaning is attributed to particular biological features of human beings, as a result of which individuals may be assigned to a general category of persons that reproduces itself biologically. This process has a long history in precapitalist and capitalist societies. (Miles and Brown 2003: 102–103)

Racism "presupposes" racialization but is construed as a more general concept. After asserting that racism should be "identified by its ideological content rather than function," Miles and Brown argue, "The distinguishing content of racism as an ideology is, first, its signification of some biological and/or somatic characteristic(s) as the criterion by which populations are identified ... Second, one or more of the groups so identified must be attributed with additional (negatively evaluated) characteristics and/or must be represented as inducing negative consequences for (an)other group(s). Those characteristics or consequences may either be biological or cultural" (Miles and Brown 2003: 103–104).

From race to class: the Marxist contribution to the study of race

One characteristic of racism as ideology, as defined by Miles and Brown, is significant for our purposes.

Therefore, racism can successfully (although mistakenly) make sense of the world and provide a strategy for political action. It follows that, to the extent that racism is grounded in economic and political relations, strategies for eliminating racism should not concentrate on trying *exclusively* to persuade those who articulate racism that they are "wrong", but on changing those particular economic and political relations. (Miles and Brown 2003: 107)

This assertion that racism is less a problem of thought – of ideology in itself – than of practice – the continuation or the transformation of the relations of production – echoes the critical standpoint on ideology that is found in *The German Ideology*. In other words, there is in the analyses of Cox and Miles the claim that there is no *empirical object* that can be called race from a scientific (i.e., non-ideological) standpoint; therefore, any effort to correctly comprehend race as an empirical object is not only bound to fail, it is also bound to reify the idea of race. What needs to be comprehended, however, are the social relations (of class) that give rise to the ideology of race and the practices of racism. Race, racism, and race relations are all features of societies structured by class relations; as entities, they are *nothing* apart from these relations. Race has a reality only in a qualified sense, it has reality (but only as an ideology) in relation to economic relations and the political arrangements that are built upon them.

Based on this typical form of argumentation, the Marxist tradition can rightly be held to be a radical critique of the race concept itself. On the basis of a set of empirical claims and conceptual framings, biological concepts of race are ruled out as legitimate ways to understand race from the beginning; moreover, social concepts of race and racial groups are also held to be ideological (i.e., reified). To the extent that social class relations and identities are *essential*, race and racial identities are *non-essential*. Nonetheless, what remains troubling for Marx's analysis of ideology – how unreal thoughts can exist within a historical materialist perspective in the first place – presents an equally difficult situation for the Marxist analysis of race. Why do groups of individuals understand themselves to belong to "races" and "racial groups" rather than to belong to different fractions of the class order? What explains the grip of commonsense ideas about race and racial categories on the popular imagination and on intellectuals? As we discussed above, Paul Ricœur found that the theory of class allowed historical materialism to answer the question of how ideology – the unreal and the untrue – could arise from a concrete existence whose truth should be faithfully reflected in consciousness. The imposition of the ruling class ideas caused a mystification of reality in the minds of the subordinate classes. However, this solution is premised on the underlying materialist assumption that economic relations are the basis of reality, and that thought *should* correspond directly to this reality. The contradiction between subject and object, between material conditions and the realm of ideas – the starting point for the historical materialist theory of knowledge – is, and must be, overcome and transcended – in short, resolved. Historical materialism is a theory of the unification of these two opposed standpoints: and yet, this unification occurs at the price of the reduction of the *unreal* (ideas) to the *real* (economic relations of production). Miles, more than Cox, allows for an independent manifestation of race in the common sense of ordinary people and in the reification of the bourgeois and radical sociology of race. Nonetheless, this independence is denied in the second move, which brings ideological and reified concepts of race into contact with economic relations.

Could it be possible, however, that race and racial groups are explicable independently of class (as scholars who study race in the context of the United States have argued)? Is the effort of sociologists working in the Marxist tradition to eradicate race as an analytical category inadequate to the *reality* of race itself, a reality that is fundamentally misconstrued by class analysis? We believe the answer to both questions is yes. On the one hand, race exists as a complex of classifications, feelings, and practices that are not directly dependent on the economic situation of groups for their existence. On the other hand, the contradiction between thoughts and social life that needs resolution for historical materialism is better comprehended as the object that emerges *sui generis* from the ideational force of a belief in race. At the same time, the notion of reification does not capture this type of conceptualization of race, for whereas a reified concept of race builds its efficacy out of the concept itself, we have claimed for the idea of race a co-incidence of the idea with a physical reality beyond the idea itself. Here it is possible to utilize Derrida's claim (1978) that linguistic structures lack a center – and therefore must be understood as the play between the center and the structure – to illuminate the nature of an idea that is real and unreal. In its knowledge of this reality Marxist thought, driven to reduce any contradictions, lacks the conceptual wherewithal to apprehend the means by which race comes to exist in all its contradictions.

3   British social anthropology

It is commonly accepted that "doing anthropology" in the United States and in Great Britain does not mean exactly the same thing, neither does it imply the same methodology nor, most fundamentally, the same interests and angles of approach.[1] British anthropology has largely focused on the social – hence its qualification of "social anthropology." While American anthropologists looked at cultural practices, the British were above all interested in actual social relations – which implied looking at social structure, as well as classifying and comparing. The gaze of the social anthropologist, then, is on small things, but it looks beyond, to the "social system" in the background – which is very different from the immersion for its own sake that is characteristic of cultural anthropology. Social anthropologists want to understand the actual social structure, how it works, how it functions; and so the gaze of the anthropologist focuses on the present. Keith Hart, for instance, recalls that during his days as a student in the (very) social anthropology department at Cambridge in the sixties, he "once asked in a supervision, 'Why are the Lele matrilineal?' and was told, 'We ask how, not why. That is evolutionary history. We are only interested in the functional consequences for Lele society that they are matrilineal'" (Hart 2003: 1).

A specific gaze then, both in spatial and temporal terms, clearly distinguishes social anthropology. And this is what is of interest to us in this book: the way in which race and ethnicity came to be conceptualized within social anthropology is highly dependent on its general focus on social dynamics; and it is worth noting, as will become clear in this chapter, that within social anthropology it is ethnicity that comes to be central, while the term race almost disappears; we shall see in which conditions this happened.

---

[1] Although often absent from the curriculum in the United States, British social anthropology has had a tremendous influence on social thought in Great Britain and abroad. Talcott Parsons, who attended Malinowski's seminar at the London School of Economics in 1924–1925 before studying at the University of Heidelberg, was one of the American scholars who brought back British social anthropology's version of functionalism to the United States.

Indeed it is precisely this different gaze of the social anthropologist and its theoretical frame that allowed the possibility for conceptualizing ethnicity as a dynamic, interactive social process of definition and differentiation, thereby enabling a return to a Weberian conception, strangely enough in a "style of thought" characterized by the powerful domination of functionalism and structuralism. Adam Kuper (1975) argues that British social anthropology lasted until the seventies only; we shall not enter this debate. However, we argue that a continuity can be traced from the "canonical" British social anthropology of Malinowski, Radcliffe-Brown, and Evans-Pritchard, which nurtured Edmund Leach, to Fredrik Barth in the late sixties, to the contemporary conceptualization of race and ethnicity, which is illustrated by the work of Thomas Eriksen. This continuity should be understood as an opening of successive doors, starting with the emergence of British social anthropology, which provided a specific point of view on the social world and thereby allowed a grasp of race and ethnicity that differs from the one found in sociology or cultural studies as well as in cultural anthropology. We start with the specific gaze of social anthropology, which we conceive of as a nurturing terrain constructed between, roughly, 1920 and 1940.[2] We pursue this continuity by narrowing down our focus to the specific question of race and ethnicity and providing an analysis of the work of Leach, Barth, and Eriksen.

Social anthropology and the primacy of the social

There is little doubt that British social anthropology represents an intellectual tradition (McDonald 2001: 60), which Kuper characterizes as involving "a set of names, a limited range of ethnographic specialties, a list of central monographs, a characteristic mode of procedure, and a particular series of theoretical problems" (1975: 227). Indeed, this tradition can be traced back to the beginning of the twentieth century and involves a specific approach to the social world marked by Durkheimian sociology and the essential practice of ethnography. Moreover, this tradition is inhabited by iconic figures and their no less iconic field sites and subsequent books: Bronislaw Malinowski's *Argonauts of the Western Pacific* (1922), A. R. Radcliffe-Brown's *The Andaman Islanders* (1922), Edward Evans-Pritchard's *The Nuer* (1940), or Edmund Leach's *Political Systems of Highland Burma* (1954). We shall

---

[2] Of course this is a very limited account: we hope that this will not be interpreted as a simplification. We wish here simply to provide the reader with the necessary context to our further exploration of the contributions of Leach, Barth, and Eriksen.

see in this chapter why, as well as to what extent, we can talk about it as a current of thought of its own; we shall mostly focus on the relationship between theory and practice, which will allow us to delimit British social anthropology's specific view of the social world.

At the beginning of the twentieth century, British anthropology closely followed the development of Durkheim's work.[3] This closeness in thought gradually became more than a sustained attention and interest; one only has to read the 1910 teaching notes of Radcliffe-Brown to see how much of an early influence Durkheim was on him (Stocking 1984a: 113–129)[4]: from the social division of labor to solidarity and cohesion to the profane as being "what is not sacred," one can see why Stocking (1984a: 110) sees there "the beginning of British anthropology's long affair" with the Durkheimian school. This influence is also obvious in the work of Bronislaw Malinowski, the Polish anthropologist who was appointed at the London School of Economics in 1921, following his return from the Trobriand Islands and the publication of his famous *Argonauts of the Western Pacific*.[5] But Malinowski also developed his own approach, which, according to Goody (1995: 37), was characterized by:

(a) The elaboration of "a sort of inventory of the elements of culture,"
(b) A belief in the "wholeness of culture," none of the elements receiving any special emphasis,
(c) The idea of "fieldwork as experimental testing of a theoretical approach."

In Malinowski's view, "culture" was synonymous with tradition and society (Goody 1995: 36); looking at culture implied an inventory of practices ("the elements of culture") through intensive fieldwork, and included the study of the social structure, law, and religion as well as kinship systems or political institutions. Malinowski emphasized the equal importance and necessary interconnectedness of all elements of culture, which together form a whole; there was also the idea that this whole is in some way "larger" than the sum of the parts. Nothing can

[3] See Stocking (1984a, 1984b) for more details on the early reception of Durkheim's work.
[4] It is worth noting that the intimate relationship between British and French social thought was never to be found at this degree between German and French social thought. Durkheim reviewed Tönnies's *Gemeinschaft und Gesellschaft* as early as 1889, and Simmel published a paper in the first volume of the *Année Sociologique*, although Durkheim was not thrilled by his work (see his letter to Mauss of June 1897 in *Lettres à Marcel Mauss*, 1998: 59).
[5] He was appointed as lecturer in 1921, and then to the first chair in social anthropology at LSE in 1927.

be analyzed outside of its context, everything has to be analyzed in relationship to the whole.[6] While this could have led to a better apprehension of the relationship between societies, it was not the case: as McDonald notes, it led instead to "an unfortunate bounding of societies as islands" (2001: 62). Nevertheless, one has to understand the rupture that Malinowski represented in the field of anthropology. His functionalism and his insistence on intensive fieldwork fiercely opposed both evolutionism and diffusionism, which so far had dominated the field. By focusing on the present, Malinowski argued two essential points. First, that "primitive" societies can (and should) be understood like "civilized" ones and therefore in their own terms, in relation to their own context and categories, not to Western ones – hence his insistence on the ultimate goal of understanding "the natives" from their own point of view through immersed fieldwork (Malinowski 1922: 25; see also Radcliffe-Brown 1932). Second, that the social structure should be observed as such, in its actual and present functioning, as opposed to observing it strictly as the result of the past and as a step towards "civilization": the explanation of social structure is to be found in function, not in historical causality.

Malinowski was dominant in British social anthropology until his death in 1942. Evans-Pritchard had estranged himself from his venerable (and tyrannous) professor; after the war, Evans-Pritchard and his close friend Meyer Fortes made the social anthropology department at Oxford more prestigious than the London School of Economics program.[7] And the difficult relationship he had with Malinowski,[8] associated with the appeal of structuralism and the critique of Malinowski's functionalism, brought Evans-Pritchard closer to Radcliffe-Brown. Radcliffe-Brown is usually given credit for the emergence of "structural functionalism" as well as being considered the other founding father of British social anthropology. McDonald offers

---

[6] "[Culture] obviously is the integral whole consisting of implements and consumers' goods, of constitutional charters for the various social groupings, of human ideas and crafts, beliefs and customs. Whether we consider a very simple or primitive culture or an extremely complex and developed one, we are confronted by a vast apparatus, partly material, partly human and partly spiritual, by which man is able to cope with the concrete, specific problems that face him" (Malinowski 1944: 36).

[7] Radcliffe-Brown was appointed at Oxford in 1937 (he had been at the University of Chicago since 1930). Until 1951 (when Fortes left for Cambridge), both Evans-Pritchard and Fortes were there as well – Evans-Pritchard was appointed to the Chair in 1947. For more details see Goody (1995) and Stocking (1998).

[8] "Evans-Pritchard was already in conflict with Malinowski before he met Fortes. The dislike seems to have been instantaneous and mutual" (Goody 1995: 69).

an enlightening metaphor in her comparison of Malinowski and Radcliffe-Brown:

> If *Argonauts* had some literary affinities with Joyce's *Ulysses* ... the analogy for Radcliffe-Brown's approach was the anatomy textbook. Where Malinowski conceptualized society rather as one of the Kula necklaces he wrote about – a chain of one thing leading to another, which could potentially continue round in circles for ever – Radcliffe-Brown was clear that it was a rather mechanically conceived organism. (McDonald 2001: 64)

Radcliffe-Brown, indeed, had embarked upon a more systematic and systemic analysis, which saw society as an integrated body that tends toward equilibrium; each element participates in maintaining this equilibrium and the social order therewith. Whereas Malinowski was concerned with "needs" and how institutions meet them as being the basis of social structure, Radcliffe-Brown was concerned with the social structure itself, and how it functions with the ultimate goal of maintaining equilibrium.[9] His approach, indeed, has often been characterized as heavily influenced by the Durkheimian theoretical frame, as opposed to the "simple" functionalism of Malinowski. Moreover, in quite a structuralist move, he defined social anthropology as "the study that seeks to formulate the general laws that underlie the phenomena of culture" (Radcliffe-Brown 1958 [1923]: 8).[10] The "dry approach" of Radcliffe-Brown was to some extent well married with Malinowski's more sensual approach in the work of Evans-Pritchard: the latter, despite his repeated claims not to be "an intellectual," nonetheless took theory seriously; in *The Nuer* for instance, he asserts that "facts can only be selected and arranged in the light of theory" (1940: 261). The development of his own thought, in simultaneous opposition and connection to both Malinowski and Radcliffe-Brown, is very visible in his work, especially in the early *Witchcraft, Oracles and Magic among the Azande*, which argues that Zande magic is a meaningful social system of knowledge that organizes the world (an argument that prefigures symbolic anthropology).[11] His claim that witchcraft, oracles, and

---

[9] Malinowski distinguished different levels of needs, the most basic of which engendered a much more complex and vast system in order to maintain the social system over time. For instance, the need for food is met by gardening, which in turn necessitates an economic and social organization, which in turn will have to be transmitted to the next generation, etc.

[10] Fortes sees the founding moment of this structuralist turn in Radcliffe-Brown's paper "Patrilineal and Matrilineal Succession," in which he argues for the existence of laws, against the "anomalie" and "deviance" theories then prevalent in American ethnology (the paper was written in 1935, while he was in Chicago; see Stocking [1998: 356–357]).

[11] As found in the work of his student Mary Douglas.

magic, as interdependent elements forming a coherent system, provide a rational explanation of misfortune and thereby order the world in a meaningful and efficient way, represented a fundamental rupture with the Western conceptualization of rationalization, which was to play a central role in the latter's redefinition.[12]

Evans-Pritchard's departure from Radcliffe-Brown's position, however, is not to be found in his switch from function to structure to systems of meaning as much as it is to be found in his overarching view of the anthropological field and his definition of social anthropology. He strongly believed that social anthropology was closer to the humanities than it could (and should) ever be to the natural sciences. And indeed, this is of course linked to the fact that he was interested in meaning, value, and symbolic systems: to him, although the process of ordering the world through rationalization is universal, there is no single rationalization system and therefore no universal law to be found; anthropological inquiry, then, cannot be modeled on natural sciences: it necessarily involves understanding and interpretation, and the adaptation of the anthropologist to a system of values that is different from his or her own. Notwithstanding the crucial difference with the "scientific" view held by Radcliffe-Brown that this move represents, it also led to a major consequence: the possibility of reintroducing historical analysis within social anthropology. Evans-Pritchard, indeed, drew a close resemblance between anthropological and historical inquiry; anthropology, according to him, involves three steps: first, the anthropologist has to understand the society he studies, to "enter" its symbolic system; second, the collected data is the basis of a sociological analysis of social structure; third, the analysis of a particular society's social structure is compared with that of other societies (Evans-Pritchard 1950: 121–122). One can see here the parallel drawn with historical inquiry (although one fundamental difference lies in the way the data is collected) and a strong humanist view of anthropology. But there is also a double move operated by Evans-Pritchard: from Malinowski's isolated islands to the possibility of (and need for) comparison, and from Radcliffe-Brown's present-focused view of social structure to the reintegration of historical processes – and thereby the possibility for explaining social change. As we shall see, this departure from a spatial and temporal vacuum will prove to be absolutely essential in the history of social anthropology.

British social anthropology therefore built an intellectual tradition that involved a specific gaze on the social world. This gaze is influenced by

---

[12] See Habermas's commentary on Evans-Pritchard in *The Theory of Communicative Action*, volume I (1984 [1981]), in particular pages 55–57.

the methodological choices that define the anthropologist's observation of the social world – the intensive fieldwork à la Malinowski, which implies participant observation of an immersed observer over a long period of time – as much as by the theoretical choices that frame this methodology. Indeed, the dialectical relationship that exists between method and theory is particularly well illustrated in the case of British social anthropology.[13] Theory shapes what questions one asks; in the case of British social anthropology, it is undeniable that the unique combination of functionalism and structuralism also gave birth to a set of questions that were absolutely dominant in the field: in particular, the question of the interconnectedness of cultural elements and their contribution to a greater whole, and questions related to systemic organization and its goal of maintaining equilibrium. The lumping together of scholars as different as Malinowski, Radcliffe-Brown, Evans-Pritchard, and Fortes in the same current of thought is both justified and an over-simplification. A current of thought always contains both homogeneity and heterogeneity; in the case of British social anthropology, one can observe in the 1950s strong dissensions within a tradition that, obviously, also shared a no less strong commonality. The latter can best be described as the specificity of the gaze of the social anthropologist, which produced not only a specific angle on the social world (which, as any other, is necessarily selective), but also a way to explain what one sees and the questions one asks about it. This dialectical relationship between the theoretical framework, methodology, and the object, produced what we would call a nurturing terrain, which allowed the focus on the *social* world to be held in a specific way: in a way, British social anthropology "socialized culture," which represented a funda-mental break from evolutionism. This switch is especially visible in the work of Radcliffe-Brown, who almost completely replaced the term "culture" with the terms "social structure" and "social system": culture is fundamentally social, and anthropology therefore has the task of understanding the social system. This nurturing terrain allowed a new apprehension of, and crucial focus on, the interconnectedness of cultural elements and the process quality of social structure, which in turn made possible the work of Edmund Leach in Burma (which represented a significant moment for the further conceptualization of ethnicity). This nurturing terrain, then, should be seen as having allowed subtle but crucial displacements to occur: from cultural content to social process, from origins to laws, from isolated islands to interaction, without

---

[13] Some have gone as far as saying that monographs had become for British social anthropologists only a pretext, a useful vehicle for theory.

forgetting the considerable change that it brought in terms of methodology. These displacements literally made possible a new and original apprehension of race and ethnicity, from the sixties onward.

From Edmund Leach to Fredrik Barth: the dynamism of ethnic groups

A key moment in the conceptualization of race and ethnicity in social anthropology is found with Edmund Leach's monograph on the Kachin, *Political Systems in Highland Burma* (1954); interestingly, this classic in political anthropology also represents the reintroduction of historicity and social change into the field (see in particular 1954: 282–283). While undertaking fieldwork in Burma in the late forties, Leach quickly realized that he was facing a system in which "ethnicity" and "culture" posed many problems to the observer: the region in which he worked was composed of several "ethnic groups" that could not be clearly distinguished in the traditional way, that is, by using cultural content or physical features. Indeed, these ethnic groups might share language, religion, or dressing code (in various combinations), as well as space; their boundaries were also particularly permeable, as individuals could move back and forth between the groups quite easily. Leach acknowledges the difficulty, or even impossibility, of applying the usual method to his field: "A study of Kachin social organisation cannot therefore proceed in the classical manner which treated culture groups as social isolates" (1954: 60) because, in this case, there is no coincidence between one uniform culture and one uniform social system.

Within the somewhat arbitrarily defined area which I called the Kachin Hills Area the population is culturally diverse and the political organisation is structurally diverse. The variations of culture do not fit the variations of structure, nor do the variations of either culture or structure fit consistently with variations in ecological background. (Leach 1954: 63)

Instead of studying the Kachin culture and its social system as a stable, fixed unit, Leach argues that the Kachin Hills area contains one single system composed of three interactive and interdependent subsystems of political and social organization (*Shan*, *Kachin gumsa*, and *Kachin gumlao*) that work as ideal types in the Weberian sense. The Shan, who live in the lowlands, have a highly hierarchical political system, with hereditary princes; the Kachin *gumlao* form is egalitarian and acephalous; finally, the *gumsa* form lies midway between the *Shan* and *gumlao* forms. Hence there is a diachronic and synchronic variation: the social and political organization of Kachin villages might change both over time (tending toward either the *Shan* or *gumlao* pole) and in the present, since individuals might switch from one system to the other. This discovery opened Leach's work to an account of both historical change and the interactive character of "ethnic identity":

I assume that the system of variation as we now observe it has no stability through time. What can be observed now is just a momentary configuration of a totality existing in a state of flux. Yet I agree that in order to describe this totality it is necessary to represent the system as if it were stable and coherent. (Leach 1954: 63)

This represents a major theoretical break: Leach claims that the anthropological "photograph" of social structure is but one in a succession of photographs that, put together, form a movie, that is, a changing, moving, evolving whole. This "photograph of the present," this *instantané*, therefore cannot be considered atemporal; nonetheless, it allows a glimpse at the whole, at the system itself. This view supports the methodological basis of social anthropology while criticizing it: instead of rejecting its present-focused approach, it claims to use it as a heuristic device while acknowledging its limitations (1954: 283–285). The anthropological photograph therefore has to be seen as a highly contextualized social structure, or rather as an instant view of social relations; it opens up the possibility to *reach* the social structure while not claiming to *represent* it in a static way.[14]

Kachin identities, then, are seen as flexible and changing rather than rigid and static; and this leads Leach to challenge the assumption that culture and structure coincide: for him, this coincidence is absent most of the time (1954: 282). This of course challenges the traditional unit of analysis in anthropology, which had so far been the "tribe" or the "clan," and which assumes a stable coincidence between culture and structure: the group "possesses" the culture, and the stabilities of its boundaries remain unquestioned. In the conclusion of his book, Leach asserts that

The ordinary ethnographic conventions as to what constitutes *a* culture or *a* tribe are hopelessly inappropriate ... I would claim that it is largely an academic fiction to suppose that in a "normal" ethnographic situation one ordinarily find "tribes" distributed about the map in orderly fashion with clear-cut boundaries

---

[14] A similar, though different, view is found in the Durkheimian school's insistence on practice and in its conception of methodology as being what allows the scholar to rise out of practice. As social individuals, we are embedded in practice; and practice is the nexus of social structure. However, while social structure is present in social practice, it does not allow itself to be seen readily; as long as we are in practice, social structure is elusive. Here, in the case of Leach, there is this idea that the moment can tell us about structure, without being confounded with it.

between them ... Many such tribes are, in a sense, ethnographic fictions. (1954: 281, 290–291, emphases in original)

It is therefore not only the notion of tribe but also the very "naturalness" of its existence that is challenged by Leach, who goes as far as claiming that the "tribe" unit, homogeneous, stable, and clear-cut, is an ethnographic fiction, an assumption that the anthropologist applies to reality in order to make sense of it. Hence with Leach, the "tribe" becomes a fluctuant and flexible identity that is susceptible to change not only over time, but also in the relationships it is part of within a system. It is *in relation to each other* that the people in the Kachin Hills think about themselves; it is *within a system of social relationships* that the groups are established, modified, and maintained. But Leach goes further. The political fact becomes conceived within a relationship between the actual and the ideal, both by the anthropologist and by the Kachin themselves. The gap between the actual and the ideal is dynamically inhabited by what Leach calls an intellectual process of "as if," which clearly becomes, in the conclusion of *Political Systems*, the heart of his reflection on ethnicity, culture, and the political.

In practical field work situations the anthropologist must always treat the material of observation *as if* it were part of an overall equilibrium, otherwise description becomes almost impossible. All I am asking is that the fictional nature of this equilibrium should be frankly recognized. (Leach 1954: 285, emphasis in original)

This is the way in which Leach offers to solve the problem raised by the "fictional tribe"; indeed, what is left of anthropological descriptive and theoretical aims if culture is a fiction, if no stability exists, and if fluidity is found on both a diachronic and synchronic level? The solution lies in the way in which both the Kachin and the anthropologist think, that is, articulate conceptual categories *as if* there were indeed an equilibrium. Both are aware of a fundamental relationship between "actual behaviour" and "ideal behaviour" (1954: 292). There *is* some order; the order lies within the conceptual realm, in which categories are articulated in a dynamic way, within "the grammar of ritual action" (1954: 101) that is shared (and negotiated) by everyone.

The people may speak different languages, wear different kinds of clothes, live in different kinds of houses, but they understand one another's ritual. Ritual acts are ways of "saying things" about social status, and the "language" in which these things are said is common to the whole Kachin Hills area. (Leach 1954: 279)

Fundamental to Leach's thought, then, is the distinction made between the actual (or the practical) and the ideal (or the conceptual), a distinction that runs throughout *Political Systems of Highland Burma* (see in particular pp. 103–104). This, interestingly, is not the main path followed by subsequent anthropologists who study ethnicity; rather, what they retain from Leach is the inadequacy of stable and fixed categorizations in the analysis of "ethnic groups," the idea that instability can be "built in" at the structural level, and the dynamic character of ethnicity.

Fredrik Barth was one of the anthropologists who stepped through the door opened by Edmund Leach: he asserted that ethnicity is a social process that has to be clearly distinguished from cultural content, which he called the "cultural stuff." The introduction he wrote to his edited volume *Ethnic Groups and Boundaries* (1969) remains a foundational step in anthropological approaches to ethnicity, and this is mainly because of an assertion that completely changed the way in which ethnicity (and therewith, notions such as ethnic group, tribe, culture, or identity) was conceptualized: Barth indeed asserts that *it is not within groups that ethnicity resides, but in between them*; in other words, ethnicity is a relational process situated within social interactions. Barth starts his argument with the traditional anthropological assumption that "there are discrete groups of people, i.e. ethnic units, to correspond to each culture" (1969: 9), an assumption that he wishes to demonstrate as being inadequate (1969: 9) as well as producing unwanted theoretical consequences by rendering ethnicity and ethnic groups impossible to analyze. In particular, Barth has in mind phenomena that appear puzzling when one starts with the assumption that culture and ethnic groups coincide in a stable and clear-cut way: if this were the case, how can we explain that ethnic boundaries are maintained in situations of cross-cultural contact and of ethnic membership flows? The keyword in Barth's approach to ethnicity is *boundary*: ethnic boundaries, rather than the ethnic group, are meaningful in the analysis of ethnicity.

First, we give primary emphasis to the fact that ethnic groups are categories of ascription and identification by the actors themselves ... Second ... we attempt to explore the different processes that seem to be involved in generating and maintaining ethnic groups. Third ... we shift the focus of investigation from internal constitution and history of separate groups to ethnic boundaries and boundary maintenance. (Barth 1969: 10)

These emphases represent a tremendous change in the anthropological conceptualization of ethnicity, because they treat ethnicity as a *process* rather than as a *content*. Barth rejects not only the importance of culture – as a cultural content that is possessed by the groups in a stable way. He also shifts the causality relationship between culture and ethnicity: instead of defining, or producing, the ethnic group, the culture of the group comes into play as a result of ethnic group organization (1969: 11). The fundamental shift is made from the cultural to the social: what Barth calls "the cultural stuff" (1969: 15) serves only as a marker that functions within the definition, delimitation, and maintenance of ethnic boundaries.

> Some cultural features are used by the actors as signals and emblems of differences, others are ignored, and in some relationships radical differences are played down and denied ... The critical focus of investigation ... becomes the ethnic *boundary* that defines the group, not the cultural stuff that it encloses. (Barth 1969: 14–15)

In other words, culture is used dynamically to produce sameness or difference in the space that exists between ethnic groups. Within the group, sameness is produced, but it is produced only in relationship to another group. Hence ethnicity is not defined by the cultural elements that are enclosed within the group: it involves the cultural traits that function in between the two groups, traits that are used in the construction and maintenance of the symbolic boundaries between the two groups. One can see here the connection with Edmund Leach's criticism of pre-war anthropology: where Leach speaks of "anthropological butterfly collectors" (1966: 68–69), Barth asserts that the assumption that culture and ethnicity coincide has as an unwanted consequence that the differences between groups become "differences in trait inventories" (1969: 12). Indeed, notwithstanding deep differences between them, both Leach and Barth place an emphasis on social processes, and on interactions within a social system. What matters is not the cultural trait in itself, but the way in which it is played and displayed (to remain in the register of the "game" evoked by Barth) within a sphere of social interactions in which groups define themselves in an active manner. In Barth, anthropology is wholly conceived as the study of the social; culture does not disappear, but it is of secondary interest, and comes into play only insofar as it is part of social relationships; within this frame, ethnicity is about *culture made socially significant*, it is not about cultural traits. Hence the ethnic group is not a homogeneous, stable, and clear-cut cultural unit: Barth switches from the static "tribe," which was dear to the early anthropological tradition, to the ethnic group as "a form of social organization" (1969: 13).

The early interrogations of the notion of "ethnic group" posed by Leach in *Political Systems of Highland Burma* and the subsequent publication of Barth's *Ethnic Groups and Boundaries* have spurred a very dynamic reflection on ethnicity in the field of social anthropology in the past three decades. Barth's short introduction, in this sense, really revolutionized the field: scholars then embarked on numerous studies of the dynamism of ethnic groups and the active and moving definition and maintenance of their boundaries, and they also started to reflect on ethnicity as a symbolic process; they looked at the way groups actively *build* difference and sameness, *select* cultural traits that matter in a given situation, and *interact* within themselves and without. At the turn of the twenty-first century, the view of ethnicity as a relational process of social interaction is widely accepted within social anthropology; it has also challenged broader anthropological concepts, in particular culture and social units, and the assumption that there is a one-to-one correspondence between culture and ethnicity: most social anthropologists today, although their work might not deal with ethnicity per se, do not take their field for granted, and ask a series of questions. How is the group defined? How does the group define itself? Does the definition of the anthropologist coincide with the self-definition of the group, and with the definitions imposed upon it by its neighbors? Stability has ceased to be taken for granted, and the symbolic processes that are a part of ethnic identity are being given more and more attention. This was made possible, to a great extent, by Barth's assertion that ethnic groups are social, not cultural units; that ethnic identity is above all a question of boundaries negotiated between the groups; and finally that the content enclosed by these boundaries (the "cultural stuff") matters only insofar as it is used within the process of boundary erection and maintenance.

Contemporary conceptualizations: Thomas Eriksen

Since the publication of Barth's edited volume, numerous anthropological studies have focused on ethnicity, and its intersections with various social processes such as nationalism, religion, or music.[15] Ethnicity indeed has become a widely used term, and one of the major concepts in social anthropology. Among this great number of studies, the work of one anthropologist stands out not only because of its quality but also its resilience: Thomas Eriksen, a social anthropologist from the University of Oslo, has published extensively on ethnicity since the beginning of the nineties.[16] Eriksen's work explicitly claims an anthropological approach to

---

[15] See for instance Jenkins (1997), Yelvington (1995), and Anthony Cohen (1985). Earlier, the work of Abner Cohen (1969, 1981) also marked the conceptualization of the intersections between ethnicity and politics.

[16] See Eriksen (1992, 1993, 1998).

ethnicity (Eriksen 1993: 1–2). Both terms of this definition are important here, because they lay out the possibilities and the limits of Eriksen's work: there is a focus on the "ethnic phenomenon" using the conceptual and methodological tools of social anthropology. And indeed race is largely absent from Eriksen's work, due to his dismissal of both race's empirical reality and conceptual utility.

Ideas of "race" may or may not form part of ethnic ideologies, and their presence or absence does not generally seem to be a decisive factor in interethnic relations ... Race or skin colour as such is not the decisive variable in every society. (Eriksen 1993: 6)

On the basis of fieldwork in Trinidad and Mauritius, Eriksen indeed shows that the same phenomenon can be *called* racial somewhere but not elsewhere (1993: 6; see also 1992 and 1998); and it is here that the overarching frame of his work appears clearly: through anthropological fieldwork, Eriksen is more interested in what people do, think and say, than in the identification and definition of social processes imposed on individuals and groups. Hence, there is no conceptual possibility of defining race if the concept appears to be variable, depending on its use and signification in different societies. One can feel here not only the inscription of his thinking into the social anthropological tradition, but also the influence of Fredrik Barth: what matters is what happens within social interactions, at the (micro) level of both practical use and ideal conceptualization. In other words, Eriksen offers one possible solution to the empirical puzzle offered by race and ethnicity: "race," "community," "religion," and "color" are different forms, different modalities taken by the ethnic phenomenon in different societies. Therefore, the multiplicity of forms evidenced in empirical reality actually refers to one single phenomenon, which Eriksen chooses to call "ethnicity." It is ethnicity that can, and should, be conceptualized. Eriksen does so by using the framework put forth by Barth (1969), placing the utmost importance on the *in between* character of any ethnic relationship:

For ethnicity to come about, the groups must have a minimum of contact with each other, and they must entertain ideas of each other as being culturally different from themselves. If these conditions are not fulfilled, there is no ethnicity, for ethnicity is essentially an aspect of a relationship, not a property of a group. (Eriksen 1993: 12)

Hence ethnicity is not about culture or cultural difference per se; it is about the *use* of culture *within* social interactions. There is a very clear opposition to static views of ethnicity as being some sort of differentiation made between cultural contents. Following Barth, ethnicity is a question of *between*, not a question of *inside*. And this conceptual position is both cause and consequence of a more general concept of culture found within social anthropology: in a way, it is almost as if culture did not matter, although its existence is not denied. Culture is significant only to the extent that it is dynamically used within social interactions (Eriksen 1993: 58). The pertinence of this approach is justified on two very different levels. First and foremost, the secondary presence of culture – almost like a shadow in the background, present and seen and yet not really defined or cared for – is legitimate because culture is in no way the primary object of study. The primary object is the *social world*. Hence it seems rational to look at this shadowy culture *only to the extent that it enters the life of the social world*. Second, the secondary presence of culture in the specific conceptualization of the ethnic phenomenon is made legitimate by the fact that it offers a solution to what seemed to be a conceptual dead-end. The "content" approach (exemplified in very different ways by currents of thought such as racial science, American racial relations, or early anthropology) is unsatisfying not only because it is conceptually inadequate but also because it contradicts the empirical evidence gathered in the field.

In other words, ethnicity is neither a conflict of cultures nor a clash of civilizations. It is the use, in social interactions, of various and changing cultural elements. Hence it is not culture, or cultural difference, that produces ethnicity; but culture might become part of a social relationship at a certain time and in a specific situation, a relationship which is called "ethnic." As Eriksen points out, "Ethnicity is thus constituted through social contact" (1993: 19). At this point, we touch upon the question of tradition and transmission. The main merit of the social anthropological conceptualization of ethnicity, indeed, is that it is closely aligned with the empirical reality observed through fieldwork and provides a way to understand this reality (a reality found to be multiple, variable, changing, and, all in all, quite puzzling). Following Barth, taking the use of culture, as opposed to its inherent content, as a point of departure allows for an understanding of the dynamism found in empirical reality. The French national anthem provides an illustrative example. In April 1792 Rouget de Lisle, an officer, composed the song following the French declaration of war on Austria; a few months later, in August, it was sung during the insurrection at the Tuileries, by citizens from Marseille; it then took its current name *La Marseillaise*. In 1795, it was declared national anthem by the Republic. Under the Empire and Restauration, the song was banned, but was claimed again during the Revolution of 1830; finally, in 1887, the song became the national anthem once more, and still is today. Hence the history of the song points to its interpretation as the symbol of the republican ideals and, therefore, of the Republic; but in the second half of the twentieth century, this revolutionary song was progressively appropriated by the extreme right and came to symbolize nationalism and racism. But after the victory of the French soccer team in the 1998 World Cup, it was sung by all, and the media widely relayed this "reappropriation," through which the national anthem and the French flag were becoming the (re)new(ed) symbol for a nation of citizens of all colors and creeds, in the image of its national soccer team. One sees clearly here that it is not the song itself that matters, but its changing meanings and the way it is made significant within social relationships: a song written as the King of France declared war on Austria successively became the symbol of the French Revolution, of the young revolutionary Republic, and of the French Republic, before being associated with the extreme right and finally re-claimed by a cosmopolitan France, despised by the extreme right. How can the same object come to symbolize such different, and sometimes even opposed, political and social views? Precisely because "culture" does not statically belong to a group, but rather works dynamically through the meaningful use of which it is the object.[17]

Hence, for Eriksen, there is no systematic coincidence between ethnicity and culture. Ethnicity is a way in which culture is made a part of social interactions (1993: 58). Eriksen's definition of ethnicity stresses the relational and situational characteristics of ethnicity. It is at this point fruitful to mention Richard Jenkins, whose book *Rethinking Ethnicity* (1997) is an elaborate attempt at further conceptualizing ethnicity in the aftermath of Barth's *Ethnic Groups and Boundaries*. Here too there is an emphasis on ethnicity as a relational process; but more interestingly Jenkins also tends toward making ethnicity a modality of the broader concept of social identity (the latter being the subject of another of his books, *Social Identity* [1996]). The same idea is found at the end of Eriksen's book, when he wonders:

Is it still analytically fruitful to think about the social world in terms of ethnicity? Perhaps a wider term, such as "social identity", would be more true to the flux and complexity of social processes, and would allow us to study group formation and alignments along a greater variety of axes than a single-minded focus on "ethnicity" would. (Eriksen 1993: 173)

---

[17] In 2007, incidentally, the national anthem was part of the political program of the socialist candidate Ms Royal: she wanted it to be sung in French schools, and this precisely to "reclaim" its Republican character. What the national anthem stands for, indeed, is a highly contested element of French political life, as the very short history presented here has shown.

And indeed the way in which ethnicity has been conceptualized within social anthropology permits it to be seen as one modality of social identity, or even as social identity itself. Indeed, if we take the definition proposed by Eriksen (or Jenkins), a certain number of phenomena can fall under the ethnic category. For instance, Harvard alumni have all shared a collective experience during their studies, which was clearly delimited both in physical space (within the Harvard campus) and in symbolic space (from tangible markers such as school gear to symbolic markers such as language); they are part of a group with clearly and exclusively delimited boundaries (not everyone is, or can be, a Harvard alumnus); they belong to a network formed by all Harvard alumni, which might offer them support at the professional or individual level; their belonging gives them exclusive privileges not accorded to outsiders; they claim this belonging in a positive way ("we are all from Harvard") and in a negative way ("we are not like Princeton or Columbia alumni"). Hence a series of questions arise. Does this mean that "Harvard" is an ethnic group? Is not culture, in this case, made significant within social interaction? And further, are not the interests of the group related as much to politics and economics as they are to identity? In a similar fashion, Abner Cohen has asserted that London stockbrokers can be said to be an ethnic group (1974).

Hence, while providing the anthropologist with a pertinent conceptual tool grounded in empirical reality, the social anthropological theorization of ethnicity, which has tended to evacuate "race" and retain "ethnicity," also implies a theoretical problem akin to dissolution: race becomes a modality of ethnicity, and ethnicity a modality of social identity.[18] And needless to say, "social identity" is a vague concept that suffers from its broadness.

---

[18] Anthropologist Peter Wade (whom we discuss at various points) works explicitly on race, and in doing so distinguishes himself from the mass of social anthropologists who work on ethnicity and practically ignore the concept of race.

4   British cultural studies

We cannot end our examination of various conceptualizations of race without including British cultural studies, which here will be synonymous with the so-called "Birmingham School." Indeed, here is a school of thought that has made race, racism, and post-colonialism the central features of its inquiry – coupled with class. Its unique combination of Marxist theory, post-structuralism, and political engagement have led the Birmingham School to make a distinctive contribution to social theories of race and ethnicity, which we shall illustrate with the work of Stuart Hall and Paul Gilroy.[1]

The Centre for Contemporary Cultural Studies (CCCS) was opened in 1964 at the University of Birmingham; after 1968, under the leadership of Stuart Hall, it quickly became the center of the emerging cultural studies field. Hall was to stay almost ten years at the CCCS; along with his colleagues and students, he revolutionized the new field by theorizing and practicing a new social science: fundamentally interdisciplinary, opposed to what was at the time a very static and empiricist British sociology, the Birmingham School was also practically engaged and oriented toward social change in a concrete way. Most of the important figures in the development of the CCCS – such as Richard Hoggart, Raymond Williams, and Stuart Hall – were active in leftist politics and in particular in the New Left. Hence the focus of the work at the center was not "culture" but rather "cultural politics," that is, the intersections between culture and politics, particularly in relationship to popular culture and the media.

As Hall has pointed out, cultural studies as a field is difficult to define. It should not be forgotten that Hall was educated as a sociologist; and the creation of cultural studies was precisely aimed at filling a gap left by British sociology in the sixties: a very monolithic, static, empirical

---

[1] Scholars who have either studied at or been a part of the CCCS include Richard Hoggart, Raymond Williams, Stuart Hall, Paul Gilroy, Angela McRobbie, Dick Hebdige, David Morley, and Paul Willis.

sociology. One can surely see cultural studies as answering a desire for dynamism, freedom, and innovation: the idea was not only to look at culture in its own right, it was also to cross disciplinary boundaries and engage the discipline in concrete reality.

It might also be helpful, since the focus of the preceding chapter was social anthropology, to situate cultural studies negatively, by using the contrast it offers with anthropology. The most obvious distinction lies in the focus of the field: while social anthropology is interested in culture only insofar as it plays a role within the social realm, cultural studies look at culture in itself and for itself. And the definition of culture given by Stuart Hall says a lot not only about the object of inquiry, but also about the angle chosen to look at it:

By culture ... I mean the actual, grounded terrain of practices, representations, languages and customs of any specific historical society. I also mean the contradictory forms of "common sense" which have taken root in and helped to shape popular life. (Hall 1985: 439)

Hence the different way in which social anthropology and cultural studies conceive of culture is apparent – for the social anthropologist, the "grounded terrain" is eminently social; there does not exist any practice or representation that lives outside the social realm. This is also the case for cultural studies, which views culture as a social phenomenon. But instead of relegating culture to the background as does social anthropology (which places social interaction in the foreground), cultural studies makes it the central focus, and then – and only then – is culture's social character brought into the analytical frame. A second difference is the almost exclusive emphasis on power that is found in British cultural studies. Rather than a "social culture," it is a "political culture" that is the focus. Furthermore, culture is seen as fundamentally dynamic; it is a "changing same" (Gilroy 1991b) that inhabits a constantly changing space of construction:

Culture is a production. It has its raw materials, its resources, its "works-of-production." It depends on a knowledge of tradition as "the changing same" and an effective set of genealogies. But what this "detour through its pasts" does is to enable us, through culture, to produce ourselves anew, as new kinds of subjects. It is therefore not a question of what our traditions make of us as much as what we make of our traditions. Paradoxically, our cultural identities, in any finished form, lie ahead of us. We are always in the process of cultural formation. Culture is not a matter of ontology, of being, but of becoming. (Hall 1999: 16)

Hence both cultural studies and social anthropology depart from the fixed notion of the "tribe," of the "ethnic group," from a view of culture as an immutable entity. In the course of this chapter we shall see, however, how this departure was made in different terms in the case of cultural studies, and how it led the field to different consequences regarding the conceptualization of ethnicity and race.

Interestingly, the intellectual evolution of the CCCS, in particular the angle it used to look at culture, is reflected in the way in which ethnicity has been conceptualized over the years. From the use of Marxist theory – especially Antonio Gramsci, who proved to be extremely influential in the work of Stuart Hall – in the seventies and early eighties to a gradually more "diaspora-focused" apprehension of ethnicity in the work of Hall and Gilroy, one indeed can observe the shifts operating within the broader field of cultural studies.

From Gramsci to new ethnicities

Hall entered the conceptualization of ethnicity within a Marxist framework that gave a central place to the writings of Gramsci (as well as, to a lesser extent, the work of Louis Althusser and Étienne Balibar). What Hall found in Gramsci was a Marxist theoretical approach that stressed the importance of the superstructure (i.e., the realm of ideas, values, and beliefs), which was seen as independent, at least to some extent, from the economic base of society (i.e., the mode and relations of economic production). Hence, Gramsci's emphasis on the role played by cultural hegemony in the reproduction of a capitalist system and its social relations offered Hall a means to avoid reductionism (i.e., the reduction of culture to the terms of the economic base); it thereby also allowed cultural studies to exist within a Marxist framework.

Inserting a Marxist framework within the very foundation of British cultural studies – what Hall called the "break into a complex Marxism" (1980a: 25, 26) – was an enterprise of utmost importance for the CCCS in the seventies; the keyword of the works produced then was indeed ideology.[2] By using Gramsci and reinterpreting Marx, in conjunction with post-structuralist scholars such as Foucault, the CCCS produced an extensive conceptualization of ideology, which included Hall's very famous piece "Encoding/Decoding" (1980b) as well as numerous articles on television and Marxist theory. Hence Hall was able to develop a Marxist approach that not only justified the focus on culture, but also allowed a new analysis of cultural politics in British society. Hall used Gramsci's notion of hegemony to develop a framework that could

---

[2] A collective volume was published in the Working Papers series of the CCCS in 1977: *On Ideology* (London: Hutchinson/CCCS, 1978).

situate ethnicity, ethnic identity, and racism upon a chessboard on which culture becomes dynamic and inserted within politics; this approach is summarized in the article "Gramsci's relevance for the study of race and ethnicity" (1985), in which he applies Gramsci's ideas to the notion of ethnicity.

Of course, this new Marxism had to address extensively the relationship between race and class. As we discussed in the second chapter, this has been a major question within Marxist thought that was usually answered by showing that what appears at first to be a "racial" or "ethnic" situation is actually a class-based situation; race and ethnicity are ideological illusions (among others) that hide the reality of class conflict. British cultural studies, on the other hand, showed that representations (hence the sphere of the ideological) matter in themselves, and that analysis has to take this into account. In other words, it is not simply a question of positionality within the system of production, hence an economic question: there is something else, there is the fact that representations themselves, symbolic processes, are inherent to power and domination. Hall's insistence on historicity is linked to this latter point: it is precisely in the historical configuration of one specific situation that one can situate representations. For this reason, a deterministic Marxism, which focuses its analysis solely on the position towards the means of production, has to be abandoned. Instead, each situation must be seen as a specific configuration, like a game board on which class and representations intersect without superseding each other. These representations include all kinds of "culture," for instance ethnicity, gender, working-class culture, or subcultures. Hence the symbolic is not a simple consequence of one's economic position; it is a second layer, a texture that cannot be ignored.

The way in which Hall conceptualizes ethnicity until the mid-eighties obeys different exigencies, all of which can be answered with the aid of Gramsci. There is first the need to justify the exclusive focus on culture claimed by the emerging field of cultural studies, and this is made possible with the use of "cultural Marxism." Second, culture is fundamentally viewed as a symbolic process – in which the keyword is "representation"; here again, Hall finds assistance in Gramsci. Third, this symbolic process is eminently political; cultural politics are a field of battle between hegemonic ideologies and cultures of resistance, and there Gramsci's notions of hegemony and counter-hegemony and his metaphor of the "war of position" (i.e., the struggle waged on the terrain of the institutions of civil society by a counter-hegemonic "historical bloc") provide Hall with the most fertile framework.

This foundational view of representation and ideology, strongly grounded in Marxist thought, gradually led to Hall's interest in "identities." We argue that there is no break between a Marxist and a non-Marxist period, but rather a shift that allowed Hall to articulate both the dynamism of fluid identities and structural constraints. Hence it is not as if Hall had been Marxist and later on became "something else." This articulation, as Floya Anthias argues, might well be "the very strength of his position" (1998: 560). During the eighties, he published more and more on the question of "black cultural politics" in Great Britain, and this led him to address the issue of diaspora and diasporic processes as well as "ethnicity," "black identities," and "Britishness." In these writings, Hall stressed the constructed character of color, thereby dismissing "race":

What is at issue here is ... the recognition that "black" is essentially a politically and culturally *constructed* category, which cannot be grounded in a set of fixed trans-cultural or transcendental racial categories and which therefore has no guarantees in nature. (Hall 1989: 443)

Hall argues against the "natural" character of race; "black" is a signifier, and hence is inserted within a discourse, not within a "natural guarantee." From this point of departure, Hall argues for the reconstruction of the concepts of race and ethnicity in a way that departs from essentialism, which can be seen as the major project of British cultural studies as a whole. Hall proposes to abandon the term "race," which wrongly naturalizes a discursive category, and to adopt the term "ethnicity," which grasps the constructed character of a relational and contextualized signifier:

If the black subject and black experience are not stabilized by Nature or by some other essential guarantee, then it must be the case that they are constructed historically, culturally, politically – and the concept which refers to this is "ethnicity". The term "ethnicity" acknowledges the place of history, language and culture in the construction of subjectivity and identity, as well as the fact that all discourse is placed, positioned, situated, and all knowledge is contextual. Representation is possible, only because enunciation is always produced within codes that have a history, a position within the discursive formation of a particular place and time. (Hall 1989: 446)

As we have seen in the preceding chapter, the abandonment of the term "race" and the adoption of "ethnicity" as a working concept also occurred within social anthropology. Hall calls for a reconceptualization of ethnicity in a manner that radically de-essentializes it; this means "we will have to re-theorize the concept of *difference*" (1989: 446). Ethnicity is constructed; it is dynamic, changing, unfixed, and contingent upon both the historical context and the individual dimension of experience. This formulation also implies the recognition of the *positive value* of ethnic identity:

What is involved is the splitting of the notion of ethnicity between, on the one hand the dominant notion which connects it to nation and "race" and on the other hand what I think is the beginning of a positive conception of the ethnicity of the margins, of the periphery. That is to say, a recognition that we all speak from a particular place, out of a particular history, out of a particular experience, a particular culture, without being contained by that position. (Hall 1989: 447)

What Hall articulates is the fundamental problem posed to any conceptualization of ethnicity as well as the anti-racist struggle, in which British cultural studies were actively involved: how can one deconstruct a concept ("race" or "ethnicity") based on difference without indeed negating difference? How can one fight racism while recognizing difference? The solution offered by Hall is to make a value judgment upon ethnicity – by de-essentializing it, Hall also makes available a way to conceive of "ethnic identity" as something that is not necessarily negative: to a negative (racist) conception of ethnicity, Hall opposes a positive conception. By arguing that ethnicity is constructed, he also argues that it is historically contextualized; most importantly, he argues that ethnicity can be seen as a force of resistance within the struggle for power. Within the configuration of contemporary British society, articulated around colonialism and capitalist hegemony, Hall views "new" ethnic identities as subversive and counter-hegemonic. The most important passage in the above quote is the last sentence: here is found the quintessence of Hall's thinking. We are all different, each of us is unique and particular – this is ethnic identity. But he adds to this "without being contained by that position"; this latter point represents Hall's effort to avoid any essentialism. Here one sees clearly the difficulty of his task, and the way in which he attempts to solve the problem: a positive ethnic identity and anti-essentialism can be combined, articulated in a way that allows the subject to simultaneously claim his or her difference without being *contained* by it.

It is precisely this difficult articulation between claiming difference and de-essentializing it, accompanied by the politically engaged character of British cultural studies, which led Stuart Hall towards the notion of diaspora. We catch a glimpse of it at the end of "New ethnicities" (1989), in which Hall introduces the term "diaspora-ization" as a response to a series of "black" films produced in Britain in the 1980s (among them *My Beautiful Laundrette*).

The final point which I think is entailed in this new politics of representation has to do with an awareness of the black experience as a *diaspora* experience, and the consequences which this carries for the process of unsettling, recombination, hybridization and "cut-and-mix" – in short, the process of cultural *diasporaization* which it implies. (Hall 1989: 447)

Hall is trying to show that something has changed or is changing in the "politics of representation"; if these "new ethnicities" are unsettled, unfixed, and still claimed and *to be claimed*, it is because they have to do with a "diaspora experience." Hall uses the reggae term "cut-and-mix," which refers to the process of cutting, erasing, and keeping, and then remixing, which originally belongs to the vocabulary of reggae sound-systems.[3] Hence to him, ethnicity is a process of selection, which depends on the situation and specific moment in both individual and collective life; it is a dynamic process, eminently political, able to simultaneously claim and disclaim, by which individuals can be both on the inside and on the outside. Hall argues for the positive possibilities opened by these new, diasporic ethnicities: to be Briton and yet be different; to be from elsewhere and still be from here; to combine in multiple ways the multifaceted possibilities of "Britishness." This moment in Hall's conceptualization of ethnicity is crucial, and what is interesting in its genealogy is that it springs from his interest in "black popular culture." When looking at "black cultural repertoires" (1992: 471), Hall argues that:

There are no pure forms at all ... Always these forms are impure, to some degree hybridized from a vernacular base ... They are not the recovery of something pure that we can, at last, live by. In what Kobena Mercer calls the necessity for a diaspora aesthetic, we are obliged to acknowledge they are what the modern is. (Hall 1992: 471)

Thus it is by looking at the diasporic character of "black popular culture" that Hall constructs a view of ethnicity that emphasizes the simultaneity of dynamic identifications within a view of cultural politics largely inherited from Gramsci – that is, in terms of a struggle against hegemony in which the latter is never complete, never stable.

Blacks in the British diaspora must ... refuse the binary black *or* British. They must refuse it because the "or" remains the site of *constant contestation* when the aim of the struggle must be, instead, to replace the "or" with the potentiality of an "and". That is the logic of coupling rather than the logic of opposition. You can be black *and* British ... "Black" ... is not a category of essence, and, hence,

---

[3] This term was used by Dick Hebdige (1987) a few years earlier as the title of his book on reggae music: *Cut'n'Mix: Culture, Identity and Caribbean Music*.

this way of understanding the floating signifier in black popular culture will not do. (Hall 1992: 472, 473)

Diasporized identities – Hall goes even further, referring to identities that have been "twice diasporized": once from Africa to the Caribbean, and a second time from the Caribbean to Great Britain. This process to which "black popular culture" has been subjected makes it fluid by nature; it makes it multiple, dynamic, multi-sited. Moreover, Hall argues for the necessity of this process, for its *positive value*. There is something in these "diasporized ethnicities" that makes them not only archetypical of modernity (Hall 1992: 471) but also valuable within the struggle against capitalist hegemony. Indeed, the very nature of diasporic identities makes them subversive: they come from the margins, from the dominated positions of the colonized, and the "logic of coupling" more than one identity that they imply allows them to destabilize cultural hegemony almost inherently.

Diaspora against race

Hall developed the notion of diaspora at a conference in 1998,[4] at which he described the diasporic articulation between ethnicity and modernity. Hall argues that there is a new dimension of diaspora, which is archetypically found in "Caribbean culture": his analysis, which refers to Derrida's notion of *différance* (Hall 1999: 7), shows that the Caribbean diaspora does not function within a closed binary between two terms; in other words, it is fluid, syncretic, creolized; it allows multiple passages within a multifaceted identity, instead of a closure based on a static binary of difference. Hall uses the term "impurity" again and again to define this new diaspora; against an old diasporic identity based on purity (and here the chief case would be the Jewish diaspora) is opposed a new diasporic identity based on impurity.[5]

Caribbean culture is essentially driven by a diasporic aesthetic. In anthropological terms, its cultures are irretrievably "impure". This impurity, so often constructed as a burden and loss, is itself a necessary condition of their modernity. (Hall 1999: 8)

One sees clearly here the outcome of Hall's new analysis of the Caribbean diaspora: to construct impurity as a positive quality, as an adequation to

---

[4] Lecture given at the fiftieth anniversary of the University of the West Indies, Cave Hill campus, Barbados, 1998. Published as "Thinking the diaspora: home-thoughts from abroad" in *Small Axe*, 1999.

[5] There is a very interesting parallel to make here with Irene Gedalof's book *Against Purity: Rethinking Identity with Indian and Western Feminisms* (2000).

modernity, as a cultural asset – as opposed to its traditional construction as a burden and a loss. The inadequacy of the nation-state model in the analysis of the Caribbean diaspora, as much as in the political practice it can develop, leads Hall to emphasize that "this diasporic perspective on culture [is] subversive of traditional nation-oriented cultural models" (1999: 10). Hence Caribbean culture becomes a positive, fluid, diasporic position that is subversive of both the nation-state and cultural essentialism. The conclusion of Hall's lecture leaves no doubt:

This is the path of "diaspora", which is the pathway of a modern people and a modern culture. (Hall 1999: 18)

By the end of the nineties, Hall was therefore arguing that the diasporic process was inherent to ethnicity in modernity; and not only were these "new ethnicities" adapted to the modern world, they were seen as a positive, subversive alternative to the essentialism that had so far accompanied ethnicity and its role in cultural politics. It is important to understand here that Hall's theory constantly plays on two levels of inquiry: a conceptual level, at which he is constructing a theoretical concept, and a practical level, at which he is examining the concrete possibilities and limits of ethnicity within cultural politics. In other words, Hall is operating both at the level of the issues posed by an essentialized concept and at the level of the concrete consequences of this concept in everyday life. It is not only about what ethnicity is; it is also about what ethnicity should be. This simultaneity of the conceptual and practical levels is particularly obvious in the work of Paul Gilroy.

Since the 1980s, Gilroy's work has challenged the concept of race through an examination of terms like "ethnicity," "culture," "authenticity," and "tradition." At the root of this work lies Gilroy's interest in music and, more specifically, in "black music." What is "black music"? What makes its authenticity? How is it played and displayed in relationship with the identity of the group? These questions concerning culture and race are a red thread running through Gilroy's book *The Black Atlantic* (1992), in which he uses the metaphor of a ship to show that "black culture" has to be conceptualized around the notion of passage; this choice refers as much to the ship (in general) as to the slave ship, and therefore has the advantage of being meaningful both on the general level of modernity and on the particular level of "black culture" (1992: 4, 17). The Atlantic becomes this dynamic and multifaceted space of crossings which, Gilroy argues, has shaped modernity:

I want to develop the suggestion that cultural historians could take the Atlantic as one single, complex unit of analysis in their discussions of the modern world and use it to produce an explicitly transnational and intercultural perspective ... A concern with the Atlantic as a cultural and political system has been forced on black historiography and intellectual history by the economic and historical matrix in which plantation slavery – "capitalism with its clothes off" – was one special moment. (Gilroy 1992: 15)

Hence Gilroy argues for an analysis of "black culture" (and of modernity in general) that is organized around the multiple movements that define it; and this implies not only the displacements traced along the triangle formed by Europe, Africa, and the Americas during the slave trade, but also the multiple movements that have occurred *a posteriori* through immigration from and within each of these poles. This theoretical move echoes Hall's emphasis on a "twice diasporized" black culture: Gilroy argues that the Black Atlantic is a complex diaspora, formed both out of an original displacement and out of subsequent movements. Gilroy's analysis allows for a conceptualization that insists not only on the "origins" (or not on the origins *only*) of black culture but also on the multiplicity of subsequent exchanges – geographical, material, and symbolic – that took place within the Atlantic space; and this will form the keystone upon which the displacement from "race" and "ethnicity" to "diaspora" is progressively articulated. Indeed, by refuting the sole structuring power of African origins, Gilroy emphasizes the dynamism and constant construction of the cultural "changing same"; and he also argues for a simultaneous unity and multiplicity of "black culture" and against the reification of African origins found in what he would later on call "black fascism." Thus *The Black Atlantic* provides the foundation for Gilroy's subsequent work, in particular opening a path to his book *Against Race* (2000). *The Black Atlantic* was an academic best-seller as much as a mainstream success; the term has become widely used, inside and outside the academy.[6] And indeed, this book worked both as an intellectual revolution for scholars who work on "black culture" and as an argument that immediately made sense. But the very struggle against essentialism pursued by Gilroy poses problems, which are better crystallized in *Against Race*. Indeed, this book explicitly seeks to destroy

---

[6] A couple of examples among many: *Studiosound: The Black Atlantic Project*, a musical collaboration between musicians in the USA and the UK sponsored by the British Council; and *The Black Atlantic Website*, a "dedicated resource of research, knowledge and archive that helps the viewer to achieve an overview of the interdisciplinary that constructs the Black Atlantic discourse," hosted by the House of World Cultures in Berlin (www.blackatlantic.com).

"race" on the conceptual level, and on the practical, political level. In Gilroy's own words,

This book addresses some of the continuing tensions associated with the constitution of political communities in racialized forms. It considers patterns of conflict connected to the consolidation of *culture lines* rather than color lines and is concerned, in particular, with the operations of power, which, thanks to ideas about "race," have become entangled with those vain and mistaken attempts to delineate and subdivide mankind. (Gilroy 2000: 1)

Gilroy proposes to analyze this "entanglement" of race and power, and to show that there is an urgent need to go beyond the color line – hence beyond Du Bois's conceptualization of "black culture" – and to give up racial thinking – which he calls "raciology" – completely. The task at hand is clear:

To demand liberation not from white supremacy alone, however urgently that is required, but from all racializing and raciological thought, from racialized seeing, racialized thinking, and racialized thinking about thinking ... However reluctant we may feel to take the step of renouncing "race" as part of an attempt to bring political culture back to life, this course must be considered because it seems to represent the only *ethical* response to the conspicuous wrongs that raciologies continue to solicit and sanction. (Gilroy 2000: 40–41)

Therefore Gilroy calls for the abandonment of "race" altogether. He denounces the "absurdity" of race (2000: 42) on the conceptual level and stresses its negative, contaminating effect on politics. Indeed, Gilroy argues that fascism is not the sole appanage of Europe; and the strongest critique in *Against Race* targets "black identity politics" and what he sometimes calls "black fascism."[7]

By positioning himself "against race," Gilroy goes further than most scholars in the field of race and ethnic studies. As we have seen in the preceding chapters, there is a wide consensus today about the inadequacy of race as a concept, at least at the level of objective science. Hence, race is largely conceived as a historically and culturally dependent object, and it is mostly its consequences that are studied. This consensus implies that scholars agree that race is a changing object, a dynamic social process that places boundaries between groups in a manner that is variable both on the diachronic and synchronic levels. Race then becomes the meaning attributed to physical difference and/or

---

[7] After the publication of the book, the term "black fascism" provoked violent critiques. See for instance the reviews written by Molefi Kete Asante (2001) and by Carole Boyce Davies (2002).

the concrete consequences it has at a social level. But very rarely is race itself questioned; on the contrary, scholars contest the placement of the boundaries (for instance Davis 1991) or work on racism (for instance Bonilla-Silva 2003). This is the major interest of Gilroy's book: he is not concerned with racial equality, but with the disappearance of race. For Gilroy, no work can be done without a radical refusal of essentialism – not only at the theoretical level, but also at the practical, political level. In other words, it is not where the boundaries are, what they mean, and what consequences they have that matters: it is the very existence of the boundaries that must be challenged. He argues for what he calls a "planetary humanism," which cannot be envisioned with race.

In taking this position, Gilroy is diametrically opposed to most American sociologists of race, and his book can be seen as a radical critique of their "realism." Howard Winant for instance argues that "to be without racial identity is to be in danger of having no identity" (2002: 184), since American society is so deeply defined by race: "Will race ever be transcended? Will the world ever 'get beyond' race? Probably not" (2002: 316). Gilroy does not direct his critique at American scholars, because his concern is first and foremost the "cultural politics" of black culture, and not American sociology. But his book can be read otherwise. Indeed, many scholars within American sociology have replaced a radical questioning of race with the analysis of its concrete consequences, as if the only thing that mattered was concrete inequalities. This position is well illustrated by an exchange between Eduardo Bonilla-Silva and Mara Loveman. In response to her critique of his conceptualization of racism,[8] Bonilla-Silva states:

Race ... is *always contingent* but it is also *socially real* ... As long as "reified" blacks in the United States are still lynched by individual whites ... and as long as black Puerto-Ricans have little access to political, economic and social resources, I, a "reified" black-looking Puerto Rican, will continue to study racial structurations throughout the world. (Bonilla-Silva 1999: 905)

This upside-down causality – the hard, concrete reality of race makes it a permanent, essential, structural component of social reality – is precisely what Gilroy denounces in his book. As Ien Ang (2000) noted, the most disconcerting paradox of race is found in the fact that although it does not exist, it still *feels* like it is natural, essential; but *it is not because*

---

[8] In 1997, Bonilla-Silva published an article called "Rethinking racism: toward a structural interpretation." Loveman reviewed this article in "Is 'Race' Essential? A comment on Bonilla-Silva" (Loveman 1999). Bonilla-Silva responded in turn with "The essential social fact of race: reply to Loveman" (Bonilla-Silva 1999).

something is experienced that it exists. And further, it is not because discrimination is based on skin color that race is real. The danger, according to Gilroy, lies precisely in the intellectual consequences of this theoretical problem. Indeed, by analyzing exclusively the social consequences of race then this absurd concept[9] is naturalized further, and maintains its grip on social relationships. In other words, Gilroy denounces the utilization of racial thinking (i.e., "raciology") in the name of anti-racism itself; and he also denounces the dangers of the partial acknowledgement of race that can be found in cultural politics as well as in the academic world. Gilroy does not deny the powerful effect and consequences of race in everyday life; however, he argues that a radical refusal of "racial thinking" is necessary if these consequences are to be alleviated.

It is no wonder that the most violent reactions to Gilroy's book were to be found within the African-American afrocentrist current, an example of which is Asante's review of *Against Race* (2001). Asante reacted to Gilroy's book by taking offense at his attempt to treat "racial thought" (including fascism) as a generic concept applicable both to "blacks" and "whites." Asante argues that "fascism's most daring and dangerous manifestation has always been in white racial domination and white supremacist notions" and that therefore it is incorrect to analyze white and black nationalism on the same level. According to Asante, Gilroy's project is to destroy the African subject, to render African identity invisible, with the exact same result sought by white supremacists; this is, to him, what the rejection of race entails. Interestingly, Asante at this point echoes scholars like Bonilla-Silva or Winant: he argues that the reason why he disagrees with Gilroy's vision of a "raceless" future is precisely the fact that this would mean losing identity altogether:

I do not look forward to such a colorless, heritage-less, abstract future, and do not see why anyone should look for it. Only those who have a need to escape from their own histories have a need for such a raceless future. (Asante 2001: 851)

Race is equated with heritage, with concreteness, and with history; renouncing race would mean renouncing all of this, it would mean renouncing identity altogether – in somewhat the same fashion as Bonilla-Silva's argument against Loveman, that her "sociology of 'group-making' entails the abandonment not only of race (and ethnicity) but of *all* sociological categories of analysis" (1999: 904). And this, of course, is at

---

[9] "The founding *absurdity* of 'race' as a principle of power, differentiation, and classification must now remain persistently, obstinately in view" (Gilroy 2000: 42).

the heart of the afrocentric paradigm: the all-importance of race, and its displacement from a negative to a positive meaning, accompanied by the reification of culture. In Asante's view, to lose race would imply the loss of both identity and culture. This argument has to be replaced within the fundamental premise of afrocentrism, that is, the centrality of Africa as a cultural, political, and social referent; Gilroy's emphasis on the equal importance of both the origin and the subsequent movements can only participate in what Asante calls the Colored American thesis (Asante 2001), that is, in a process of alienation that denies the centrality of a superseding Africa in the black – or rather African – identity. According to Asante, this already was the project of *The Black Atlantic*; and it is developed and refined in *Against Race*. To the denigration of the African origin, to the discrimination endured by African-Americans precisely because of this African origin, the only possible answer is to claim this very same origin, to charge it with a positive value. It is only logical then to see Gilroy's attempt to undo the binary by eliminating the main signifier in the equation (race itself), rather than fighting for the recognition of the positive value also contained in the "black" pole of the equation, as a frontal attack against the main referent of afrocentrism. It is only logical, because it is exactly what Gilroy is doing: he argues that *any* racial thought is fundamentally dangerous.

Gilroy's project, then, is to go beyond race – to go without race altogether. How can this be done? Interestingly, the solution that Gilroy offers is the diaspora. This term is not new in his work; but what is elaborated in *Against Race* is a complex attempt to construct the diaspora as the most pertinent position from which essentialism in the modern world can be abandoned. Diaspora becomes *an ethical alternative to racial thinking* (2000: 41). Gilroy starts with "identity," emphasizing the diluted content and conceptual "slipperiness" of the term (2000: 107). Identity can take on different ethical colorations; it can be positive or negative; it can be an open communication or a fixed entrenchment, as in the case of Rwanda evoked by Gilroy:

It becomes a thing to be possessed and displayed. It is a silent sign that closes down the possibility of communication across the gulf between one heavily defended island of particularity and its equally well fortified neighbors, between one national encampment and others. When identity refers to an indelible mark or code somehow written into the bodies of its carriers, otherness can only be a threat. Identity is latent destiny ... No longer a site for the affirmation of subjectivity and autonomy, identity mutates. (Gilroy 2000: 103–104)

The alternative to this fixed identity, "to the metaphysics of 'race', nation, and bounded culture coded into the body" (2000: 123), is precisely diasporic identity. Diasporic identities stand against fixed culture, "petrified forms," "fossilized identity," and "ethnic absolutism"; it is through diasporization that identity can become "a noun of process" (2000: 253). Indeed, diasporic identities are fluid and multiple by nature, open and transnational, and they exist only within and through crossings – geographical, cultural, and social.

Diaspora is a useful means to reassess the idea of essential and absolute identity precisely because it is incompatible with that type of nationalist and raciological thinking ... Diaspora disturbs the suggestion that political and cultural identity might be understood via the analogy of undistinguishable peas lodged in the protective pods of closed kinship and subspecies being. (Gilroy 2000: 125)

Because they are by definition multidimensional, diasporas do not remain tied to absolute concepts such as race or nation. Hence Gilroy sees in diasporic identity an alternative – maybe the only alternative? – to the fixed identities that one can so often observe in the contemporary world. The Black Atlantic, which is an eminently modern diaspora, provides Gilroy with an illustration of the possibility of abandoning essentialism altogether and it allows him to observe

The workings of those complex cultural circuits that have transformed a pattern of simple, one-way dispersal into a webbed network constituted through multiple points of intersection. (Gilroy 2000: 131)

Gilroy's utopian feelings transpire through the example of Bob Marley (2000: 130–133). It is not only that diaspora – the impure, fertile, multidimensional, open diaspora – can offer a concept in the fight against essentialism. It is also that there is something unscientific about it; a texture, a feeling: "We can discern the power of identity based, not on some cheap, pre-given sameness, but on will, inclination, mood, and affinity" (Gilroy 2000: 133). Diasporic identities, unlike "sameness," are not "cheap" or "pre-given"; they allow a creative dialectic between collective identity and individual identity, a recognition of the uniqueness of each individual juxtaposed with the solidarity produced by collective identity; in this, for Gilroy, there is power. We are reminded here of Hall's fundamental idea about "new ethnicities":

A recognition that we all speak from a particular place, out of a particular history, out of a particular experience, a particular culture, without being contained by that position. (Hall 1989: 447)

For Gilroy, diasporic identity allows for the recognition of difference without binding the individual to it. And this is indeed the fundamental distinction made by Gilroy between fixed and diasporic identities: while the first acts as a closure for the individual, the second provides individual freedom. Diasporic identity is something to fight for relentlessly, not only because of the harmful character of racial thinking, but also for the sake of humanity. Gilroy calls upon a moral duty, the moral and political responsibility to refuse essentialism under any of its forms (Gilroy 2000: 277).

Another diluted concept?

The conceptualization of race and ethnicity found within British cultural studies therefore has to be seen in a broader and yet absolutely fundamental context: the refusal of essentialism. Both Stuart Hall and Paul Gilroy have been especially clear about the centrality of this project; and their struggle concerns not only the theoretical conceptualization of identity, culture, and politics, but also the practical, politically engaged side of cultural studies. In other words, essentialism is considered as not pertinent on the conceptual level, and also as dangerous in the social sphere. This articulation between theory and practice, between social sciences and politics, is characteristic of British cultural studies. This struggle against essentialism has accompanied a conceptual displacement within the field: from race to ethnicity in the work of Stuart Hall, and finally to "new" or "diasporized" ethnicities; from "fixed identities" and "ethnic absolutism" to "diaspora" in the work of Paul Gilroy. For the latter, diasporic identities are articulated as a viable alternative to essentialized identities and culture in the modern world. From a conceptual standpoint, this displacement allows for the recognition of the fundamentally modern hybridity of identities; from a political standpoint, it allows a radical struggle against the equally modern essentialism engrained in race and nationalism.

It is important to note that the displacement of race is highly localized; Hall develops it from the specific case of the Caribbean and Great Britain. Gilroy's displacement is situated in the larger space of the "Black Atlantic." Hence, neither Hall nor Gilroy claims any sort of universality, although they see in the modern world a constant increase in prominence of the process of diasporization. Hall treats the case of the Caribbean diaspora as an archetypical example of what a modern diaspora is, or can be; the Black Atlantic provides Gilroy with the framework for his argument against essentialism.

This displacement of race is highly seductive, because it is helpful in understanding the social world as dynamic, just as social anthropology allowed for a comprehension of the dynamic character of "ethnic groups" that are not, in reality, isolated or static. It is also seductive because it offers a weapon in the struggle against racism and provides a new way of conceiving of cultural politics. But one important problem remains, which is to some extent similar to the problem that arises with regard to the social anthropological concept of ethnicity: a problem of dilution. Does the term "diaspora" offer more conceptual precision than the term "ethnicity"? In the next chapter, we shall question this displacement, not only at the level of its conceptual precision, but also in terms of the struggle against essentialism. In other words, does the concept of diaspora really escape all traces of essentialism?

5   Intermediate reflections on essentialism

Life with its irrational reality and its store of possible meanings is inexhaustible. The concrete form in which value-relevance occurs remains perpetually in flux, ever subject to change in the dimly seen future of human culture. The light which emanates from those highest evaluative ideas always falls on an ever changing finite segment of the vast chaotic stream of events, which flows away through time.

(Weber 1949: 111)

Today we mock at the strange ratiocinations that the doctors of the Middle Ages constructed from their notions of heat and cold, humidity and dryness, etc. Yet we do not perceive that we continue to apply the selfsame method to an order of phenomena which is even less appropriate for it than any order, on account of its extreme complexity.

(Durkheim 1982: 66)

The fundamental premise of classical sociology is the recognition of the elusive character of reality. For Émile Durkheim, reality is not a given; ideas and feelings are impressed upon it; in Durkheim's felicitous words, "we are the victims of an illusion which leads us to believe we have ourselves produced what has been imposed upon us externally" (1982: 53). For Max Weber, reality is irrational and chaotic (1949: 111); it is multiple, and made of infinite possible combinations. It is in order to grasp this reality, and thereby be able to understand and explain it, that Durkheim and Weber each developed a "sociological method": the problem of the sociologist is not only to make sense of this reality, it is also to see it; and it is only by using a specific methodology that the elusive object – whether chaotic or hidden – can be reached, thereby allowing sociological analysis. To make reality intelligible, Weber offers a methodological tool which he calls ideal-types. Ideal-types are a rational construction used to make sense of and explain an irrational reality.

For the purpose of a typological scientific analysis it is convenient to treat all irrational, affectually determined elements of behavior as factors of deviation from a conceptually pure type of rational action ... The construction of a purely rational course of action ... serves the sociologist as a type (ideal type) which has the merit of clear understandability and lack of ambiguity ... Only in this respect and for these reasons of methodological convenience is the method of sociology "rationalistic." (Weber 1978: 6)

The ideal-type is not a normative model; Weber is concerned with finding a way to make something out of the multiplicity of social reality, to go beyond the infinitely unique quality of the actions of men. Hence the ideal-type is, in Weber's words, "a methodological convenience." The term "ideal" here does not refer to a normative judgment, which would deem certain types of action better than others. It means that the ideal-type is an abstraction, an accentuated "idea" that enables the sociologist not only to see reality through ordering but also to understand and explain it. Therefore, ideal-types do not exist in reality in their pure form; in Weber's own words, they are a "utopia":

An ideal-type is formed by the one-sided accentuation of one or more points of view and by the synthesis of a great many diffuse, discrete, more or less present and occasionally absent concrete individual phenomena, which are arranged according to those one-sidedly emphasized viewpoints into a unified analytical construct. In its conceptual purity, this mental construct ... cannot be found empirically anywhere in reality. It is a utopia. (Weber 1949: 90)

The "real object" is distinguished from the "object of knowledge": the former – social reality – can only be analyzed through the latter – a construction. The idea that sociology has to use an abstraction extracted from reality, precisely in order to be able to see this reality through an operation of ordering and to understand and explain this reality, is common to both Weber and Durkheim – although the methodologies they develop to achieve that goal are different. For Max Weber, sociology "seeks to formulate type concepts and generalized uniformities of empirical processes" (1978: 19); the ideal-type allows for the construction of a theoretical concept: there is no sociological concept without an ideal-typical elaboration (1978: 21). The idea is to extract ideal-types from the multiple combinations of concrete, unique actions that shape social reality. Theoretically, the ideal-types order reality, they make it intelligible and enable the sociologist to actually see it; but they cannot be found in reality in their pure forms: no social action can be oriented only by one single type. Ideal-types are not an end, they are a means; they are extracted out of reality in order to understand and explain it. Therefore the ideal-typical methodology is not a unilateral movement built from reality to the ideal-type, but a bilateral movement that occurs from reality to the ideal-type and back to reality (see Figure 3).

The methodological pertinence of the ideal-typical construction is obvious. The empirical data provides the "reality" from which are

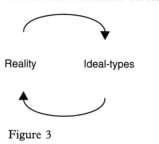

Figure 3

extracted a certain number of types. These ideal-typical abstractions, in turn, are applied to reality in order to understand and explain it. Hence the ideal-typical construction evolves within a circle that should be repeated until the types work, that is, until they prove to be as adequate as possible to social reality on the level of understanding and interpretation. This circular movement, repeated until the highest adequacy is found, is reminiscent of Gadamer's hermeneutic circle (1989).

This precision is obtained by striving for the highest possible degree of adequacy on the level of meaning ... [ideal types] are always constructed with a view to adequacy on the level of meaning. (Weber 1978: 20)

We shall construct ideal-types for the different styles of thought on race considered so far. Although Weber primarily employed ideal-typical constructions as a methodological device for comparison of various types of action, we shall apply them to patterns of thought. Our intention is to draw out the direction of these patterns "in the sense of logical or teleological 'consistency'" (Weber 1958: 324) as they relate to the conceptualization of race.

A typology of displacement

In the preceding four chapters, we have offered an analysis of the way in which four "currents of thought" have conceptualized race in the twentieth century. This in turn now allows us to distinguish a process common to those four distinct modes of inquiry: namely, a process of *displacement*, itself ascribed within the broader project of *opposing essentialism*. Indeed, those four fields can all be credited for their attempt at de-essentializing the most essentialist concept of race, inherited from the nineteenth century's scientific racism. The process of displacement that has occurred in each of these fields is made on terms specific to each, and takes different modalities.

Marxist thought displaced its inquiry from race to class. The solution offered to the puzzle of race is straightforward: race does not exist as a biological fact; but it does not exist at the social level either. Indeed, any apparent racial situation is actually a class situation in disguise. Race becomes an invention used by the ruling class in order to exert its domination; race is only an idea, which in fact can be traced back to the economic structure and the position of individuals and groups in relationship to the means of production. Race is displaced because race is not *real* in the Marxist framework.

In American sociology three forms of displacement of race developed over the course of the twentieth century. The first form, visible in the work of Du Bois and Park, displaced a purely biological conception of race by adding culture (i.e., language, history, cultural inheritance, etc.), but did not reject biology *in toto*. Hence, these scholars took the first step towards a sociological conception of race. The second form of displacement is more generally seen in the wholesale replacement of biology by culture. This move, exemplified in the writings of Omi and Winant, rejects the efficacy of any biological account of race (and racial groups). Phenotypical difference is merely utilized to distinguish between groups. A third form of displacement involves the substitution of racism for race. Structuralist accounts of racism found in the work of Wilson and Bonilla-Silva often do not conceptualize race at all; instead, the emphasis of inquiry is on the manifest effects of racism: discrimination, violence, and statistically measured inequality in a variety of domains of social life.

British social anthropology displaced its inquiry from race to ethnicity, or, to be more exact, from the fixed unit of "ethnic groups" to the dynamic process of "ethnicity." Race does not exist as a biological reality; and within the social world, it is a construction made within the symbolic charge of social relationships. It becomes only one of the different modalities that can be taken by the broader concept of ethnicity, seen as a dynamic process of boundary erection and maintenance that exists between groups and not within them. From a fixed content, social anthropology therefore switched to a dynamic process. Interestingly, this displacement could also be characterized as occurring from "culture" to the "social"; culture indeed becomes something that participates in, but does not constitute, the ethnic process.

Finally, British cultural studies displaced its inquiry from race to ethnicity to diaspora. It is probably in this field that the struggle against essentialism is the most explicit, because it is part of an explicit political project. It is also in this field, logically, that the dismissal of race has been most complete. Hence, diaspora does not simply replace race; it is set in

Table 2 *A typology of displacement*

	From	To
Class for race	Race	Class
Culture for race	Race	Culture
Racism for race	Race	Racism
Ethnicity for race	Race	Ethnicity
Diaspora for race	Race	Diaspora

opposition to race. Race is a "floating signifier"; it bears the mark of an essentialism that is not only non-pertinent from a conceptual point of view but also dangerous at the political and social levels. Diasporic identities are seen as an eminently modern way of conjugating "identity" that allows individual freedom; race, its eminently modern antithesis, conjugates identity in a way that produces closure. The displacement operating within cultural studies is ascribed within the recognition of a field of tension considered to be characteristic of modernity: the tension between fixity and fluidity. Ultimately, it is through a normative judgment that "diaspora" is deemed preferable to "race."

The typology of displacement (Table 2) illustrates the different modalities that can be taken by a conceptualization of race ascribed within the struggle against essentialism. We distinguish five ideal-types, which can be used to analyze the modalities in which a conceptual, or at least discursive, displacement has taken place within social thought during the twentieth century, in an attempt to abandon essentialism. In each of these types, a different term was substituted for the term "race," a substitution that was accompanied by a reconceptualization of the term. We shall call these five types: "class for race," "culture for race," "racism for race," "ethnicity for race," and "diaspora for race."

The first type, *class for race*, considers race as an ideological invention that hides what is in fact class domination. Hence any analysis of a so-called "racial situation" has to be made in economic terms; ultimately, the conclusion is that race does not exist: the only reality is economic. Marxist scholars who work on race obviously fit this ideal-type well, but one can find tendencies as well in most works on the intersections between race and class or, more interestingly, gender. Indeed the superseding importance of gender over race, found in some second-wave feminist theory, can be analyzed along the same lines as the primacy of class over race found in Marxist thought.

The second type, *culture for race*, either adds culture to biology or replaces biology altogether with culture. In this case a biological definition of the group is replaced by a cultural definition; or, a correspondence is made between "blood" and culture at diverse degrees. Tendencies towards this type can take multiple forms, and they are found in multiple conceptualizations. One illustration of the "addition option" is found in both Park and Du Bois, for whom culturally differentiated groups may more or less closely map with biologically differentiated groups; in this case, there is more than biology to the definition of the groups. Another illustration is found in the definition of ethnic groups on the basis of the "cultural content" seen as belonging to them; from Leach's "butterfly collectors" (1966: 68–69) to Ruth Benedict's *Patterns of Culture* to the common metaphor of an American multicultural "salad bowl," the ethnic group is seen as a clear entity that owns specific cultural practices and traits which define it. Finally, some conceptions of the group actually assume that there is an explicit link of causality between "race" and culture; some of the tendencies within afrocentrism, for instance, conceive of culture as being completely juxtaposed with "race" and go as far as arguing that it is, at least partly, biologically produced (as in the "melanin" argument). The interesting dimension in this type, however, is that each and every modality it can take leads to an automatic assumption that there is some sort of correspondence between race and culture. Indeed, to define the group by the culture it carries ineluctably produces an essentialist fixity, which sees culture as something that is passed on – either through genes, blood, kinship, or even "symbolic" kinship – from one generation to the other; this passed-on culture is seen as defining both collective and individual identity; and loyalty is due to it. This is precisely the danger that Gilroy sees in what he calls "raciology." Ultimately, race "matters" and is seen as defining individual and collective experiences in a deterministic way – whether race "matters" because it exists (as in scientific racism or afrocentrism), or because society has been living with the idea of race for the past centuries (as in Bonilla-Silva's or Winant's pessimistic statements). We shall return to this point later in this chapter.

The third type, *racism for race*, brushes aside the concept of race to focus its inquiry on racism. The premise here is that what matters is how a contemporary society is structured; if it happens to be racially structured, then analysis has to focus on mechanisms of discrimination against one (or more) groups that take place at the economic, political, social, and cultural levels. Here, contrary to the first type, it is not that race does not exist: what matters more, from an analytical standpoint, are solely the concrete consequences of racial thought. One sees clearly the paradox: race is made central in analysis, whereas scholars would deny it exists. Very different scholarly works tend towards this ideal-type: those of Wilson, Bonilla-Silva, Winant, and also to some extent works by certain British "race relations" sociologists.

The fourth type, *ethnicity for race*, abandons race on the premise of its conceptual inadequacy. A static, fixed conception of identity is replaced by an active and dynamic "ethnicity," considered as a relational process. At the same time, the term culture takes on a new dimension: it is not a fixed corpus of habits (the French *us et coutumes*) which belongs to one given group any more, but becomes a reservoir of symbolic markers that matter only insofar as they are used by the group in relationship to other groups. Obviously, British social anthropology tends towards this ideal-typical treatment of race; but interestingly British cultural studies also fit this type quite well, at least at the level of the switch from "fixed identities" or "ethnicities" to "new ethnicities."

The fifth type, *diaspora for race*, does not negate race, but opposes diaspora to it. Both race and diaspora are conceived of as products of modernity, and are pitted against each other as antitheses. Race, in this case, exists only as a discursive system that organizes the social world in a deep and resilient way; this implies that only its consequences upon the actions of men are concrete, and therefore that it is reversible: the society can exist without it. There is the hope that another eminently modern phenomenon, diaspora, can overcome race and eventually lead to its disappearance. British cultural studies tend towards this type, especially with the later phase of Hall's work, and with Gilroy; but this tendency can also be found in an altered way in many post-modern works, within diaspora studies, and in feminist theory; the idea here is that "diaspora" or "diasporic identities" are a source of empowerment in the struggle against racism.

This typology therefore allows a deeper look at, and understanding of, the complex reality of thought about race. Indeed, it is helpful to inquire into other theories of race – we have mentioned afrocentrism, feminist theory, or diaspora studies, but the list could be lengthened. Addition-ally, the five types elaborated above can be combined in multiple ways: cultural studies, for instance, combine a replacement of race by both ethnicity and diaspora. Indeed we would like to go back to our own material – the way in which four currents of thought have conceptualized "race" in the twentieth century. It is our understanding that the most fertile outcome of our typology is to shed light on the broader project common to all four conceptualizations: the struggle against essentialism. The issue we would like to explore now, with the help of the ideal-types we have built, is the following: while there has been a displacement at both the discursive and conceptual levels, does this imply that, at the conceptual level, a break with essentialism has really occurred? In other words, is the outcome of the anti-essentialist enterprise a displacement of signifiers or a displacement of the signified?

The question of essentialism: displacing signifiers or displacing the signified?

Essentialism is a standpoint that holds that people can be categorized into separate groups whose intrinsic differences mark off the boundaries between groups – hence that *essence* is stronger than *existence*. The intrinsic differences are conceived as *natural* or *naturally occurring* among individuals within these groups.[1] Race can be understood as the epitome of essentialist thought, both for conceptual and historical reasons. Conceptually speaking, the idea of race has been highly naturalized, grounded in what seemed an uncontestable visible and invisible biological truth. The racial science of the nineteenth century used various techniques to show the essential character of race: from readily available physical differences such as skin color, hair texture, or facial features, to "deeper" measurements such as the size of the crania or diseases and anomalies more widespread among a given group than another. Historically, race became a structural element in European expansion and the rise of colonization; it participated in defining the humanity (or lack thereof) of colonized people and their level of civilization. Hence with the definition of race as a type, which came to be dominant by the middle of the nineteenth century, we face essentialist thought taken at its highest degree: biologically grounded, discursively fixed, and ingrained in social, political, and cultural policies.

When essentialist concepts are applied to social groups, they can be criticized from two distinct directions. They can be challenged empirically, as being inadequate to reality; and they can be criticized from a moral standpoint, for denying individuality and human autonomy. Both challenges are visible in the humanities and social sciences during the twentieth century. In the humanities, a critique of essentialism has been mounted for gender (Spelman 1990; Fuss 1990). In the area of sexuality, Foucault (1980) described and deconstructed the discursive process in which the "homosexual," as a person with a past, a case history, and a physiology, became defined by sexuality, as a way of being, as a

---

[1] This vision of the social world as being comprised by a variety of *natural kinds* is commonly held today among socio-biologists and evolutionary psychologists. For a discussion of essentialism in the natural sciences see Ellis (2002); for a discussion of the utility of the concept of natural kinds in the social sciences see Haslam (1998); for a discussion of essentialism in philosophical semantics see Kripke (1980) and Putnam (1975).

new species. In feminist philosophy Judith Butler has articulated the logic of a de-essentialized conception of sex and gender:

> If gender is the cultural meanings that the sexed body assumes, then a gender cannot be said to follow from a sex in any one way. Taken to its logical limits, the sex/gender distinction suggests a radical discontinuity between sexed bodies and culturally constructed genders. Assuming for the moment the stability of binary sex, it does not follow that the construction of "men" will accrue exclusively to the bodies of males or that "women" will interpret only female bodies. Further, even if the sexes appear to be unproblematically binary in their morphology and constitution (which will become a question), there is no reason to assume that genders ought also to remain as two. The presumption of a binary gender system implicitly retains the belief in a mimetic relation of gender to sex whereby gender mirrors sex or is otherwise restricted by it. When the constructed status of gender is theorized as radically independent of sex, gender itself becomes a free-floating artifice, with the consequence that *man* and *masculine* might just as easily signify a female body as a male one, and *woman* and *female* a male body as easily as a female one. (Butler 1999: 10)

By taking the body and same-sex desire as entities that required de-naturalization, feminist and queer theory has moved a long way towards a de-essentialization of concepts and categories of gender and sexuality. As the preceding chapters indicate, efforts have also been made in the social sciences to de-essentialize the race concept. Marxism, American sociology, British social anthropology, and cultural studies have each undertaken a project of de-essentialization, from an empirical and moral standpoint. Each, as we have argued, has displaced race as a means to this end. Our primary concern, however, is that despite their intentions, an essentialist conception of race has not been fully eradicated, in the main because of the inadequacy of the substitute concepts, class, culture, racism, ethnicity, and diaspora, to the paradoxical reality of race. We posit that whereas the movement away from biological accounts of race (which view races as natural kinds) towards alternative concepts has been characterized as a shift away from biological essentialism, biology and essentialism are not entirely overcome.

American sociology

Essentialism has posed a serious problem for sociological thought about race. In the case of scholars working in the United States in the early twentieth century, two issues related to racial essentialism were confronted. First, biological essentialism was employed by Social Darwinists to explain the alleged racial inferiority of blacks and Chinese workers (among others), as exemplified by the different empirical circumstances in which the different races existed. If members of the white race commanded the most influential positions in society, and were viewed as the sole contributors to the unfolding of Western civilization, then these outcomes could be explained by race as a biological fact. Confirmation of this essentialist view of social life was made manifest during the 1893 World's Columbian Exhibition in Chicago, in which the evolutionary path of civilization was represented spatially in the exhibition: the "White City" filled with the technological achievements of European nations stood at the far extreme from the re-creation of a "Dahomey Village," which depicted "natives" engaging in "native pursuits" (Bederman 1995). Second, biological essentialism was invoked to justify political and legal measures that separated the races in the public sphere (e.g., the segregation of blacks and whites in a variety of public facilities, in railway travel, and in educational institutions in southern American states) and to argue against the amelioration of the social conditions in which subordinate racial groups lived.[2]

Thus it is understandable that insofar as W. E. B. Du Bois's writings on race stood as a critique of essentialism, they also address both dimensions of the biological conception of race. In these writings – by an author whose education was steeped in German historicism and whose practical politics were confronted by the "color line" – can be found an analytical and ethical displacement of biological essentialism with culture (i.e., history and language). On the one hand, Du Bois revalorizes the *content* of the cultural attributes associated with the black race, reflecting a Herderian and religious sensibility towards the contribution each nation and its people make to the history of the world and the glory of god. Against the negative view of black cultural achievements, he poses the positive qualities of black culture. On the other hand, Du Bois adds culture to the concept of race by arguing insistently that mere physical differences are not sufficient to account for the culture of groups. Yet racial cultures still refer back, with greater and lesser empirical accuracy, to discrete racial groups. Consequently, while Du Bois struck a blow at biological essentialism through the valorization of black culture and the claim that biology does not alone account for culture, his dependency on biological essentialism remains strong. In effect, Du Bois's use of culture primarily tempers the consequences of a racial-essentialist worldview (that both denigrates non-white cultures and justifies their socio-political subordination) rather than rejecting biological essentialism itself as an entirely false concept of race. Du Bois

---

[2] For a discussion of the impact of biological essentialism (i.e., scientific racism) on the shaping of public policy in late nineteenth-century America see Lofgren (1987: 93–147).

relies on a notion of natural kinds of races to distinguish between races and to correlate these races with different cultures.

The history of the American Negro is the history of this strife, – this longing to attain self-conscious manhood, to merge his double self into a better and truer self ... He would not Africanize America, for America has too much to teach the world and Africa. He would not bleach his Negro soul in a flood of white Americanism, for he knows that Negro blood has a message for the world. He simply wishes to make it possible for a man to be both a Negro and an American, without being cursed and spit upon by his fellows, without having doors of Opportunity closed roughly in his face. (Du Bois 1986b: 365)

This passage from *The Souls of Black Folk* illustrates Du Bois's theoretical dependency on, and movement away from, essentialism. Biologically distinct white and black races exist. Yet, for Du Bois, this empirical fact should not lead to a negation of the distinctiveness of the black race – which has a special message for the world – by assimilation into "white Americanism" or the imposition of discrimination that prevents the "American Negro" from embracing his American-ness. Du Bois recognizes that mere blood relations do not create a unified race: only a shared language and history can do that. At the same time, he understands race to require blood relations. Thus an essentialist conception of race is a constant feature in Du Bois's thought despite his emphasis on culture.

As we have seen, Du Bois is not alone with respect to the turn towards culture to explain group differences between the races. Horace Kallen, who was primarily concerned with immigrant groups and the process of cultural assimilation, and Robert Park, who directly analyzed the problem of race in society, both invoke culture to describe groups and their relations. For Park, each individual is a "bearer of a double inheritance" that is part biological and part social. The social inheritance comprised what would today be called culture: "habits, accommodations, sentiments, attitudes, and ideals" (Park 1950: 282). For Kallen, the *natio* (nativity) of an individual is the "inherited organic set" of earlier ancestors. Nothing can change this familial connection to one's cultural ancestors, and not even intermarriage could succeed in producing a new race on the North American continent: "older types persist, and there is nothing to keep them from so continuing on any principle of the relation of heredity to environment that may be applied to them" (Kallen 1924: 177). In Park's view blacks might transform their cultural inheritance based on their proximity to whites, but this transformation would not touch their biological inheritance. Kallen took the opposite position concerning immigrant "races" from eastern and southern Europe: not only were they unassimilable culturally and ancestrally, they should not be forced to assimilate (an act that would damage their ability to achieve a "perfection that is *proper to* [their] *kind*" (Kallen 1924: 121). In both Park and Kallen's conceptualization of social groups, these groups are held to be dependent on some type of essential biological (i.e., racial or ancestral) inheritance, although the future prospects of racial and ethnic groups in relation to assimilation are held by both to be a matter of culture.

In the race concepts of Du Bois, Park, and Kallen, an ideal-typical displacement of race is situated within a continuity of race (as a biological essence) and culture (the social characteristics of groups). Culture is emphasized for both analytical and moral reasons against the strict biological essentialism of racial science; nevertheless a biological concept of race remains a relevant part of the understanding of society. In contrast to these earlier race theories, Omi and Winant break entirely with biology. Winant (2002) has offered a relatively concise, *social* concept of race as "a concept that signifies sociopolitical conflicts and interests in reference to different types of human bodies." However, in the two editions of *Racial Formation in the United States*, Omi and Winant provide more expansive formulations. In the first edition, after stating that "the social sciences have come to reject biologistic notions of race in favor of an approach which regards race as a *social* concept," the authors then merely confirm this view rather than arguing directly against biology:

Race is indeed a pre-eminently *sociohistorical* concept: racial categories and the meaning of race are given concrete expression by the specific social relations and historical context in which they are embedded. Racial meanings have varied tremendously over time and between different societies. (Omi and Winant 1986: 60)

Omi and Winant give a clear definition of racial categories, such as the "black/white color line" in the United States; however, one can ask what are the racial meanings that vary? It is difficult to locate exactly what the authors mean by racial *meanings*, although they state that the meaning of race is contested: it is formed, transformed, destroyed, and re-formed (Omi and Winant 1986: 61). In the second edition of their book, Omi and Winant link racial categories and racial meanings to racial formation, the "process by which social, economic and political forces determine the content and importance of racial categories, and by which they are in turn shaped by racial meanings" (Omi and Winant 1986: 61). Is this lack of a definition of racial meaning problematic? Again, the two main goals of their writing are (1) to demarcate the specificity of *race* and to argue against the reduction of race to other factors and (2) to refute the idea that race can be given up. Referring to the latter goal, they argue in the first edition that

The continuing persistence of racial ideology suggests that these racial myths and stereotypes ... are, we think, too essential, too integral to the maintenance of the US social order. Of course, particular meanings, stereotypes and myths can change, but the presence of a *system* of racial meanings and stereotypes, of racial ideology, seems to be a permanent feature of US culture. (Omi and Winant 1986: 63)

However, they do define race in relation to culture (racial categories and meanings) and political movements (racial projects). Racial projects form and reform the racial order of society: "race [is] *an unstable and 'de-centered' complex of social meanings constantly being transformed by political struggle*" (Omi and Winant 1986: 68).

If race is permanent and yet changing, what sort of "meaning" might be adequate to such a complex social fact? A sense of circularity ensues from this effort to define race in non-biological terms. Omi and Winant's bloodless race concept implies that racial categories and racial meanings are produced and contested by racial projects, which invoke racial categories and meanings. They reject the idea that race can be thought of as "an essence, as something fixed, concrete and objective" (Omi and Winant 1986: 68). However, what precisely is racial about racial meanings, categories, projects, and formations? There is in this cultural account a lingering essentialism. The social concept of race, which is described in essentialist terms vis-à-vis society (i.e., it is an intrinsic feature of American society), retains a patina of the biological concept of race. Reference to phenotype, which is the only way racial differences can be identified, remains an unarticulated condition of possibility for this ostensibly cultural concept of race (for both the analysts and the commonsense view of race). Moreover, racial meaning and categories are defined as given features of modern racialized societies, which means, concomitantly, that the racial identity of individuals and groups is given, no matter how much room for contestation of identity might exist. A cultural concept of race that proceeds on such a basis (or a basis similar to the one employed by Omi and Winant) corresponds to what can be called social essentialism. The socially essentialist concept of race asserts the inevitability of race and races without referring to an idea of intrinsic biological differences that the concept presupposes.

Social essentialism appears in its most logically consistent form in the social structuralist account of race, in which racism is substituted for, or displaces, race. For social structuralists, racism – defined in terms of measurable forms of racial inequality – impacts subordinated racial groups, yet the nature of race is not accounted for. Instead, race is understood as a social fact linked to racialized social orders. Insofar as these racial orders are viewed as durable, racial groups are unavoidable features of societies so constituted. "The core of my theorization ... was my argument that after race-based structurations emerge, definite socially existing races arise, which develop distinct objective interests" (Bonilla-Silva 1999: 899). Races arise after racial structurations – while this claim is suspect from the standpoint of the logical sequence it stipulates, it does have the analytical advantage of shifting the focus from the thorny problem of defining race (that is, the thing that transforms groups of people into races) to the more certain ground of power relations between groups and the conflicts they generate. However, in comparison to the early theories of race in American sociology, the social structuralists skirt the problem of the reality of race that was taken on directly by Du Bois, Park, and, in a related way, by Kallen.

Marxism

As a style of thought, Marxism, in contrast to the sociology of race relations, is advantaged by being grounded in a theory of knowledge, which stands behind the practical application of class analysis to phenomena such as race. As a parsimonious theory of social relations, Marxist analyses of race exhibit a high level of logical consistency since they are based on a few key principles derived from Marx's texts. Class analysts treat race as a socially significant but epiphenomenal entity. Because class theory defines social reality as being fundamentally comprised of economic relations, the problem of the biological concept of race does not arise. Moreover, rather than entertaining the possibility that biological concepts of race are relevant for understanding race relations, class theorists such as Cox and Miles treat biological concepts as one feature of the epiphenomenon that is race. The problem is not that biological concepts are scientifically incorrect vis-à-vis the conceptualization of race (a position which presupposes that biology *might* contribute to knowledge of race – a position entertained by Du Bois and Park); for class analysis, race itself is nothing more than an ideological category. In other words, *any* conceivable concept of race is constitutionally inadequate to empirical, social reality (as defined within the Marxist framework).

Race is *ideological* in class analysis because it is conceived of as serving the function of enabling the ruling economic class(es) to consolidate and maintain control over an exploited class of laborers (whether slave labor or free labor), by promoting racial conflict and suppressing class conflict. In the Marxist theory of knowledge, race is *ideological* because it is an idea that distorts consciousness of the true empirical reality, which is comprised of economic relations and not race relations; the latter are illusory because they are predicated by the former. As a consequence, race relations have no reality independent of economic power relations. This has led Robert Miles to reject the ideas of races and race relations.

There are no "races" and therefore no "race relations." There is only a belief that there are such things, a belief which is used by some social groups to construct an Other (and therefore a Self) in thought as a prelude to exclusion and domination, and by other social groups to define Self (and so to construct an Other) as a means of resisting that exclusion. Hence, if it is used at all, the idea of "race" should be used only to refer descriptively to such uses of the idea of "race." (Miles 2000: 135)

The emphasis on the *use value* of race as a key component of power relations in the modern world has meant, concomitantly, that race is not treated as an "object" that presents a unique problem of conceptualization. Ultimately, race and race relations are not *real*.

The logical consistency in class analysis makes Marxism a formidable paradigm for the study of race. It is intuitively satisfying to a view that emphasizes the unreality of race. Even if the insistence on the dominant class's political project is softened and the notion of class struggle is nuanced (as it is, for instance, in Wilson's "test" of orthodox and neo-Marxist class theory in *The Declining Significance of Race*), class analysis is the most rigorous critique of biological essentialism. Biology is not simply replaced by the "social," it is replaced by a very specific vision of the social, which offers a standpoint from which not only to denounce the *injustice* of racism as it mediates class exploitation but also to insist on the absolute *falsity* of biology. Anyone seeking a break with essentialism, therefore, would find in Marxism a congenial style of thought.

Nonetheless, two conceptual problems exist in the Marxist analysis of race. The first has to do with the fact that class analysis refuses to address the *reality* of race (and not simply its ideological unreality): it does not address race as a phenomenon in its own right. This critique can be found in the cultural and structural accounts of race (and racism) discussed above. Omi and Winant argue that there is little in class analyses "which comprehends class formation in broad enough terms to suggest a theory of racial dynamics" (Omi and Winant 1994: 35). Yet the problem presented by the refusal of class analysis to confront the idea of race-in-itself lies at a deeper level. Class analysis seeks to resolve the contradiction of thought and reality. However, rather than conceiving the paradoxical relationship of race's reality and unreality as *reflective* of an actual material condition, it reduces race to one pole, that of unreality. This materialist reduction of race to immateriality reveals a second related problem. Class analysis misconstrues the *material conditions* that give rise to race: as we shall argue in subsequent chapters, it is an "idea" that is imbricated in reality (the reality of physical difference) but this reality is not biological per se. In other words, race is neither pure thought nor is it reducible to a biological essence. It is related to a different type of material condition, that combines physical differences that are initially race neutral, a process of categorizing these differences *as race*, and a belief in the significance of these differences. This condition, which is *contradictory* to the Marxist theory of knowledge, can be resolved neither by a bridging concept such as the ruling class's imposition of an ideologically distorted concept nor by transcending the dualism of thought and empirical reality through the metaphysical guarantees of a historical materialist perspective. The second problem of class analysis, then, is its failure to comprehend the *specificity* of racial reality. In the final analysis, rather than submerging race within class relations, the Marxist displacement of race actually leaves racial essentialism in place insofar as it is unable to explain the obstinate persistence of race as anything other than illusion.

British social anthropology

With the post-Barth conceptualization of ethnicity, it seems evident that social anthropology has been able to replace the essentialist concepts of race and ethnic group. There is no denial of the use, and therefore existence, of fixity and essentialism within social relationships; but conceptually speaking this is only a symbolic tool, a belief used by individuals and groups. Hence what might feel natural to the people is actually a construction used dynamically within social interaction – whether this is "race," "culture," or "nationalism"; ethnicity becomes a situational and relational process, ascribed within specific historical and social contexts, and culture becomes a resource used as a social marker. This is not to say that culture does not matter; it *does* have significance for individuals and groups; but conceptually speaking it is nothing more than a tool.

However, one problem that arises is the danger of conceptual dilution, which is expressed in two different dimensions: first, ethnicity seems to dilute into the broader concept of social identity; second, race is brushed aside without really being addressed while remaining something that "happens" in some societies. Both dimensions express conceptual fuzziness, and they are linked in the sense that it is precisely the desire to brush race aside that allows the dilution of the concept. Indeed, ignoring "race" implies that the notion of physical difference is taken out of the definition of ethnicity. Richard Jenkins (1997: 13–40) defines ethnicity as follows:

1. ethnicity emphasizes cultural *differentiation*, within a dialectic between similarity and difference;
2. ethnicity is *cultural* – based in shared meanings – but it is produced and reproduced in *social* interaction;
3. ethnicity is to some extent *variable* and *manipulable*, not definitively fixed or unchanging;
4. ethnicity as a social identity is both *collective* and *individual*, externalized and internalized.

We can consider each of these points separately. First, ethnicity is not about cultural elements, it is about relationships of cultural differentiation: it is the process by which both "us" and "them" are defined and distinguished, as Eriksen emphasizes in his work. This process takes place within a dialectic of both positive and negative practices; that is, the validation for ethnicity always arises from both identification and opposition, from similarity within the group and difference outside it. Second, the cultural difference between two groups is not the decisive feature of ethnicity: what is decisive is the fact that the groups have at least a minimum degree of contact and *entertain ideas of each other as being different*. This was actually the point of departure of Edmund Leach's reflection: in Burma, he realized that groups that considered themselves different from each other actually spoke the same language or had the same cultural practices. Hence, *ethnicity is an aspect of a relationship, not the property of a group*. In fact, culture can be considered not as the cause of the social production of difference between the groups, but as its outcome (Jenkins 1997: 13), because it is constantly being redefined through social interaction. Therefore, "neither culture nor ethnicity is 'something' that people 'have', or, indeed, to which they 'belong'. They are, rather, complex repertoires which people experience, use, learn and 'do' in their daily lives, within which they construct an ongoing sense of themselves and an understanding of their fellows" (Jenkins 1997: 14). It is actively created, recreated, modified, conserved, or forgotten within social relationships. Third, ethnicity is not definitively fixed; it is not immobile. It is a social process of cultural differentiation that can vary (and usually varies) both diachronically and synchronically. Jenkins's use of "to some extent" (1997: 40) hints at the fact that the manipulation of ethnicity, however, occurs within certain limits: there needs to be a logic at the level of meaning, as Jenkins reiterates in the conclusion of his book:

Although ethnic identity is socially constructed, it is not infinitely variable, malleable, or negotiable ... That there are limits to the plasticity of ethnicity, as well as to its fixity and solidity, is the founding premise for the development of an understanding of ethnicity which permits us to appreciate that although it is imagined, it is not imaginary. (Jenkins 1997: 169)

This emphasis on both the constructed character of ethnicity and its limits has also been emphasized by Peter Wade (1999). Fourth, and finally, ethnicity implies a dialectic that ineluctably links two distinct processes, categorization and identification (Jenkins 1997: 22, 23), and exists within the interplay between the individual and the collective.

What springs from this definition is that ethnicity is an aspect of social relationships between individuals who consider themselves culturally different from members of other groups with whom they have a minimum of regular interaction. As Thomas Eriksen argues, when cultural differences regularly make a difference in interaction between members of groups, the social relationship has an ethnic element. Interestingly, race becomes only one of the possible ways in which difference can be articulated between groups, and physical difference only one of the possible markers engaged within the ethnic process, as argued by Eriksen: "Ideas of 'race' may or may not form part of ethnic ideologies, and their presence or absence does not seem to be a decisive factor in interethnic relations" (Eriksen 1993: 5).

And, in turn, ethnicity becomes only one among many "social identities," as is made quite clear in Jenkins's *Social Identities* (1996; see for instance page 91). The work of Kevin Yelvington (1995) on ethnicity, gender, and class in a Trinidadian factory illustrates this point. Although he notes that the term "race" was usually used on his field site and that the concept of ethnicity was "played out ... under the rubric of the colonial term race" (1995: 25), the anthropologist chooses to use the term "ethnicity" for conceptual reasons:

Because "race" is based not on biological fact but on the construction of reality, and because the notion of ethnicity usually implies this social and cultural construction, I prefer to subsume the notion of "race" under the rubric of ethnicity for purposes of analysis. In this way identity ... can be seen as contingent and changing, depending on culture, history, and relations of power. (Yelvington 1995: 25)

Yelvington's choice illustrates quite well the conceptual displacement that occurs in social anthropology, which simultaneously recognizes the use of "race" in social relationships and its non-pertinence at the conceptual level. In other words, it is fundamental for the anthropologist to make a distinction between what people say, do, and think on the one hand, and the analytical level on the other: this echoes Eriksen, who points out that the same process is called "racial" in some societies but not in others. The process that the anthropologist analyzes is ethnicity; even when people use "race," it is constructed, dynamic, and ultimately grounded not in intrinsic qualities of the group but in the social relationship developed between at least two groups. Hence race is only a dimension that ethnicity can take; it is a belief that can be used within the ethnic process. Yelvington, however, does not completely evacuate "physical" or "biological" difference. Ethnicity can be defined as social identity characterized by metaphoric or fictive kinship according to which people "see each other, not exactly as kin, but as 'possible kin'" (Yelvington 1995: 24–25). There is here a very interesting way to reinsert "race," albeit in a non-essentialist way: ethnicity is about individuals and groups *imagining some sort of fictive kinship* that does not necessarily rest on actual kinship.[3] This position is helpful to distinguish ethnicity from the broader notion of social identity; ethnicity becomes one of the modalities of the process of social identity, hence excluding other identity formations such as Cohen's stockbrokers or Harvard alumni. The resilient problem, however, is that even in the latter cases an argument could be made for the elaboration of a "fictive kinship" that would function on the model of symbolic kinship, of which other examples are Christian godparents or the prominence of the maternal uncle over the genitor in some matrilineal societies.

And so the question that arises is the following: if race is one of the dimensions that ethnicity may take, what dimension exactly is it? There is a good deal of blurriness on this point as evidenced by the very small amount of space devoted to "race" in the works of Eriksen, Yelvington, or Barth. The consensus seems to be that race is about physical difference, about the phenotype – hence ascribed in the aspect of the body that is visible immediately, and which, of course, might not correspond exactly with "deep" difference, that is, the level of the genotype. Sandra Wallman, like Thomas Eriksen, argues for the "minimizing" hypothesis: race is just a different type of marker, one based on physical difference.

But there is an interesting discussion in Jenkins, which uses as a point of departure the distinction of ethnicity and race along the lines of a double distinction, identification / categorization, and culture / biology, which is very common inside and outside the academy. Hence

---

[3] This strongly echoes Max Weber's definition of ethnicity (1978: 385–397).

John Rex (1986: 20–22) distinguishes "racial situations" based on phenotypic differences, and "ethnic situations" based on cultural differences. Notwithstanding the fact that, as Peter Wade (1993a: 21–22) points out, the way in which individuals perceive phenotypic differences is itself culturally variable, the association of ethnicity with culture and of race with phenotype (and/or genotype) raises numerous problems, of which the most acute is probably the normative judgment implied in this distinction. Indeed, it is as if ethnicity were a sort of "positive" race: ethnicity would be about choice, about cultural inheritance, about multiculturalism, and would not necessarily imply a hierarchy of ethnicities; on the other hand, race would be about imposition – and, consciously or not, about violence, domination, and hierarchy, with an inevitable reference to genocide and apartheid. Furthermore, ethnicity would be about a cultural inheritance deemed authentic and legitimate, while race would be about some false and illegitimate physical features charged with meaning. Ultimately, then, ethnicity is "good" and race is "bad." But is there really a way to "transform" race into something positive? And are not both race and ethnicity precisely about the dialectic between categorization and identification anyway? Jenkins extricates himself from this problem by a complicated circumvolution, which leads him to argue that ethnicity is ubiquitous, while race is a historically located abstraction:

If ethnic identity is basic to the human condition . . . "race" is not. And if ethnicity is arguably a basic, universal facet of the human cultural repertoire, ideas about "race" are not. "Racial" categories are second-order cultural creations or notions; they are abstractions, explicit bodies of knowledge that are very much more the children of specific historical circumstances, typically territory expansion and attempted imperial or colonial domination. (Jenkins 1997: 77)

Nonetheless, Jenkins is led back to the argument that race indeed constitutes one dimension among many that ethnicity can take.

The most that can be said is that, at certain times and in certain places, culturally specific conceptions of "race" – or, more correctly, of "racial" differentiation – have featured, sometimes very powerfully, in the repertoire of ethnic boundary-maintaining devices. (Jenkins 1997: 79)

And from this point Jenkins finally argues for race to be conceptualized as the outcome of historically specific ethnic situations, marked by domination and hierarchy, an outcome in which difference is construed as being immutable and fixed:

My argument is that racism(s) and categories of "racial" classification and differentiation are most usefully conceptualized as historically specific allotropes of the general, ubiquitous, social phenomenon of ethnicity. They arise in the context of situations in which one ethnic group dominates, or attempts to dominate, another and, in the process, categorizes them in terms of notional immutable differences, often couched in terms of inherent inferiority and construed as rooted in different biological natures ... It is socially constructed *immutable difference* ... which lies at the heart of the matter. (Jenkins 1997: 83)

Interestingly – and this brings us back to the "social identity umbrella" – this enables Jenkins to simultaneously argue for the radically distinct character of race and ethnicity (1997: 79) and for a continuum, which he builds from kinship to co-residence to ethnicity to nation all the way up to race (1997: 85). Hence Jenkins speaks of "ethnicity and its allotropes: locality, community, national identity, nationality ... and race" (1997: 169). In the end, the process at hand is social identity, fundamentally understood within the dialectic between identification and categorization; and in this Jenkins demarcates himself from the common understanding of a "good" chosen ethnicity versus a "bad" imposed race. "There are no groups," he says, "ethnic or otherwise, without categorization" (1997: 166). What distinguishes race from ethnicity is the ubiquity of the latter, and the fact that the former tends more strongly towards the pole of categorization than towards the pole of identification; but both take place within the space of the symbolic construction of boundaries between groups, which itself cannot exist outside of the dialectic between identification and categorization.

Thus there is a tendency in social anthropology to brush race aside as one modality of ethnicity, and to dilute ethnicity as being one modality of social identity. A direct consequence of this is the lack of anthropological studies of "race" or even "racism," as pointed out by Jenkins (1997: 48–50), although this is changing with Peter Wade's series of publications on race, culture, and nature (1993a, 2002, 2004). Indeed, while the departure from essentialism is obvious in the social anthropological construction of the concept of ethnicity – a dynamic, relational concept that emphasizes the symbolic construction of difference and its use within social interaction, while shifting from cultural content to social boundaries – there remains a cost: the fact that the concept of ethnicity becomes a dimension of social identity, thereby diluting itself to some extent. Race is seldom analyzed – it becomes a modality taken by the ethnic processes in specific circumstances, or something that people "use" within the "ethnic repertoire" and that relates to phenotype – and yet it does not disappear. The tendency within social anthropology, therefore, is to pay little attention to race by focusing on ethnicity; but there seems to remain an unquestioned link made between race and phenotype. Interestingly, British cultural studies has taken a completely different position: it makes race central, while showing that it does not exist.

Cultural studies

Indeed, anti-essentialism has been a defining project within British cultural studies, a project for which Stuart Hall even "preaches":

And we ought to sort of preach on this occasion, no, not only to give up the bad habits of smoking and drinking and whoring and gambling, but to give up certain forms of political essentialism and the way in which it makes you sleep well at night. (Hall 1997: 290)

In fact, this anti-essentialist project has to be understood within British cultural studies' analysis of modernity – it is not circumscribed within the analysis of race and ethnicity. In a co-edited book on modernity (Hall *et al.* 2000), Hall argues that modern societies emerged as the result of a complex process of interaction between distinct political, economic, social, and cultural processes that "worked on and transformed traditional societies into modern ones" (2000: 9). Characteristic of cultural studies is, of course, the importance given to the "cultural process," viewed not as a reflection of the other spheres but as constitutive of modernity (2000: 15); culture is defined as "meanings, values, symbols, ideas, knowledge, language, ideology: what cultural theorists call the symbolic dimensions of social life" (2000: 15).

Hence the conceptualization of race and ethnicity has to be understood as a part of an anti-essentialist project, which itself is a part of an analysis of modernity. And fundamentally, "race" is understood as part of the cultural formation of modernity: what Hall famously called the gradual elaboration of a discourse of "the West and the rest" (2000: 184–227), a system of representation that draws on a dichotomy between two poles of a binary. This discourse, for Hall, has been the most powerful and structuring discourse in the formation of modernity:

The West produced many different ways of talking about itself and "the Others." But what we have called the discourse of "the West and the rest" became one of the most powerful and formative of these discourses. It became the dominant way in which, for many decades, the West represented itself and its relation to "the Other" ... We analyzed it as a "system of representation" – a "regime of truth." (Hall 2000: 225)

In *Against Race* Gilroy examines several manifestations of this "regime of truth" and traces the resilience of race (or "raciology") from its crudest form found with nineteenth-century racial science to Black nationalism to the advent of genomics and new media. He concludes,

The order of active differentiation that gets called "race" may be modernity's most pernicious signature. (Gilroy 2000: 53)

Thus for Hall, as for Gilroy, there exists a "close connection" (Gilroy 2000: 58) between race and modernity. Further, Gilroy's book establishes the persistence of essentialism at the heart of modern democracies, which he envisions as a process of encampment: there is a tendency to establish "camps" which, whether they actually have positive premises (such as collective solidarity) or negative consequences, all ultimately rest on absolutism and closure. Hence Gilroy asserts, "modernity is besieged" (2000: 93), and he claims the need for taking position "between camps" (2000: 84) and for "refiguring humanism" (2000: 53) against all forms of essentialism and absolutism. As we have seen in the preceding chapter, this project takes the form of the diaspora: to absolute identities that tend towards closure, both Gilroy and Hall oppose multifocal identities that tend towards freedom.

Interestingly, the conceptual argument that they bring forth establishes *both race and diaspora* as direct "signatures" of modernity. The issue here becomes eminently political: after demonstrating that race does not exist outside of the discursive space (hence that it is a non-object, or rather, that it is an object that does not exist in nature), both Hall and Gilroy shift towards demonstrating that *identity* can take different forms: some are essentialist – race – and some are not – Hall's "new ethnicities" or Gilroy's "diasporic identities." Both forms are eminently modern – resting on the essentialist thought that accompanied the formation of modernity, or on the multiple movements, both geographic and cultural, that have existed during the formation of modernity and especially at the end of the twentieth century. "Race" and "diaspora" are pitted against each other as two paradoxical, but nonetheless characteristic, features of modernity; they are considered as two antagonistic alternatives in modern societies. The struggle against the former is politically legitimized; it is not only a question of the *reality* or *unreality* of race; rather, it is a question of its *nefarious consequences* upon society – upon politics, upon thought, upon individual freedom as much as collective solidarity.

There is tremendous merit in this approach. First, there is conceptual soundness in the sense that both race and diaspora, essentialism and anti-essentialism, are grounded in modernity itself, as well as in the fact that they are considered as discursive practices, within a broader conception of the symbolic sphere brought forth by cultural studies as a field. Second, there is a genuine attempt to get rid of essentialism, by frontally engaging with it: race is not evacuated from analysis, as it might have been, in different forms and to different degrees, in American sociology, Marxism, and British social anthropology. Third, this frontal engagement with race bears witness to an intellectual struggle *without guarantees*, to use Hall's famous words. Gilroy's position, in particular, given the cultural and political context at the turn of the twenty-first century, shows courage and integrity. These three points converge towards the general theory developed by cultural studies, which ties the "ideal" and the "material" and affirms that the symbolic – meaning, representations, ideas, language – not only is a part of society, but also plays an active role in social action. It is not that ideas form "the world," and it is not that "the world" can be shaped according to whatever one thinks of it; but "the world" is made of the interaction between ideas, social action, and social structure. Hence, race does not disappear behind its concrete consequences (as in American sociology), it is not set aside at the level of analysis (as in British social anthropology), and it is not discarded as an "ideology" (as in Marxist thought).

Such a sound approach, however, still bears danger within. And to show this, we need to turn to the alternative to race that both Hall and Gilroy see in "hybrid" or "unfixed" identities born out of a process of "cultural diasporization." Both of them ground these identities in multiple belongings; in the complex dialectic between different places found in the "Black Atlantic" (Gilroy) or the Caribbean diaspora (Hall). By definition, diasporic identities are multifocal, and thereby open and fluid; they alone are able to disrupt essentialism and to maintain individual freedom. However, both Gilroy and Hall fall back on something that can be said to be "essentialist." When Hall argues that one can be "black and British" without having to choose between the two (1992: 473), there remains the idea that there *are* two entities – "black" and "British" – which, although they can be combined and "hybridized," still bear some sort of existence individually. Similarly, Gilroy's emphasis on a shared *experience*, albeit multidimensional and not centered around the origin, can be interpreted as a displacement from the biological (the "origin") towards the cultural (subsequent movements). Both scholars grant a central importance to the crossing of the Atlantic and the experience of slavery; this is what defines the commonality of the group, but it is not the only thing that defines the group. Hence what Gilroy calls "the rootless comospolitanism of the Black Atlantic" (2000: 115) can also become *fixed in its very lack of fixity*: no matter how negotiable or transformable the "black experience" is, it still remains the "black experience." The "black subject" still exists, both in Hall and Gilroy: and "sameness" rather than "difference" therefore remains at the heart of "diasporic identities" – a critique that has been already made by Floya Anthias (1998). But this fundamental commonality – despite the multiple possibilities and layers that "identity" can take, it remains "black" – is the product of a highly complex negotiation, which requires another reflection on the comparison between race and diaspora: according to Gilroy, there are positive dimensions to the very dangerousness of race, and those, of course, include its ability to bring people together, albeit against others. Indeed, race is a powerful symbolic cement for the group, which builds solidarity. For both Hall and Gilroy, it is therefore important to resolve the paradox of "new ethnicities" or "diasporic identities," or, in other words, to not construct individual freedom and difference at the expense of community. We say here "construct" because, as always, the conceptual and the political levels are intermingled in their work: it is important both conceptually and politically to show that collective solidarity can exist without, and outside of, race. And so the black subject is made of difference, of alternativeness, of multiplicity; and although its very existence is to a certain extent essentialized, it is, ultimately, the preservation of individual freedom that matters, and allows Paul Gilroy to claim the "in-between camps" position of diasporic identities.[4]

The attempt at conceptualizing race by avoiding essentialism is interesting; it is also probably among the most successful of the four currents of thought we have observed so far. By associating multiplicity and individual freedom with collective solidarity, Gilroy indeed is able to engage race but also to dismiss it – without making it disappear, without discarding it by omission, and without denying its concrete consequences. The use of the term "experience" throughout Hall's and Gilroy's work, of course, is another problem that remains. Because in the end, there is the assumption of a commonality of experience between certain individuals that cannot be shared by others, on the basis of historicity. The point here is not to deny the commonality of individuals confronted by the same history; indeed "experience" can be shared, at

---

[4] We do not want to criticize Gilroy's analysis from the standpoint of case studies of "diasporas" that would invalidate it, because he develops a multicentered model that comes in opposition with the common view of diaspora as being centered around the origin (be it real or imaginary). Indeed, there is no reason why "diasporas" should avoid an essentialist rigidity and be immune to nationalistic or racist thought – examples of which are found throughout history as well as in Gilroy's own work. In a way, Gilroy can be said to develop his diasporic alternative to race in opposition not only to racial or ethnic absolutism, but also to diasporic absolutism itself. Hence it is both pointless and unfair to criticize his model by using existing examples of "diasporic essentialism."

least more closely with some individuals than with others. But to claim the existence of a collective experience shared by all brings one very close to denying that some might not share it. What is experience? Can there be any "shared" experience between two human beings? Can two persons, no matter how close, "experience" the same situation in a similar way? And does the lack of common "experience" evacuate an individual from the group? The real essentialism, hence, lies not in the "black" epithet, but in the fact that an "experience" is assumed to be shared by people who have been through the same process (Hall's "diasporization"). This, in our view, forms the strongest paradox in the work of Stuart Hall and Paul Gilroy. And although they can be credited for attempting to de-essentialize both identity and "experience," there remains enough essentialism to allow for a misinterpretation that could lead to a reification of experience such as is found in the United States, where introductory courses in Black Studies departments are entitled "The Black Experience," as if there were a unique "way" to be black, radically foreign to a unique "way" to be "something else." Consequently, we are led back to the very binary of radical difference that Stuart Hall has fought so relentlessly.

As the day of the publication of *The Interpretation of Dreams* approached, Freud described his understanding of the book to his friend Wilhelm Fleiss:

The whole thing is planned on the model of an imaginary walk. First comes the dark wood of the authorities (who cannot see the trees), where there is no clear view and it is easy to go astray. Then there is a cavernous defile through which I lead my readers – my specimen dream with its peculiarities, its details, its indiscretions and its bad jokes – and then, all at once, the high ground and the open prospect and the question: "Which way do you want to go?" (Freud 1900: 155, note 1)

At the end of these intermediate reflections, in which we have sought to shed light on the different ways the four styles of thought remain linked to essentialist definitions of race, the way forward is not self-evident. Insofar as these styles of thought have constituted what can be said about race, the direction to be taken presents certain risks, which are associated with the need to build from scratch a new perspective that does not repeat the pitfalls of past approaches, albeit in a new way. Therefore, we will find a new direction in analytical frameworks that permit us to hold the paradoxical reality of race before us as an object of analysis. These frameworks were not built for this specific purpose; yet, they are fortuitous because they allow our analysis to remain on the high ground that opens onto a new point of view on race.

6   Belief and social action

One could see an automatic relationship between biology and essentialism as an overarching, defining structure for the analysis of race within the social sciences; indeed, it is against a dominant "racial science" that the social sciences of race have stood since the beginning of the twentieth century. The struggle to be fought, hence, has been simple: while it was left to scientists to show the inaccuracy of racial science, social scientists took on the task of reshaping a concept not grounded in any biological reality, while analyzing a "social reality" that perdured. But the very simplicity of the project – the liberation of social science from the scientifically corrupt inheritance of the nineteenth century, an act of intellectual decolonization – has been repeatedly challenged. The contemporary resilience of race can be explained by the duration of its participation in both discursive practices and the social structure; in other words, its pervasiveness can be analyzed as a consequence of the fact that it has proved difficult to erase race from the way individuals, groups, and societies live, because it has participated too closely, and for too long, in social organization as much as in thought. What seems at first sight simple begins to appear as an insurmountable difficulty.

In the first five chapters of this book, we have looked at the efforts produced by four types of inquiry, which all share difficulties in successfully liberating the concept of race from essentialism. But we would like to argue that, while in the *social world* the resilience of race can be read as the discursive and structural resilience of a system of thought that participated heavily in the organization of social life over the course of centuries, at the *conceptual level* the resilience of race as an essentialist concept can be read at least in part as the result of an epistemological error, which lies *precisely* in the *overarching organizing assumption that biology equates with essentialism.*[1] By rejecting biology altogether on the

---

[1] See Wade (2002: 112) for a commentary on this assumption. However, Wade's critique focuses on the association between biology and fixity, which he demonstrates is not automatic, although it is commonly viewed as such. Our critique focuses on the

ground of its mechanical association with essentialism, social thought throws the baby out with the bathwater; and this radical refusal has led to the inability of theories of race clearly to analyze the paradox of an object that is both real and unreal. Denying biology altogether, indeed, implies that "physical differences" are either denied or ignored; but ultimately "physical difference" remains present in the vague, underlying assumption that race has to do with physical features. Hence we end up with a situation – analyzed at length in the first five chapters – defined by the simultaneous denial or rejection of the biological and its implicit, shadowy presence. For the conceptualization of race to become more adequate, the issue of physical difference (i.e., the phenotype) needs to be explored.

Ironically, the equation of biology with essentialism and the subsequent efforts to reject biology did not remove essentialism from certain ways of conceptualizing race *without* biology. The biological is replaced by the social in the contemporary social science of race. Yet this social concept of race retains the logic of essentialism by fixing different kinds of intrinsically different social groups and incorporating individuals into groups based on these intrinsic differences. Moreover, a trace of the biological infects the social concept of race insofar as the conceptual distinction between racial groups refers back to – as an empirical support – the commonsense definitions of race that circulate in society. Whereas the racial science of the nineteenth century brought biology in through the front door, twentieth-century social science allows biology to slip in through the back entrance. Thus, the equation of biology with essentialism has led to a deeply paradoxical outcome concerning race. On the one hand, the rejection of biology has led to conceptual confusion about the "object" that is race. On the other hand, the assumption that essentialism and biology go hand in hand has not eliminated essentialism from social scientific concepts of race; this unrecognized essentialism is often grounded in commonsense views of race that are consistent with the biological concept of race.

Clarifying the question of the object

In this chapter, we elaborate on our initial claim that race is a thing of belief, that there has been up to this point a confusion between two objects of inquiry: "race" and the "belief in race." We start from the premise that races do not exist within humankind; what exists, though, is

consequence of this assumption, that is, the evacuation of any biological reference from the conceptualization of race – which ironically actually allows biology back in.

Table 3 *The three objects in the conceptualization of race*

Object A	Object B	Object C
Phenotype	Perception of the phenotype	Belief in race

physical variation and human beings' perception of physical variation. In other words, there *is* a biological object – the *phenotype* – which should not be confused with the *perception of the phenotype*, which is, if not entirely, at least in a great part a social process (as demonstrated by Peter Wade). Hence what we suggest here is that *the fact that we "see" physical differences in a specific way that is dependent on social life does not imply that these physical differences are completely ideal.* It only means that we accommodate a biological reality on the basis of the social life we share together.

Additionally, we argue that there is *also* a social object – *racial belief.* There is no object called "race" outside of the social object we call "racial belief." Therefore, instead of one vague object called "race," three objects can be distinguished (see Table 3).

The first object, which we call *phenotype*, concerns what in an organism is readily observable. The phenotype cannot be defined without its companion the genotype (which could be added as a fourth object to Table 3): indeed, there is a relationship between the genotype and the phenotype, although there is no automatic correspondence. The genotype is the indicator for the genome; it is partly expressed, and partly not expressed, in the phenotype. For example, someone might have a gene for blue eyes, and still display brown eyes, leaving the former gene unexpressed. For our purpose here, it suffices to say that nineteenth-century racial science was based on the phenotype, that is, on the variations found in the physical appearance of individuals; and our perception of physical difference is also based on the phenotype: it is what one sees. The problem of categorizing individuals by phenotype has been demonstrated on numerous occasions.[2] Indeed, the genetic variation found *within* so-called "racial groups" is actually as high as, if not higher than, the variation found *between* them.[3]

---

[2] Nineteenth-century scientists could not agree on the number of "races," dividing humankind into anywhere between three and sixty-three groups. See Smedley (1999).

[3] Interestingly, there actually exists a debate, within genetics, about the existence and/or significance of "race." However, it is fair to say that a dominant consensus agrees to the non-existence of race at the genetic level. We shall go back to the non-unified discourse of genetic science about race in Chapter 7.

Hence there exists an object A, the phenotype, which equates with physical appearance. Each of us looks different, while some of us share more physical resemblance than others. This first object is a natural object, subject to measurements, observations, and demonstrations. However, the description of the phenotype as "natural" does not mean that it is stable: the phenotype (as well as the genotype) is subject to changes provoked by the environment (among other factors). It is also susceptible to modifications linked to individual life, whether we speak of diet (weight changes, which are also accompanied by "deeper" consequences at the metabolic level, for instance), of accidents (e.g., amputations, fractures), of voluntary surgery (e.g., surgery that reconstructs or enhances physical appearance), of various diseases (especially skin related), or of voluntary transformations (e.g., skin tanning or bleaching, hair frizzing or straightening). Thus the phenotype is a natural object that, nonetheless, is not completely fixed, whether it is in its relationship to the genotype (the same genotype can be associated to different phenotypes, and vice versa) or during the lifetime of a given individual.[4] What must be recognized, however, is that it *does exist* outside of the social realm, although the social realm can also modify it; however, modifications are also limited – a tall woman with dark skin and blue eyes cannot turn into a short man with white skin and black eyes, at least not with the current state of science. This natural object – the phenotype – is not the object we are most concerned with (the *belief in race* is the central focus). However, it needs to be recognized as a distinct object in order to situate it in relation to other objects that pertain to what is called race.

The second object, which we call the *perception of the phenotype*, is a social object, although it does rely on biological features as well (namely, the sense organs). What we see, hear, smell, touch, and feel is highly dependent not only on our sense organs (which make us "see" differently than would a cat or a fly, for instance) and the ways in which this "standard" perception can be modified (for instance through drug use, according to our mood, or because of diseases or "defects" such as Daltonism). But perception is also dependent on the social world.[5] Hence we arrive at an essential object in the study of the belief in race. We argue, with Peter Wade, that the perception of the phenotype, the perception of physical differences, is largely a cultural and social

---

[4] An interesting discussion of the unfixed character of "human nature" can be found in Wade (2002).

[5] See, among others, the work of psychologist Jameson (2005) on the relationship between perception, cognition, and culture in "color-naming."

product. The impact of the perception of the phenotype can be found on at least two levels, in what we see and in how we perceive what is seen.

At the first level, we do not perceive all the physical attributes of a given individual at once. Our perception initially focuses on *specific* physical attributes, which implies a specific selection or choice of which attributes matter immediately and take precedence over others. These attributes could be as diverse as the color of the eyes, the figure, skin tone, or the way one dresses. It is not that we do not physically "perceive" other attributes, it is that we exercise selectivity within this process of perception. There is no way to explain the prevalence of the perception of skin color, accompanied by secondary traits such as hair texture or the shape of the nose or lips, over other physical features, other than by a cultural and social habituation through which we come to see these traits as being more important and more significant than others. In other words, beliefs and collective representations held in a given society have an influence on this selective perception process, evidenced by the emphasis placed on certain traits as compared to others. It is not a coincidence that skin color has become the one element that dominates all others; and it is only in those cases that are not clear-cut enough for us to categorize immediately that we rely on other physical attributes to either invalidate or validate our first impression: facial structure, hair texture, etc. The way we perceive physical appearance is not simply a mechanical "photograph" taken by the retina: it is also an *act of cognition*, intimately connected to socially inflected mental categories as well as individual emotions, which influence the dry, physical perception of what stands before our eyes.

Hence the second level concerns the fact that there is an unavoidable meaningfulness of what we perceive. In other words, there is actually no dry perception, that is, there is no perception that does not rely on meaning. Human beings are condemned to see the world through the lenses of the social world they inhabit; the *biological* perception of an object is necessarily embedded in *meaning*. Studies in cognitive psychology have demonstrated that cognitive processes constantly build up on the basis of continuous experimentations. When we see a fire, we do not think further to associate what we see with "heat" and with "touching it means getting burnt," for instance. The association between what we see and what we know of it has become automatic and immediate. We do not need to experiment with fire twice to always associate "fire" with "heat" and with "burnt"; some of us actually never experiment with fire at all, trusting what another human being tells us about the experiment.

What does all this say about race? We argue that there are in reality *two different objects* in what is commonly referred to as "phenotype" or

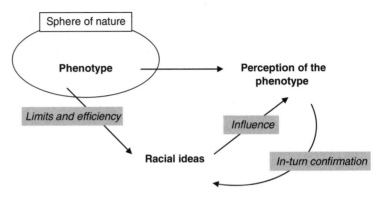

Figure 4

"physical difference" in social studies of race. The first of these objects is the actual phenotype – that is, the set of attributes and processes of the genotype that are expressed. In the case of race, this has to do mostly with readily observable anatomical traits. The second of these objects is the human perception of the phenotype, which becomes here much more a social object than the first. Indeed, the perception of the phenotype is saturated with meaning; in the case of race, (selected) phenotypical traits *mean* something specific. Someone who has dark skin is not simply going to be *seen* as such; she is going to be *meaningfully seen* as the member of a specific group – let's say, "Negro" in New York in 1910, or "African-American" in 2001 – and this belonging to a group also implies a set of consequences: for example, "such a person cannot enter this restroom" or "such a person could be the object of racial profiling." Hence as Peter Wade argues,

Certain biological differences exist among humans and are themselves in reality socially meaningless in that they do not determine or even influence social differences. But people build ideas about race onto chosen perceived biological differences and the object of social analysis is these ideas. (2002: 43)

However we disagree with Wade on one point. We agree that the racial ideas that saturate perceived biological differences are the object of social analysis; but they are not *built onto* perceived biological differences. They *produce* a specific perception of biological differences. Hence we distinguish *three* objects (see Figure 4).

As Wade argues, the phenotype is not pregnant with race; it is not pregnant with socially constructed racial meaning. It *only concerns* physical diversity, which does *not* call forth racial categories. The only way in which the phenotype comes into play in this racial ensemble is the manner in which it is taken up – through *coincidence* – by racial ideas. Hence, the phenotype does limit the efficiency of a racialized system of thought. But that is *its only participation in the ensemble.* And we say "participation" because it is not *necessary* to the existence of the ensemble. In other words, there is no doubt that a racial system could exist that operated on the basis of boundaries *not found in nature.* However, our claim – influenced by a Durkheimian perspective – is that a minimal coincidence between racial ideas about physical variation and the actual existence of physical variation is needed in order to ensure the social efficacy of such a collective representation.

Second, the *perception* of the phenotype *is not pregnant with race either;* it is only transformed into a perception of race by its association *with racial ideas.* We shall not enter into the debate within cognitive psychology – for instance, Hirschfeld's claim that there are specific "cognitive devices" upon which "race" is grafted (1998) and hence that there is some sort of cognitive need for "natural taxonomies" – but rather we simply state that the perception of the phenotype *can* be impressed by racial ideas but that it does not *have* to be. In other words, it is possible to imagine, with Stuart Hall or Paul Gilroy, a world in which individuals would perceive physical appearance in a totally different, and non-racial, way, and in which physical difference would mean nothing less and nothing more than that: diversity in appearance. Hence specific anatomic traits would not be more prevalent than others in our perception, other than for their higher level of "visibility" (the shape of feet, for instance, is somewhat difficult to perceive when one is wearing boots), and they would not bear within, in an automatic manner, a set of meanings and practical consequences for the individual.

This leads us to the third object, which we call *racial ideas* or *belief in race.* It should seem obvious that this is where the traditional understanding of "race" is predominantly located. We want to redefine this object as being a belief: it has no reality outside of being an abstraction, the product of thought; hence race is, above all else, something that one believes in, and its only reality is found within this belief. The claim that race is an object of belief should not be confused with the view that race is ideological or the view that racial ideas are equivalent to ideology. These perspectives, which can be found in the racial formation theory of Omi and Winant as well as in the Marxist tradition, treat racial ideas as political objects or as purely *epiphenomenal* and, in the case of Robert Miles, conclude in the argument that the analytical category of race is ideological. In contrast, the object "belief in race" should not be conceived either as the efflux of the relations of production, or as the primarily political project of a dominant group and the resistance of racially subordinate groups. Consequently, we do not find satisfactory the view that the analytical category of race inevitably reifies and reproduces race (Miles 1988, Miles and Brown 2003). At the same time, belief in race should not be taken to imply this object is purely ideational or discursive; it should not be confused with the strong post-structuralist position "*il n'y a pas de hors-texte*," that there is "nothing outside of the text" of racial ideas.[6] Indeed, our purpose is to present a de-reified and de-essentialized concept of race that articulates the double movement of belief towards the world and towards a feeling of significance that transcends that world. As we conceive it, the idea of race attends to something *in the world*; it attends to the phenotype (object A). To do otherwise would transgress the conditions of efficacy for the idea itself: a referent in the sphere of nature. What matters, however, is not the sphere of nature in itself, which is a necessary limit condition on belief, but rather the relations between the racial ideas on the one side, and the phenotype and perception of the phenotype on the other side. Hence, the belief in race entails this double movement towards the phenotype and towards racial meanings (the perception of the phenotype) that exceed whatever the phenotype offers as an empirical referent. We argue that this conceptualization of three objects (racial ideas, perception of the phenotype, and the phenotype) and their relations to each other is more adequate to the simultaneous reality and unreality of race than concepts such as class (i.e., Marxism) or other substitute concepts (racism, culture, ethnicity, or diaspora).

However, it is necessary to go one step further: we must also situate "racism" in relation to these three objects since there is more to "race" than ideas, thoughts, and words. This requires a redefinition of the relationship between the ideal and the material. Individuals act upon ideas; institutions implement policies that incorporate these ideas; groups commit or suffer physical violence because of these ideas. Hence as we discussed in the introductory chapter, one could argue that recognition of this concrete reality is more important than a discussion about the reality, or lack thereof, of race as an idea. But *practice*, such as the implementation of policies or the use of violence that is identified with *racial experience*, is *only* a consequence of a system of thought; and it cannot – and should not – be construed as *producing* race. *The reality of race cannot be inferred from its concrete consequences*, no matter how

---

[6] "That is why the methodological considerations that we risk applying here to an example are closely dependent on general propositions that we have elaborated above; as regards the absence of the referent or the transcendental signified. There is nothing outside of the text [there is no outside-text; il n'y a pas de hors-texte]" (Derrida 1974: 158).

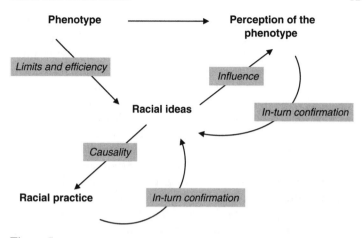

Figure 5

momentous they might be. In other words, the analysis of race cannot begin with the practice of racism. However, we also argue that there is more to the relationship between an idea and a practice than a unilateral causal link running from ideas to practices: the existence of a racial practice in the life of societies and individuals also acts upon racial ideas by legitimizing and reinforcing them. *While practice is not a proof of the reality of the ideas, over time it does become perceived as such.*[7] But before we deepen our analysis, we can add our fourth object, *racial practice*, to our descriptive diagram (see Figure 5).

The fourth object, *racial practice*, refers to the concrete consequences of racial ideas in social life. Some of these consequences can be measured, more or less well – from the number of hate crimes to the degree of segregation of a society – but others cannot: the "looks" one receives, feelings, emotions, covert discrimination, etc. It is only logical, therefore, that many sociological and social-psychological studies of race focus not on racial ideas, but on racial practice, because the latter is much more easily measurable.[8] While we argue that the conceptualization of race should focus on, and begin with, one specific object which is found at the

---

[7] An analogous interpretation of the materiality of ideology can be found in Althusser (2001).

[8] Here is not the place to enter a nonetheless important controversy: indeed, even what is measurable in racial practice is subject to ambiguity; it is difficult, although possible, to prove that someone did not get a job, or was abused, *because* of racial reasons. Hence the legal defense can be organized around the attempt to show that discrimination was not racial: for instance, the Paraguayan government, accused of genocide against the Ache people in the 1980s, claimed that there was no ground for a "racial crime" trial since the Ache had been killed for land and not because they "were Aches."

ideational level and refers to a process of believing, we also argue that this conceptualization cannot be satisfactorily elaborated without considering the relationship that this ideational object entertains with other objects. The clarification of these relationships can happen only by carefully distinguishing four objects which, taken together, form the *racial ensemble*: the phenotype, the perception of the phenotype, racial ideas/ belief in race, and finally racial practice. While this racial ensemble has to be taken as a totality, which means that any conceptualization of one object in the absence or neglect of the others is unsatisfactory, it remains true that race is located primarily within the third element of this series: at the ideational level. And that is the peculiarity of race. Race is not just an idea and neither is it just a practice; one stumbles upon the idea of race as one stumbles upon a hard rock – and the consequences of stumbling upon this idea are often more serious than those of stumbling upon a rock.

Belief

How then can social theory handle such a vexing thing as race? How can it avoid the dead ends into which various efforts to conceptualize and measure race have led? How might it best approach this sticky idea of race, which adheres to people and things but is not an essential part of them? We shall turn to what at first might seem unlikely sources to work up an adequate conceptualization of the idea of race: Weber's sociology of meaning, his concept of ethnic groups, and the sociology of religion. After all, in Weber's corpus of writings, very few pages deal with "race." Moreover, the sociology of religion has traditionally been employed to categorize and analyze objects and processes that are viewed as specifically *religious*. However, Weber's writings on meaning, ethnicity, and religion (and more recent work in this field) enable us to redirect the theory of race from a search for a concrete racial reality towards a theory of a belief in race.

In the section of *Economy and Society* that deals with "sociological concepts," Weber defines sociology as a field of study of social action. He gives social action a particular construction: "We shall speak of 'action' insofar as the acting individual attaches a subjective meaning to his behavior . . . Action is 'social' insofar as its subjective meaning takes account of the behavior of others and is thereby oriented in its course" (Weber 1978: 4). Weber, of course, seeks a *causal* explanation of action oriented to subjective meanings and, as discussed earlier, uses ideal-typical constructions to differentiate types of action and their meanings. Social action is motivated and guided by cultural values, which supply the subjective meanings that are attributed to actions. Therefore, meanings and actions are interconnected: individuals act in particular ways because they believe it is meaningful to do so; meanings gain legitimacy through acts of recognition. If race is considered in Weber's framing of the relation between belief and social action, the relation between the idea of race and the reality of race comes into clearer focus. On the one side, the belief in race depends on the recognition of the authority of racial meanings about individuals and groups in society. On the other side, this belief spurs social action, in which race is taken to be the primary mode of interaction. Our concern lies with the belief in, and recognition of the authority of, race. Both belief and recognition entail action: believing in something and recognizing the authority of that something that is the object of belief brings into being ways of maintaining belief and modes of routinizing the authority of those beliefs. The elucidation of these ways and modes of believing and legitimizing race is crucial for understanding race, which, as we have argued, has no reality apart from a belief in the idea of race.

In our view, the belief in race among individuals reinforces social relationships that are construed along the lines of race. Consequently, an explication of the conditions of belief is essential for an adequate conceptualization of race; in contrast, a conceptualization of race that begins with the existence of social relationships among *racial groups* cannot adequately work back to the constitutive processes of the belief in race. In other words, the social (that is, meaningful) existence of racial groups depends on the belief in race. Again, taking Weber as a point of departure, social relationships are understood as "the behavior of a plurality of actors insofar as, in its meaningful content, the action of each takes account of the others and is oriented in these terms. The social relationship thus consists entirely and exclusively in the existence of a probability that there will be a meaningful course of social action" (Weber 1978: 27). What is important in this definition is the emphasis on the *probability* that a "plurality of actors" will orient their behavior towards each other *because it is meaningful to do so*. What makes such meaningful action probable cannot be automatically deduced from *reality*. Thus, in discussing communal relationships as a type of social relationship,[9] Weber brings in the example of race:

It is by no means true that the existence of common qualities, a common situation, or common modes of behavior imply the existence of a communal social

---

[9] "A social relationship will be called 'communal' (*Vergemeinschaftung*) if and so far as the orientation of social action – whether in the individual case, on the average, or in the pure type – is based on a subjective feeling of the parties, whether affectual or traditional, that they belong together" (Weber 1978: 40).

relationship. Thus, for instance, the possession of a common biological inheritance by virtue of which persons are classified as belonging to the same "race," naturally implies no sort of communal social relationship between them . . . But even if they all react to this situation in the same way, this does not constitute a communal relationship. The latter does not even exist if they have a common "feeling" about this situation and its consequences. *It is only when this feeling leads to a mutual orientation of their behavior to each other that a social relationship leads to a mutual orientation of them rather than of each to the environment.* (Weber 1978: 42, emphasis added)

The emphasis on feeling that gives rise to social relationship and a sense of mutuality reverses the order of analysis, from the group to the conditions of *groupness*. For the analysis of race to move from an environmental to a social perspective, what Weber calls common feelings – which we construe as belief and recognition – must be the central theoretical concern.

Weber elaborates on this statement on race found early in *Economy and Society* in a chapter on ethnic groups. The theoretical difficulty he confronts is the imputation of an *objective foundation* for the existence of *ethnic groups*, that is, an objective, common descent among ethnically differentiated groups grounded in biological or cultural differences.[10] Weber notes, at the beginning of the chapter, an analytical problem, when he states that "race identity," by which he means "common inherited and inheritable traits that actually derive from common descent," is a "much more problematic source of social action than the sources analyzed above." He first argues "race creates a 'group' only when it is subjectively perceived as a common trait." However, the social action that arises from this perception is "usually merely negative," that is, it takes the form of antipathy towards "those who are obviously different" and therefore "avoided and despised or, conversely, viewed with superstitious awe" (Weber 1978: 385). Moreover, he argues that "this antipathy is shared not just by persons with anthropological similarities, and its extent is by no means determined by the degree of anthropological relatedness; furthermore, this antipathy is linked not only to inherited traits but just as much to other visible differences" (Weber 1978: 385). In other words, antipathy towards people who are different does not necessarily conform to the presence or absence of "anthropological relatedness." Referring to "several million mulattoes in the United States," Weber argues that the existence of these individuals "speaks clearly against the assumption of a 'natural' racial antipathy, even among quite different races"

---

[10] We have already seen the assertion of these two bases of racial and ethnic groups in the writings of Americans such as Du Bois, Kallen, and Park (see Chapter 1).

(Weber 1978: 386). This observation (among others) leads Weber to conclude "merely anthropological differences account for little, except in cases of extreme esthetic antipathy" (Weber 1978: 386).

However, it is not only "anthropological differences" that are questionable with regard to the constitution of social groups. Whether "conspicuous 'racial' differences" are based on *tradition* is "usually of no importance as far as [its] effect on mutual attraction and repulsion is concerned" (Weber 1978: 387). Rather than the traditional ways of living that have always been followed (that might be used to explain the formation of racial groups), Weber asserts

Any cultural trait, no matter how superficial, can serve as a starting point for the familiar tendency to monopolistic closure . . . But if there are sharp boundaries between areas of observable styles of life, they are due to conscious monopolistic closure, which started from small differences that were then cultivated and intensified; or they were due to the peaceful or warlike migrations of groups that previously lived far from each other and had accommodated themselves to their heterogeneous conditions of existence. (Weber 1978: 388)

Therefore, rather than being the result of long-standing ways of *being* (i.e., of experience and acting), so-called traditional differences are less important in the formation of ethnic and racial groups than the cultivation of small differences or the contingency of migration. It is at this point that Weber introduces the term *belief* to account for apparent traditional foundations of groups.

Almost any kind of similarity or contrast of physical type and of habits can induce the belief that affinity or disaffinity exists between groups that attract or repel each other . . . The belief in group affinity, regardless of whether it has any objective foundation, can have important consequences especially for the creation of a political community. We shall call "ethnic groups" those human groups that entertain a subjective belief in their common descent because of similarities of physical type or of customs or both, or because of memories of colonization and migration; this belief must be important for the propagation of group formation; conversely, *it does not matter whether or not an objective blood relationship exists.* (Weber 1978: 388, 389, emphasis added)

The political community, above all other conditions, "inspires the belief in common ethnicity" and "tends to persist after the disintegration of the political community" (Weber 1978: 389). What matters, then, in the genesis and persistence of ethnic groups is a *subjective belief in common descent based on similarities* (which are not necessarily *objective*), and the strength of this belief is most strongly cultivated when an ethnic group forms a political community.

Yet Weber remains troubled by this ideal-typical concept of ethnic groups, precisely because of the significant level of contingency introduced by the formation of social groups on the basis of belief. In registering his skepticism towards the concept, Weber specifies four processes that must be entertained in order to identify the influence of ethnicity on social action, the first of which is the "subjective effect" of customs that are either the product of heredity or tradition. He then distinguishes the "impact of the varying content of custom" and the "influence of common language, religion, and political action, past and present" on the creation of these customs. A third set of factors relate to "attraction and repulsion" and "especially the belief in the affinity or disaffinity of blood." Finally, one would have to study the "consequences of this belief for social action" (Weber 1978: 394–395). At the end of his discussion, Weber questions the very validity of the concept of "ethnic" group: "It is certain that in this process the collective term 'ethnic' would be abandoned, for it is unsuitable for a really rigorous analysis" (Weber 1978: 395).

Weber states the "concept of the 'ethnic' group dissolves if we define our terms exactly" (Weber 1978: 395). Yet why would an exact definition of terms necessitate the dissolution of the concept? What is the problem with the concept of ethnic groups? Viewed from the perspective of Weber's approach to concept formation, the problem lies in the difficulty that "ethnic" groups present for the formation of an ideal-type concept: it lacks the "merit of clear understandability and lack of ambiguity" that is the methodological justification for the construction of ideal-types (Weber 1978: 6). Whereas ideal-types aim at "logical or teleological 'consistency'" (Weber 1958: 324), Weber is unable to give the concept of ethnic groups clarity and logical consistency. Not only is the concept of ethnic groups an aggregate of four separate processes, but also each one of the processes could be the basis of an ideal-type of ethnic groups. It is understandable why Weber, whose concept building in *Economy and Society* is precise, suspects that ethnic groups will not meet the criterion of *adequacy at the level of meaning*; in other words, no concept of ethnic groups will be adequate to illuminate precisely the conditions of any existing ethnic group.

Besides the remarkable clarity in Weber's thought on the problems that arise when conceptualizing ethnic groups, one other thing stands out: the centrality of belief to the process he identifies with an adequate formation of the concept of ethnic groups. The existence of ethnic and racial groups is, from an analytical standpoint, rooted in subjective belief. It is our intention to take up an analysis of race as belief at this point where Weber's conceptual analysis ends.

The use of the term belief, which is drawn from the sphere of religion, to describe what are obviously profane social phenomena is the most fortuitous aspect of Weber's attempt to develop an ideal-type of ethnic groups. However, the employment of a term that is more properly linked to the sociology of religion is not explained by Weber. We find that religion and race, or rather the sociology of religion and the sociology of race, are not as different as they might appear at first glance. As objects that present themselves for sociological analysis, race and religion present similar problems: both lack a physical presence and depend on ideational processes; both are also experienced as a reality by those who are committed to faith and those who are committed to the idea of race. While the belief in the idea of race is not particularly attuned to the transcendence of earthly reality – to an afterlife or heaven – that captivates the emotions and sentiments of a religiously motivated person, it is an idea whose persistence is not impeded by the absence of scientific evidence and the frequent unreliability of efforts to identify people using racial categories. Writing in the context of a debate among sociologists of religion over the object of inquiry, Danièle Hervieu-Léger describes a problematic that is echoed among those for whom race is the object of inquiry: "The enterprise of imposing order on a social entity which by common experience is perceived as inextricably chaotic comes up against the aspiration present in every religion, considered as a system of meanings, namely to make complete sense of the world and to condense the infinite multiplicity of human experience" (Hervieu-Léger 2000: 14–15). The effort to theorize race, which is also "inextricably chaotic," runs headlong into commonsense views that also condense the "infinite multiplicity of human experience" into categories of race. Nevertheless, when searching Weber's sociology of religion for a definition of religion that might be workable for the concept of race, one meets with what would be an immediate disappointment for scholars for whom race stands as a thing rather than a belief.

To define "religion," to say what it is, is not possible at the start of a presentation like this. Definition can be attempted, if at all, only at the conclusion of the study. The essence of religion is not even our concern, as we make it our task to study the condition and effects of a particular type of social action. (Weber 1978: 399)

Weber's ideal-typical approach to religion, which centers on its peculiarity as a type of social action, treats it as the outcome of specific orientations of this-worldliness and other-worldliness.

This might appear to be a dead-end for drawing an analogy between the concept of religion and the concept of race. Fortunately, the reading of a Weberian contribution to religious sociology found in the work of Hervieu-Léger points the way towards an *analogical relation* between religion and race as objects of sociological inquiry.[11] The first reason to support this relation is derived from an interpretation of Weber by Jean Séguy. As Hervieu-Léger writes, in his attempt to understand the field of the sociology of religion, Séguy recognized that Weber's discussion of religion ranged far beyond what would ordinarily be considered religious phenomena. After identifying an ideal-typical concept of religion as "a form of collective action, accepted by society as 'other'" and as being related to "supernatural powers," Hervieu-Léger points out that "but at once [Séguy] observes that this definition fails to contain all Weber's references to religion, when he describes social or political phenomena in which belief plays a part – the instance of a political or scientific vocation in pursuit of an ideal, or of political prophecy made by a demagogue" (Hervieu-Léger 2000: 66). This, according to Séguy, is a "*metaphorical use* of religious concepts": "'We describe this religion as analogical,' Séguy writes, 'because it does not refer to supernatural powers, but possesses most of the other features of religion in the full sense of the term'" (Hervieu-Léger 2000: 66, 67 [emphasis in original]). For Hervieu-Léger, this reading of a metaphorical or analogical concept of religion in Weber leads sociology out of an apparently ineluctable choice between a substantive concept and a functional concept of religion. In her view, it opens a pathway from a preoccupation with defining belief towards an understanding of the act of believing.

While the internal debate within the sociology of religion is not of specific relevance for the concept of race, Hervieu-Léger's understanding of religious modernity as believing is illuminating:

It is vital to define what one here understands by believing. The term denotes the body of convictions – both individual and collective – which are not susceptible to verification, to experimentation and, more broadly, to the modes of recognition and control that characterize knowledge, but owe their validity to the meaning and coherence they give to the subjective experience of those who hold them. If one here talks of believing rather than belief, it is in order to include not merely beliefs in the accepted sense, but all the resources of observance and

---

[11] Analogy is a useful means to illuminate similarities and differences between objects. Durkheim (1974 [1898]: 1) offers support for this position: "If analogy is not a method of demonstration in the true sense of the word, it is nevertheless a method of illustration and of secondary verification which may be of some use. It is always interesting to see whether a law established for one order of facts may not, *mutatis mutandis*, be found to apply elsewhere. This comparison may also serve to confirm it and give a greater understanding of its implications. In fact, analogy is a legitimate form of comparison, and comparison is the only practical means we have for the understanding of things."

language and the involuntary action which such belief in its multiple forms displays: believing is belief in action, as it is experienced. (Hervieu-Léger 2000: 72)

In terms of the sociology of religion, this definition is intended to navigate around the claim that religion is in decline in the modern age while, simultaneously, extending the range of religious phenomena to include new forms of believing that take place outside the institutional and spiritual framework of the world religions. Above all, the switch from "belief" to "believing" is sought as a solution to the long-standing definitional problem of religion, which can be traced from a myriad of essentialist definitions, to the Durkheimian oppositional binary of the sacred and the profane, to the Weberian lack of a definition. For Hervieu-Léger, the definitional dead-end can be avoided by focusing on the process of believing as opposed to the content of belief, hence displacing sociological inquiry from the essence of the object of belief towards the process by which this object is put in play within social relationships.

Hervieu-Léger's intervention can be analogized to the object race. Rather than struggling to find the essence of race – whether as biology or culture – or defining race by its function in society, as racism or as a prejudicial disposition that maintains a hierarchical racial order, the object (race) can be conceived as the outcome of believing, as the object of specific types of social action that keep the idea of race in existence and also give meaning and coherence to the lives of those who believe in it. In turn, the focus of inquiry can be further displaced from the object of belief to the process of believing: ultimately, at the conceptual level, it is not the *essence* of the object of belief that matters, but the *process* by which this object is set as a part of social action. Hence one must go beyond considering race as *the outcome* of belief: race, at the conceptual level, has to be situated *within the process of believing*. In other words, the *concept* of race is found in the coupling of a specific object of belief and of the process of believing, which becomes the actual object of inquiry.

Therefore, the conceptualization of race requires three movements of clarification. First, a necessary distinction of the multiple objects that actually participate in what we have called the racial ensemble: the phenotype, the perception of the phenotype, belief in race, and racial practice. These four distinct, although related, objects are often confounded in analysis. We argue that, although they should all be addressed to the extent that *together* they form a racial ensemble, they also should be distinguished to the extent that they are not *undifferentiated* and each have a life of their own. Hence the first step of the conceptualization process is the definition of the exact terms of the object of inquiry.

Second, there needs to be a clarification at the level of the process of inquiry itself. In other words, the second step involves the definition of the exact terms of the inquiry itself: how do we look at the object? This second step evidently requires an *a priori* clarification of the object. Once the racial ensemble has been defined, not in terms of content, that is, not in terms of the essence of the object, but in terms of relationships between a series of objects, the inquiry into this racial ensemble can be displaced from content to process. In other words, the sociologist can enter a fruitful path of inquiry that finally allows theory to work *with* the paradox of race, instead of working *against* it. The object of inquiry "race" becomes *a set of relationships between different objects that operate within a process of believing*, instead of the content or outcome of belief. That is what the term race refers to in our analysis.

A third clarification is required at the level of the conditions and effects of believing in race. In the introduction, we argued that a concrete experience of race is grounded in ideation, and that race, as an idea, is felt to be natural or real. The act of believing, which makes race real, involves at least three modes of attachment to the idea of race itself: knowledge, memory, and desire. By attachment we mean a general, affective relationship to the idea of race. However, this attachment to race is not only an emotional bond, it also entails an intellectual commitment to race. This is why knowledge of race is included with memory and desire as one modality of attachment. Racial knowledge develops and reinforces a belief in the truth of race, either as a self-evident way of being or as a body of expert knowledge of race. Racial memory cements individual and collective sentiments towards an imagined racial past – such memories are the basis of identification and an emotional bond of people living in the present with the racial "experiences" of the past. Racial desire, in contrast, is manifested less consciously, as a form of pleasure derived from the racial categories themselves. These modes of attachment are, therefore, the final dimension of an analysis of race that is adequate to the object.

> Man cannot live among things without forming ideas about them
> according to which he regulates his behaviour.   (Durkheim 1982: 60)

The racial ensemble, as defined in the preceding chapter, is a system of
relations between four distinct objects: the phenotype, the perception of
the phenotype, racial ideas, and racial practice. The core or primary
object within it is what we have called "racial ideas" or "belief in race";
but we also argue that it cannot be analyzed in complete isolation.
Indeed, the failure to conceptualize this ensemble as a whole is what
characterizes the major styles of thought on race we have previously
criticized. These styles of thought fix our attention on one of the objects
in the ensemble as the basis for the conceptualization and analysis of
race: on the perception of the phenotype, on racial ideas (which are
assimilated to the concept of ideology or discourse), or on racial practice
(which is understood variously as racialization or racism). Three subsequent problems are manifested. First, naturally occurring physical
differences (e.g. the phenotype) are misconstrued *as* racial phenomena.
Second, race is understood to be an exclusively *unreal* phenomenon
(precisely because it is epiphenomenal). Finally, race is understood to be
exclusively *real* (as some aspect of experience), even if at the same time it
is held to be *unreal*. These are ideal-typical orientations: in reality, all
three might appear in a particular style of thought about race.

Hence, we devoted the preceding chapter to distinguishing different
objects of inquiry within the commonly thought-to-be monolithic object
"race"; we argue that sociological inquiry is working here with not one,
but four distinct objects. We have also argued that none of the secondary
objects (the phenotype, the perception of the phenotype, and racial
practice) *produces* racial ideas, a claim that goes against the common
assumption of a causal relationship that moves from these secondary
objects towards racial ideas. But the question that arises, then, concerns
the relationship that the three secondary objects entertain with the primary object: if this relationship is not causal, what is it, and how does it

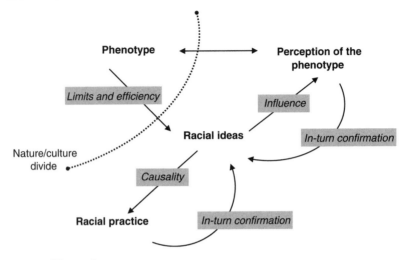

Figure 6

matter for sociological inquiry? In this chapter, we closely examine the way in which the secondary objects in the ensemble articulate with the primary object; we argue that these relationships are not causal, but take the form of relations of validity, legitimacy, and efficiency, which confirm the belief in race (see Figure 6).

We have argued that racial ideas, although they are linked to the phenotype, the perception of the phenotype, and racial practice, are not produced by any of these secondary objects. Neither the existence of physical differences in nature, nor the existence of racial practice, *produces* race. In other words, the reality of an idea does not depend upon its reality in nature; and neither does it depend upon its reality within social practice. What *does* condition the existence of racial ideas is a process of believing.[1]

If there is a belief in race, then there are conditions of validation and reproduction of this belief. Indeed, every religious movement implements some process of validation, without which believing does not last and the transmission of faith founders. Believing can be seen as a peculiar process; it postulates the existence of an object (the object of belief) for which there is no scientific evidence. Hence believing

---

[1] On the question of the reality of ideas, we stand on the ground already cleared for sociological thought by Durkheim, who demonstrated the *sui generis* reality of mental and collective representations (i.e., social facts) in *The Rules of Sociological Method*. However, to avoid misunderstanding it must be added that we are not arguing that all ideas are matters of belief (and believing).

operates within a specific regime of legitimacy, based upon the pertinence of the process *within a set of social relationships*. Religious movements use two types of validation, negative and positive, which both legitimize the specific beliefs of a given movement and delineate the boundaries of the group (i.e., by opposing an inside and an outside). Ultimately, it is precisely the process of legitimizing a given group's beliefs that also defines the group's identity and specificity. Negative validation asserts the process of believing that is specific to a group by opposing it to what exists in other groups. For example, Weber's ideal-typical charismatic leader (i.e., a prophet), who asserts "It is written . . . but I say unto you" (Weber 1978: 243), builds the legitimacy of the group's beliefs by using a process of negative validation. Positive validation, on the contrary, uses the commonality of thought and action found within the group; one's beliefs and actions are legitimized by the recognition that others do believe and act in the same way. Both processes are used simultaneously by most religious groups; and the dialectic between the two actually participates in building a dialectic between the inside and the outside, which thereby establishes boundaries between those who belong to the group, and the rest of the world. And this is the case from small independent communities all the way up to large institutionalized confessions: whether a dogma is clearly written and rigidly defined, or whether it is simply a set of ideas shared by a few individuals through daily interaction, the process remains the same.

How does this relate to the question of race? We have argued for a possible analogy between the two objects – race and religion – and also between the two fields (the sociology of race and the sociology of religion), and their modes of inquiry. Like the sociologist of religion, the sociologist of race works on an idea; this idea cannot be scientifically proven (or even, as in the case of race, has been proven unscientific), and therefore rests on a process of believing; both race and religion have no reality outside of belief, and yet they both have extremely concrete consequences, which range from individuals' daily experiences to political institutions to murder and genocide. Moreover, both race and religion require legitimation in order to acquire an existence in social life, and both also have to be legitimized in an efficient way in order to last. Ideas are fragile and, since they are supported by belief, they must be continuously reactivated. And yet – and this brings us to the paradox of race once again – ideas are also strong and persuasive; they seem natural and concrete. But the appearance of naturalness and concreteness is the result of a complex process of legitimation and confirmation that takes place within a relationship to both the natural and social worlds.

Religion does not solely implement an idea; it also relies on a series of "material" proofs found in both the natural world and the social world. We have already referred to the latter, with the mechanism of negative and positive validation of beliefs, which is eminently social. It is within social interaction that both the individual and the group confirm their belief, either through opposition or through identification. But religion also makes extensive use of the "natural world" and finds proofs that are ascribed within the physical sphere. Miracles (such as the parting of the Red Sea described in Exodus 13:17 to 15:22[2]) belong to this process of legitimacy – and here it is important to note that, because the relationship with the natural world is nonetheless ascribed within a process of belief, miracles do not need to be scientifically proven: their possibility is enough. This hypothesis – the implementation of an idea, accompanied by proofs that are not strictly ideal, within a regime of belief – is well illustrated with Weber's treatment of charismatic authority, developed in his elaboration of ideal-types of legitimate authority (1978). In contrast to bureaucratic or traditional modes of religious authority, the charismatic leader is characteristically detached from the material sphere; charismatic authority is based on the spiritual mission, on the rupture with the routine world, on the power of words. And yet even in this most detached form of authority, the leader's authority is not established only by the *words* he utters, although they are the foundational basis for his followers to believe in him. Indeed, the charismatic leader does not *possess* extraordinary skills; he is *believed* to possess them; and the only source of legitimacy for charismatic authority is *recognition*: "the mere fact of recognizing the personal mission of a charismatic master establishes his power" (Weber 1978: 1115). The words that the leader utters, and which are the foundation of belief, have to be renewed in their power, and the leader must continuously prove that it is legitimate to follow him. In Weber's words, "Pure charisma does not recognize any legitimacy other than one which flows from personal strength proven time and time again . . . The charismatic hero . . . gains and

---

[2] The song sung to the Lord by Moses and the Israelites (Exodus 15:1–18) contains the following affirmation of God's existence in relation to this miracle: "I will sing to the Lord, for he has triumphed gloriously; horse and rider he has thrown into the sea. The Lord is my strength and my might, and he has become my salvation . . . The Lord is a warrior; the Lord is his name. Pharaoh's chariots and his army he cast into the sea; his picked officers were sunk in the Red Sea. The floods covered them; they went down into the depths like a stone. Your right hand, O Lord, glorious in power – your right hand, O Lord, shattered the enemy. In the greatness of your majesty you overthrew your adversaries; you sent out your fury, it consumed them like stubble. At the blast of your nostrils the waters piled up, the floods stood up in a heap; the deeps congealed in the heart of the sea" (Coogan 2001).

retains [his authority] solely *by proving his powers in practice*" (1978: 1114, emphasis added). In other words, charismatic authority is based on the belief in an idea, that is, on the recognition that the leader has said something of the utmost importance that, in turn, requires one to follow the leader in his divine mission. And yet, this belief can be established and maintained only through a continual process of confirmation in *practice*.[3] It is precisely this paradox between the power of an idea – the sole basis of the belief that enables it to exist within social action – and its fragility that we examine in this chapter. The idea of race, like charismatic authority, draws strength *in social life*; however, it does so only as long as, and insofar as, it is *believed*. But this belief does not appear by magic, and neither is it able to last on its own. By clarifying the relationship between culture and nature, and between the practical and the ideal in the racial ensemble, the conditions of believing in race will come into focus.

The efficiency of ideas, or revisiting the nature/culture riddle

We begin with the relationship between the phenotype and racial ideas, which is the most taken for granted and least well-articulated aspect of social inquiry on race. Indeed, there is an underlying assumption, both in commonsense understandings and in (many) academic studies, that racial ideas are based on the phenotypical differences that allow for distinctions to be made between groups of people. We have argued that the strength of this assumption has led to the view that race is causally produced by the fact that we can distinguish between human beings based on their physical appearance. Consequently, even if the biological existence of race is denied, the fact that physical differences exist in nature leads to a causal interpretation of the ties between the natural world and the social world.

---

[3] There is a paradox in the way Weber conceives of the charismatic leader. On the one hand, he emphasizes the fact that the leader does not need to possess any extraordinary skills or perform extraordinary actions; what matters is that his followers believe that he does possess them and does perform them. On the other hand, Weber is unable to relinquish the notion of the charismatic leader as *being* exceptional, and possessing extraordinary abilities. The paradox is solved in the fact that *indeed* his abilities are out of the ordinary: he says things that transport his followers into a time of rupture, into a space that is located outside of the everyday, and this gives his words and actions an extraordinary character. Hence, it is not what he does, but it is the way he does it, and the fact that it is meaningfully situated within his followers' belief in their extraordinary character, that actually *transforms the ordinary into the extraordinary*.

This causal relationship is not well defined; its strength lies precisely in this lack of definition. Indeed, the fact that race (as a category produced outside of the natural world) coincides with physical difference (as a natural fact whose existence is independent of the social world) is one of the most important characteristics of its social efficiency. The fact that, in most cases, one can *see* racial (and thereby social) categories in the physical appearance of human beings renders self-evident the terms of a relationship that should be called into question; the perception of racial categories *in nature* allows the *reality* of the categories to be more easily believed.[4]

Support for this line of analysis can be found in the work of Durkheim and Mauss, who make explicit the relationship between "physical reality" and "social reality." Durkheim's strongest postulate recognizes society as an independent sphere, which does not owe its reality to either the natural world (which is the object of the natural sciences) or the individual (which is the object of psychology). The social, therefore, cannot be reduced either to nature (i.e., biological facts) or the individual (i.e., psychological facts):

Here, then, is a category of facts which present very special characteristics: they consist of manners of acting, thinking and feeling external to the individual, which are invested with a coercive power by virtue of which they exercise control over him. Consequently, since they consist of representations and actions, they cannot be confused with organic phenomena, nor with physical phenomena, which have no existence save in and through the individual consciousness. Thus they constitute a new species and to them must be exclusively assigned the term *social*. (Durkheim 1982: 52)

The definition of a social reality that exists *sui generis* is the epistemological foundation of sociological inquiry; this postulate is also shared by Lévi-Strauss: "Like language, the social *is* an autonomous reality" (Lévi-Strauss 1987: 37). However, for Durkheim, this distinction of three "realities" – the physical, the psychological, and the social – does not negate the fact that they are related to each other. So, for example, he argues that "social facts" are external to, but also influence, the individual (i.e., the collective conscience of a society exists within each

---

[4] Our use of the term "recognition" here refers to the Latin root of the term, *recognoscere*, that is, "to know again"; hence we mean "to see in nature something of which we have a previous knowledge." The term "recognition" is complex. "To recognize" means both to see something new or something we have known before on the basis of previous knowledge, and to establish and/or accept the validity of something. In both senses, there is the idea that something is known on the basis of previous knowledge. For an extensive philosophical discussion of recognition, see Ricœur (2005).

individual). But what is of crucial interest to us is the way in which Durkheim and, further, Mauss develop an analysis of the relationship between the physical world and the social world.

One of the main hypotheses in Mauss's essay *Seasonal Variations of the Eskimo* (1979) concerns the relationship between the physical environment and the social structure. Mauss questions the relationship between society and what he calls its "territorial base." He presents a double argument: on the one hand, the environment (the land and its characteristics, including flora, fauna, climate, etc.) has an influence on the configuration of a given society; on the other hand, he asserts that the influence of environment is one of *conjunction*, not one of *causality*.

We are not going to make the mistake of considering [societies] as if they were independent of their territorial base; clearly the configuration of the land, its mineral riches, its fauna and flora affect the organization of society. (Mauss 1979: 21)

However,

Land does not produce effects except in conjunction with thousands of other factors from which it is inseparable . . . For men to gather together, instead of living in a dispersed fashion, it is insufficient simply to assert that the climate or a configuration of the land draws them together; their moral, legal and religious organization must also allow a concentrated way of life. Although the geographical situation is an essential factor to which we must pay the closest possible attention, it still constitutes only one of the conditions for the material form of human groups . . . In short, the land factor must be considered in relation to a social context in all its complex totality. It cannot be treated in isolation. (Mauss 1979: 21)

This is what Mauss seeks to explain in this essay: the seasonal variations in the life of the Eskimo[5] had been demonstrated (he cites Steensby's work, published a year before in 1905), but Mauss wants to link "the land factor" to the "totality" of the "social context." As it turns out, the Eskimo society provides this enterprise with a particularly clear case study. Indeed it is an example of a "double social structure" which varies according to the time of the year. Through a detailed analysis of social life, Mauss demonstrates that the same society, based on the "settlement" unit (1979: 28), takes on a completely different form in the summer and in the winter.

---

[5] The term "Eskimo" is often considered derogatory today, and has been replaced by "Inuit." Indeed the latter means "humans" in Inuktitut, while the former was the term used by Westerners ("Eskimo" is the Anglophone variation for the French term "Esquimeau"). See Saladin d'Anglure (2006). For the sake of remaining close to Mauss's text, we will use the term "Eskimo."

We know that this [general] morphology also varies according to the time of the year . . . Although the settlement is always the fundamental unit of Eskimo society, it still takes quite different forms according to the seasons. In summer, the members of a settlement live in tents and these tents are dispersed; in winter, they live in houses grouped close to one another. (Mauss 1979: 36)

Mauss starts with the fact that the Eskimo have two places of dwelling, one in the summer and one in the winter, and then isolates not only two different habitats but also two different family structures, legal systems, and profane and sacred activities. We shall pass over the details of this analysis; what matters is the analytical conclusion reached by Mauss. The Eskimo society does not simply adapt to seasonal climatic changes, it is organized within a double social structure that revolves in time, in conjunction with seasonal changes.

In the dense concentrations of the winter, a genuine community of ideas and material interests is formed. Its strong moral, mental and religious unity contrasts sharply with the isolation, social fragmentation and dearth of moral and religious life that occurs when everyone has scattered during the summer . . . Winter is a season when Eskimo society is highly concentrated and in a state of continual excitement and hyperactivity . . . In summer, psychologically, life slackens its pace. (Mauss 1979: 76, 77)

Hence Mauss treats the seasonal variation found in this society as a complex system that forms a totality: it is a case of a double social structure that revolves in time and involves not only an adaptation to physical constraints (for instance, linked to the availability of game and the limitations it places upon hunting) but also deep structural differences. The totality of social life is marked by a cycle of apogees and hypogees: winter's concentration follows summer's dispersion; a period of heightened social actions, thoughts, and emotions follows a period in which social life has less intensity. To account for this cycle, Mauss proposes a fundamental analytical reversal, by switching from an explanation based on causality to one based on coincidence. He rejects the "natural" assumption that, *because they coincide*, seasonal changes and the social structure are *causally* linked.

Instead of being the necessary and determining cause of an entire system, true seasonal factors may merely mark the most opportune occasions in the year for these two phases to occur. (Mauss 1979: 79)

This specific example of seasonal change is very precious for us, because it provides a perfect analogy for the causality problematic posed by the relation of nature and racial ideas. Mauss must be credited for achieving an extraordinarily difficult insight: how can one not assume that seasonal change and its armada of concrete *natural facts* (such as snowfall, temperature, length of daylight, the limitation placed upon the availability of game and fishing activities, etc.) produce a different way of life by way of a *simple causal relationship*? Mauss demonstrates that this assumption is in error.

In the case of Eskimo social organization, Mauss argues for a relationship of coincidence between the natural world (e.g., seasonal changes) and society (e.g., a system of representation). Here he echoes Hubert's work on calendars (1999), published a year before the Eskimo essay, which shows that calendars are not simply a reflection of natural facts such as seasonal change and that the very reliance of calendars on "natural periodicities" involves a consensual social choice.

> In brief, the division of time entails the maximum of convention and the minimum of experience. Ultimately, concrete experience lends its additional authority . . . it is legitimate to suppose that the rhythm of time does not necessarily model itself on the natural periodicities established by experience, but that societies contain within themselves the need and means of instituting it. (Hubert 1999: 70, 71)

In Hubert and Mauss, the representation of time, and the way it is put in practice in the construction of calendars, is not caused by the natural world, although it generally coincides with it, or at least with some natural phenomena that "make sense" for a given society.[6] Hence, the relationship between the natural world and social representations is one of coincidence, not one of causality.

What does this imply for conceptualizing race? We argue that the same reversal of an assumed causal relationship found in the studies of Mauss and Hubert is also applicable: *the relationship between physical differences and racial ideas is a relationship of coincidence*. In the introduction, we formulated four hypotheses intended to clarify the relationship that exists between physical differences and racial ideas:

1. The representation is independent from the natural object, and belongs to a sphere that lies outside of, and distinct from, the sphere of the natural world.
2. There is no relationship of causality between natural reality and social reality.

---

[6] On the selection of specific natural phenomena, see the examples provided by Malinowski (1926–1927) on the Trobriand and Evans-Pritchard (1939) on the Nuer.

3. Causality is found in the social sphere, not in the relationship between natural reality and the social representation.
4. The relationship between natural reality and the social representation is one of coincidence, not one of causality; this implies that the natural world plays a role in the construction of representations, albeit not a causal role.

These four hypotheses correspond to the analysis provided by Mauss and Hubert. A term-to-term correspondence can be made between time and race, calendars and racial practice, and finally natural periodicity (day/night, seasonal change, etc.) and the phenotype. In each case, an "ensemble" links natural facts, social representations, and social practices together. However, one further step (beyond Mauss's analysis) can be taken to account for the coincidence that exists between the natural world and social representations. If, as Mauss argues, a system of representation does not need any coincidence with natural facts to exist, why *is* there a coincidence?

This question can be answered from the standpoint of the persistence of representations. Their persistence over time can be explained by the *efficiency of their articulation* with their environment (either natural or social). Robert Wuthnow has used the notion of articulation to conceptualize the duality of ideologies, which he views as both dependent on and independent of the social structure. On the one hand, if "cultural products [such as ideologies] do not articulate closely enough" with their (local) environment, they appear "irrelevant, unrealistic, artificial, and overly abstract" to their audience. On the other hand, if these products articulate too closely, they are perceived as being "esoteric, parochial, [and] time bound," and are therefore unlikely to gain a "wider and lasting audience." Thus, the "process of articulation" is "characterized by a delicate balance between products of culture and the social environment in which they are produced" (Wuthnow 1989: 3). In his study of the Reformation, the Enlightenment, and socialism, Wuthnow argues that these "cultural products" survived over a long duration because they successfully articulated with the social environment to which they were initially bound and yet transcended these specific conditions sufficiently so that they could become influential in different social environments and at later points in history.

In the case of race, it is likely that the articulation of racial ideas/beliefs with both the natural environment (physical differences) and the social environment (racial practices) contributes to their persistence over time. Indeed, such a double articulation with the natural *and* the social achieves a level of efficiency that understandably makes it difficult to perceive race, from a commonsense perspective, as anything other than a *real object*, and as a *real experience*, when, in fact, its only reality is as an idea. The fact that physical variation is "natural" provides a fantastic support for racial ideas. The mere *coincidence* of racial ideas with natural "facts" leads to a *naturalization* of ideas that are neither caused nor produced by these facts. Hence, racial ideas transcend nature, yet they are perceived as being inherent in nature. The "racial" has nothing to do with nature other than the claims made *by racial thought* that nature and culture (i.e., representations) are indeed linked. Racial practices that exist on the level of society only reinforce the efficiency of this coincidence between ideas and nature. Thus two claims are fundamental to our understanding of "race." First, nature and culture exist as two spheres that are independent from each other; to put it simply, physical differences (i.e., the phenotype) exist outside the social realm, and racial ideas exist outside nature. These two objects – physical differences and racial ideas – do not need each other to exist. But we add a second proposition to this basic hypothesis: while racial ideas are neither based on, nor produced by, nature, they nonetheless relate to it. Not only do racial ideas *refer to* something that is perceived to be *natural*, their durability is enhanced by their *recognition in nature*.

At the same time, nature also sets a limit on the efficiency of the articulation of racial ideas and nature. It limits ideas in the sense that the latter must conform, however loosely, to something that exists in nature. The limits set by the phenotype – taken as a natural fact – explain the success of some representations over others. For example, "White people" have fairer skin color than "Black people" in most cases; hence reference to the phenotype *allows* the idea of race to remain efficient in the social realm. In other words, it would be very difficult for an idea to sustain itself over time if it appeared to completely contradict nature.[7]

We are left, at this point, with an important problem. We know that ideas can exist and prosper even if they are contradicted by scientific knowledge about nature, for example the knowledge that race does not

---

[7] Our claim echoes the work of Philippe Descola (1996a, 1996b, 2005), which focuses on the relationship between culture and nature. There is a good example of the interaction between "ideas" and "nature" in *The Spears of Twilight*: Pinchu, an Achuar man, has a dream during the night, which upon interpretation prescribes hunting. But contrary to Descola's expectations, Pinchu does not set out for the forest; when finally asked about the hunting expedition, Pinchu answers, "Can't you see it's raining?" (1996b: 109). No matter how important dreams are to the Achuar, they also bend to nature. The dream – the idea – produces *the possibility for hunting*, which then bends to *the limits set by the natural world*. Had Pinchu only listened to his dream, he would have spent a day getting soaked trying to hunt, with probably disastrous results, for the rain renders hunting very difficult in the forest.

exist in nature. Why do *scientifically false* ideas of race persist? The discourse on race is highly ambiguous within science and contested without science. Briefly, within the scientific community, most statements on race made by many geneticists, including the strong stance by the Human Genome Project, assert that there is no genetically defined existence of race, only a possibility for grouping people according to any sort of genes; but there are also not only opposed statements, but above all a confusing multiplicity of discourses made at different levels (the genetic level, the phenotypical level, etc.) as well as a discrepancy between the scientific discourse on race and the practice of medicine. For instance, one only needs to step into a New York City hospital to see posters dedicated to the higher rate of prostate cancer or hypertension among African-American males; hence racial categories are being reproduced in what seems an innocuous manner, which contributes to the vagueness of the scientific discourse on race: while claiming that race does not exist on a "deep" (e.g., genetic) level, science also makes a continual use of "racial" categories at the level of its practice.[8]

An illustrative example of this problem is found in the controversy surrounding the theory of evolution. Unlike race, evolution is a concept around which there seems to be a broad consensus within science. Yet it is strongly contested outside the scientific field. There are, of course, significant differences between race theory and evolution theory: first, because the latter is the object of a scientific consensus, while the former is still the object of a scientific debate; second, because the specific relationship between evolution and Christianity has rendered the debate very intense, and mobilized energies in a way unparalleled with race. But it remains that in both cases the situation is one of a scientific theory (considered scientifically proven) that conflicts with belief; hence the conflict is articulated around a binary between the tangible character of science (and the scientific method of verification) and the intangible character of ideas (for which the only proof is found in belief). From a positivist point of view, the challenge belief presents to science is treated by the latter as of a sign of insufficient reason,[9] precisely because of the tangible/intangible binary. But from a sociological, value-free point of view, there is something to say about the way in which the confrontation takes place in society. Beliefs can survive and even flourish without, but

---

[8] This example is a witness to the difficulty of speaking of groups of people without racializing them. There are indeed elevated risks for hypertension among African-American males, as there are elevated risks for skin cancer among Caucasian individuals. This does not imply, though, that these groups are racial; but the use of the categories, albeit not necessarily in a racial way, remains systematically interpreted as being racial.

[9] For examples of scientific hostility to religion, see Dawkins (2006) and Dennett (2007).

also in spite of, science, as race and creationism/intelligent design demonstrate. As Durkheim points out

> The products of common experience, their main purpose is to attune our actions to the surrounding world; they are formed by and for this experience. Now a representation can effectively perform this function even if it is theoretically false . . . For an idea to stimulate the reaction that the nature of a thing demands, it need not faithfully express that nature. It is sufficient for it to make us perceive what is useful or disadvantageous about the thing, and in what ways it can render us service or disservice. But notions formed in this way can only present a roughly appropriate practicality, and then only in the general run of cases. How often are they both dangerous and inadequate! (Durkheim 1982: 61)[10]

Intelligent design can compete with evolution theory, not because it is scientifically provable, but because it relies on a coincidence with nature, as the "banana case" illustrates.[11] One can observe a banana and literally read (that is, interpret) its natural characteristics in a way that links it with one's beliefs: it fits perfectly in a human hand, it has a "non-slippery surface"; it opens conveniently; it is easy to digest and can be held "gracefully." Hence the natural characteristics of the banana can stand as evidence that the banana is one of the perfect creations of God, as evidence of God's "intelligent design." There is no proof that God created the banana or intended this creation to be eaten (comfortably) by mankind. But the coincidence between a natural fact (the physiology of the banana) and a social idea (an anthropocentric religious creation) *confirms* the idea of intelligent design.

In a similar fashion, race, as a "false" idea, persists in a world that highly values positivist science with the help of the relationship of coincidence with "something in nature": the phenotype. Ironically, this coincidence of racial ideas and nature allows the *social* belief in race successfully to resist contradictory scientific information. Nature is *used as a sign* of race, even when the natural sciences invalidate this sign.

---

[10] The original French is richer: "Produits de l'expérience vulgaire, ils ont, avant tout, pour objet de mettre nos actions en harmonie avec le monde qui nous entoure; ils sont informés par la pratique et pour elle. Or une représentation peut être en état de jouer utilement ce rôle tout en étant théoriquement fausse. . . . Pour qu'une idée suscite bien les mouvements que réclame la nature d'une chose, il n'est pas nécessaire qu'elle exprime fidèlement cette nature; mais il suffit qu'elle nous fasse sentir ce que la chose a d'utile ou de désavantageux, par où elle peut nous servir, par où nous contrarier. Encore les notions ainsi formées ne présentent-elles cette justesse pratique que d'une manière approximative et seulement dans la généralité des cas. Que de fois elles sont aussi dangereuses qu'inadéquates!" (Durkheim 2004: 16).

[11] A short (1:05) clip presented as "the atheist's nightmare" and widely broadcasted on the "YouTube" website (www.youtube.com/watch?v=QGMuIyBK5P4, consulted in October 2006).

Physical differences are interpreted as a sign that race does indeed exist. However, the sign becomes intelligible (as a confirmation of racial ideas) only within the logic of meaningful social action. Hence the necessity of analyzing race as an ensemble of the various relationships that exist between nature, ideas, perceptions, and practice. When the coincidence of racial ideas and nature is coupled with meaning-laden perceptions and social practices, a vague naturalization of the ideas ensues that defies what is scientifically known about race. Once racial ideas have been naturalized, they acquire a solidity that makes them difficult to dislodge from social life.

The power of ideas, or producing perception

From the relationship between nature and culture, we turn to an examination of the relationship between what we have called the "perception of the phenotype" and racial ideas. In Chapter 6, we discussed the necessary analytical distinction between two distinct objects: the phenotype and the social perception of the phenotype. The former lies in the sphere of nature; it has an existence independent of what we think of it, or feel towards it. The latter lies in the social sphere: it is influenced by a set of social processes that include an attribution of meaning. The perception of the phenotype, therefore, is a social object that owes its existence not only to human cognitive processes, but also to the range of feelings, emotions, and experiences that characterize human life. The perception of the phenotype is the process in which the phenotype is suffused with meanings that derive not from nature but from racial ideas. We have distinguished the phenotype from the perception of the phenotype for this reason: while the former is a natural fact, the latter is produced out of a "bath of meaning." Hence the perception of the phenotype is the product of the force of an idea upon what we perceive as being *real*, which happens to be different from what is *actually real*.

This point can be elaborated further. Man inhabits a world of things that are distinct from him, of things that do exist independently of him. In psychoanalytical terms, this is "the real," which imposes itself against the id and provokes the negotiation of successive steps in psychical development (such as the distinction between one's own body and the body of the mother) through the elaboration of a principle of reality, which stands opposed to the pleasure principle (Freud 1956: 335–336). According to Freud, the unconscious is governed by the principle of pleasure, that is, by the quest for the immediate fulfillment of its needs, which produces pleasure; however, this quest stumbles upon reality – the breast is not immediately presented, the mother is absent, she is the wife of the father, etc. The elaboration of the principle of reality, built progressively, is viewed as a necessary accommodation to this outside world, which does not bend to the desire of the unconscious; however, the principle of reality does not abolish the quest for pleasure: it transforms it through a process of accommodation to "things" that lie outside of the unconscious.

Our goal here is not to provide a psychoanalytical account of the relationship between the unconscious, the conscious, and "reality"; however, there is a fruitful analogy to make between Freud's theory of the unconscious and the question of social reality – fruitful because it allows for a better understanding of the relationship between "natural reality," "ideas," and their influence on the perception of "natural reality." Indeed, ideas intervene in the way we perceive "things in nature," in the sense that they come to stand between what we see and how we see it. Here "ideas" could be replaced by "meaning": *we do not perceive outside of meaning.* Hence what we see is a product of our ideas: and what we see can be different from the actual object we are looking at. Meaning operates not only as a process of knowledge – which illuminates the object with its many layers of signification – but also as a veil placed between us and the object. What we see of the world is not the world, it is what we think of the world. *And yet, things still exist.* Ideas do not make things disappear; the proof is that we still stumble upon them. That is where the analogy with Freud's principle of reality makes sense: things have to be accommodated, and even if they are not, they retain their existence nonetheless – that we do not see them does not imply that they cease to exist. It only means that they cease to exist *to us.*[12]

Because racial ideas are naturalized by the phenotype, they also modify the very perception of the phenotype. As with Durkheim's description of "vulgar notions," racial ideas *take the place of the phenotype*; they are *confounded with the real* and, as a result, we *see* our ideas instead of the things to which they relate (Durkheim 2004: 16–17). The phenotype – visible physical attributes – is replaced by a representation of the phenotype that is charged with racial meaning. It is not simply that perception is accompanied by meaning. Rather, racial meanings produce a perception of the phenotype, so that what is perceived is the

---

[12] " 'The cow is there,' said Ansell, lighting a match and holding it out over the carpet. No one spoke. He waited till the end of the match fell off. Then he said again, 'She is there, the cow. There, now.' 'You have not proved it,' said a voice. 'I have proved it to myself.' 'I have proved to myself that she isn't,' said the voice. 'The cow is *not* there.' Ansell frowned and lit another match. 'She's there for me,' he declared. 'I don't care whether she's there for you or not. Whether I'm in Cambridge or Iceland or dead, the cow will be there.' " E. M. Forster, *The Longest Journey* (1993: 3).

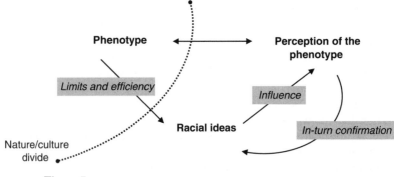

Figure 7

representation of the natural object and not the natural object – the phenotype – itself. Hence the perception of the phenotype is another "object" within the racial ensemble (see Figure 7).

Through perception, the phenotype is transformed into a set of social signifiers of race, which range from visible bodily signs (the color of the skin, the texture of the hair), to invisible bodily signs (most notably, *blood*), and, finally, to geographical regions (for example, the metaphors of Africa and Asia as the dark or yellow continents respectively). To use the title of a book by Jeanette Winterson (1994), racial ideas are "written on the body"; the phenotype becomes *racially legible* through social perceptions that derive from racial ideas. The social perception of phenotype achieves something akin to the alchemist's wish to transform lead into gold: it transforms visible and invisible bodily characteristics into well-defined social groups.

This alchemic capacity can be found in intellectual discourse; for example, at the heart of Du Bois's reflections on the races. The "grosser physical differences of color, hair and bone," while insufficient as the representation of the totality of racial groups, still contribute to the definition of "eight distinctly differentiated races, in the sense in which History tells us the word must be used . . . the Slavs of eastern Europe, the Teutons of middle Europe, the English of Great Britain and America, the Romance nations of Southern and Western Europe, the Negroes of Africa and America, the semitic people of Western Asia and Northern Africa, the Hindoos of Central Asia and the Mongolians of Eastern Asia" (Du Bois 1986a: 817–818). Although the boundaries between these groups are not always represented by an obviously *racial* phenotype, Du Bois leaves little doubt concerning the social perception of phenotype and the constitution of the racial group. Discussing the Teutons, he writes "The forces that bind together the Teuton nations are, then, first, their race identity and common blood" (Du Bois 1986a: 818). On this account, the social perception of visible and invisible signs of phenotype – racial identity and common blood – are the first determinates of a lineage, of a kinship that links individuals in a relationship to other individuals with whom there is no direct blood tie. The visible differences of color, hair, and bone (i.e., cranial measurements) become meaningful not as mere anthropological facts but as social signifiers of race; the invisible entity *common blood* transcends the ordinary intergenerational "blood" ties of family. However, whereas a family line can be extinguished, the blood that unites a race does not perish: it perdures beyond any imaginable historical limit, much as in the medieval legal theory of the king's two bodies, the mortal king might perish but his sovereign body, his body politic, remains immortal.[13] One characteristic of the social perception of the meaning of common blood is that it is timeless.

Not only is the social perception of phenotype, which arises when phenotype is saturated by racial ideas, capable of knitting together unrelated individuals – separated by time and space – into groups, it is also infused with meaning. It functions as a socially significant sign of identity. The perception of the phenotype also writes racial difference on the *social* body and these social signs of race confirm the belief in racial ideas. We can understand this circuit of the constitution of meaning and the confirmation of belief along the lines of Weber's description of the relation of "good works" to the belief structure of the early Protestants.

Totally unsuited though good works are to serve as a means of attaining salvation – for even the elect remain creatures, and everything they do falls infinitely far short of God's demands – they are indispensable as *signs* of election. In this sense they are occasionally described quite simply as "indispensable for salvation", or linked with the "possessio salutis." This means, however, fundamentally, that God helps those who help themselves, in other words, the Calvinist "creates" his salvation *himself* (as it is sometimes expressed) – more correctly: creates the *certainty* of salvation. (Weber 2002: 79)

For the Protestant believer, the significance of signs is not that they offer any absolute proof of salvation, but rather they instill *a confidence in the*

---

[13] "For the King has in him two Bodies, *viz.*, a Body natural, and a Body politic. His Body natural (if it be considered in itself) is a Body mortal, subject to all Infirmities that come by Nature or Accident, to the Imbecility of Infancy or old Age, and to the like Defects that happen to the natural Bodies of other People. But his Body politic is a Body that cannot be seen or handled . . . and this Body is utterly void of Infancy, and old Age, and other natural Defects and Imbecilities, which the Body natural is subject to, and for this Cause, what the King does in his Body politic, cannot be invalidated or frustrated by any Disability in his natural Body" (Kantorowicz 1997: 7).

belief in their own salvation. The presence of racially perceived physical characteristics (the perception of the phenotype), analogously, confirms the meaningfulness of racial beliefs. In other words, confidence in the belief in race is buttressed by an interpretive process that connects the significance of physical differences to racial ideas about those differences. However, this process is not automatic; *doubt* can arise in instances where a distinct perception and interpretation of the phenotype is less possible, for example in cases of individuals who *pass* for "white." Doubt can also be introduced when individual behaviors deviate from those racial behaviors that are associated with the social perception of the phenotype. Yet these exceptions do not undermine the validity of the general rule: the racial ideas that saturate the perception of the phenotype as a sign of race are reinforced by the interpretation of the phenotype as a sign of race.

Hence the specific physical markers used by a given racial discourse – such as skin color, facial traits, or hair texture – are given preponderance, and filter what is actually seen. These physical features are supplemented by "social features" such as language, gesture, and clothing, which form a global perception of the human body. Racial ideas are not innocuous; physical appearance becomes racialized in a way that feels natural to individuals and groups; and the combination of meaningful physical features and of social expectations influences perception, which provides another confirmation of the ideas. This constant back-and-forth movement of confirmation, over time, solidifies racial ideas to the point that they become almost impossible to dislodge – they are seen in nature, and they even come to replace nature through the way in which they shape its very perception. The outcome of a successful racial system of thought precisely lies in this replacement of the object, in its very perception, by the idea.

Ideas influence the object *not by creating it or changing it*, but by *replacing it in our relationship to it*. What appears to be a relationship to an object is actually a relationship to ideas. In a racial system of thought, if individuals see race in nature, the natural object "phenotype" is replaced by a social object "perception of the phenotype," which is directly dependent on, and informed by, ideas. What holds for individuals in society also holds true for theories of race that perceive the object by means of the same logic (see Figure 8).

Hence the problem in racial thought lies in its relationship to the object. If the object is "phenotype," then racial ideas are not only "false" (i.e., race does not inhere in the phenotype), but also impair an adequate view of the object. An interesting parallel can be made, here, between Durkheim's foundations for the sociological method of inquiry and

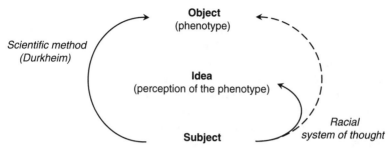

Figure 8

German hermeneutics; indeed, while these two traditions specify very different ways to attain knowledge of the object, both are nonetheless preoccupied *with the care for the object*. Whether one should discard all "vulgar concepts" in order to push the veil away from the object (as prescribed by Durkheim) or use "prejudice" within a circle of interpretation until the highest possible adequation with the object is attained (as prescribed by Gadamer), it remains that in both traditions *the object* is at the center of inquiry. We argue that when it comes to race, the phenotype is not the main object of inquiry, but rather the process by which it is assigned meaning in the social realm; but we also argue that the phenotype should neither be ignored nor dismissed in the sociological analysis of race. Natural things do not simply disappear before thought: the world is not made up *only of what we think of it*.

This claim is *methodological*: we are not preoccupied here with the question of whether racial ideas are true or false, but with the adequacy or inadequacy of the conceptualization of race as an object. Within sociological analysis, it is crucial to distinguish clearly the object(s) at hand, and the relationships they entertain with each other; as Durkheim enjoins us in his essay on the definition of religious phenomena, we have to face the object.[14] Insofar as approaches to the study of race have avoided a direct theoretical confrontation with the phenotype as an object, they fall prey to the anthropocentric illusion that things exist only insofar as we think them.

The legitimacy of belief, or revisiting the practice/ideal riddle

In order to understand how racial ideas are formed and maintained, and how they function in social life, it is necessary for the sociologist to

---

[14] "Il faut sortir de nous-même et nous mettre en face des choses" (Durkheim 1898: 2).

examine the veil ideas place between the perceiving subject and the natural world. This is also an analytical necessity because the veiling of the natural world by racial ideas is bound up in a peculiar process of the legitimation of the ideas. Race is not only thought; it is also enacted; once again, although racial ideas can stand on their own, they also entertain a relationship with actions. And so we are left with the task of clarifying the relationship between racial ideas and one final object: racial practice. This object exists within the social sphere, which, following Weber (1978: 4), we comprehend as a sphere of meaningfully oriented social action. What we call "racial practice" refers to social action to which is attached "racial meaning"; hence it is a type of action that takes into account the behavior of others within a system of racial thought (or racial value system). The lynching of African-Americans in the late nineteenth and early twentieth centuries is an extreme form of racial practice, in which race is not only the motivation of action, but also the condition for its possibility: human beings are murdered because they are thought to belong to a racial category; and their murder is rendered permissible by a broader "environment" which categorizes individuals and general qualities by race. Our intention in this section is to examine the peculiar relationship entertained by a specific type of idea – *belief* – with a specific type of practice – *racial* – in order to clarify the nature of this relationship.

The conceptualization of race must take into account its multilayered texture; race is a representation, and it inhabits a system of relationships extending in multiple directions and towards multiple objects. Indeed, it is from a relationship with something that exists in nature (the phenotype or physical difference) that the social representation gains solidity within the social sphere; but representations also interact with *practice*. Consequently, if *causality* exists, it is to be found within the social world, and more specifically within the relationship between practice and ideas. Racial ideas inform the realm of social practice in various ways, from individual action to institutions. Individuals and groups act upon their belief in race in ways which, in the negative case, range from the simple avoidance of the members of one racial group to the legally enforced separation of racial groups (as in South African apartheid and the post-Civil War American South) to the elimination of groups (as in the case of genocide). However, our focus here is on the side of the relationship between representations and practice that moves *from practice to representations*. In other words, rather than rehearsing the ways in which social structure weighs upon racial representations, we inquire into the way in which a much broader range of "practices" can act as a legitimating force in the service of the belief in racial representations. We are again arguing against simple causality: racial practices do not produce racial ideas. Rather they produce a sense of the legitimacy of the ideas.

The case of racial lynching in the United States provides a good point of departure to look at the effects of practices upon ideas. Indeed, racial lynching cannot exist without racial ideas – it is precisely because lynching is thought to be racial, and is bound to a corpus of racial representations that exist in society, that it can be described as *racial*. The act itself is only interpreted as racial when it is linked with specific representations. Hence in the United States, lynching was sometimes an act of the law, such as when a thief was hanged; an act of the law that, even when the victim was black, did not necessarily take on a racial signification. However, the combination of racial ideas and the numerical decrease in the number of whites who were lynched contributed, albeit not in a linear way, to making hanging a black person a racial act, including cases in which that person may have committed a crime.

Thus, racial lynching implies a link made between a practice – hanging – and an idea – the meaning associated with individuals categorized as black. Not only does the representation enable the practice (providing a reason for hanging a man when, in certain cases, there are no other reasons besides his "race"), it also transforms the practice into a specifically racial practice, and, by a rebound effect, it allows further practices to be interpreted as racial, whether they are or not. In other words, several processes are at work. A first process concerns the construction of an environment of permissibility, wherein ideas make a specific type of action possible. We are here in the domain of norms: collective representations allowing something to be *thought* in a certain way. When racial ideas are shared, they allow for the emergence of a set of practices that uses these ideas as a referent: avoidance, discrimination, violence, etc. The idea of race does not necessarily imply these practices; but it alone makes them possible. A second process concerns the existence of these practices: not only does the existence of racial ideas enable racial practices to emerge, it also allows for their very existence. Killing a man is not a racial act; but hanging a black man from a tree in Mississippi in the 1890s is a racial act, whether he is a criminal or not. In other words, racial meaning is attached to social practices, whether their intent is actually racial or not; and practices, therefore, become interpreted *within the realm of racial ideas*.

Thus, the sphere of practice is informed by collective representations. This, of course, does not happen with race only; but race provides a case of a very pervasive set of representations, which contaminate the sphere of practice.[15] But the link between the practice and the idea is not straightforward. It is the product of an exchange between the idea and the practice, and also between the individual and the collective; in other words, there is a complex of multidirectional confirmations, within the social sphere, between thought and practice as well as between individual behavior and collective norms. Lynching a black man for reasons of his (imagined) race can occur only in a specific context: a context where racial representations do exist, and are recognized as valid. But once it occurs, the act, as it were, rebounds back upon ideas and confirms them. If a man is lynched for racial reasons, it must be the case that racial reasons exist, and further, that race exists. Practice is not only informed by ideas, it also acts as a powerful legitimation of the existence – i.e., of the reality – of the very ideas to which it owes its life.

Analogous to our observations on the relationship between nature and ideas, there is something in practice that gives a sense of reality to the world of ideas. The act possesses a tangibility that lends credence to the idea to which it refers; someone has been *doing* it, and therefore the idea behind the action acquires a reality that it might not have had otherwise. The idea is reinforced by action, it is reinforced by the fact that it has been *tangibly enacted*. At the social level, the repetition of diverse racial practices creates an environment that reinforces the reality of racial ideas; and this reinforcement of the idea by practice is also accompanied by the reinforcement of the practice by the idea. What results from this exchange between ideas and practices is a closed circuit of mutual validation, producing a sense of the "normalcy" of both the ideas and the practices (at least, for the perpetrators in the case of racial lynching). Lynching is an exemplary case of this circuit because it involves murder, an extraordinary act that is not easily normalized. And yet the repetition of the practice and its justification in thought feed each other to produce what can seem unbelievable: the complete normalcy of killing. The possibility of both thinking about lynching and practicing lynching emerges out of an environment of permissibility created by racial ideas in nineteenth-century America (and accompanied by other factors, not analyzed here: for instance, the commonality of hanging as a form of

---

[15] This might be one characteristic feature of racial ideas: once disseminated and acted upon, they tend to invade the whole sphere of action. Hence, for instance, the quasi-impossibility of the anti-racist struggle, which faces criticism no matter what position it takes: if it refuses race, it is accused of denying the social effects of racial thought; if it does not, it remains within a racial discursive system. Another good example is the forced positioning that race imposes upon individuals, who are thereby "collectivized."

capital punishment); but in turn, the repetition of actual acts of lynching reinforces racial ideas, and establishes the practice as "normal."

Hence there is something in the repetition of a practice that normalizes it – and that normalizes the ideas it is based upon – and this even when the practice is legally reprehensible and the ideas scientifically false. People lynched and others were lynched; crowds witnessed lynchings; black men and women were left hanging from trees, bridges or poles for everyone to see. At the local level, none of these individuals was a stranger; and so one's parents, neighbors, or friends were part of this act, thereby legitimizing murder, and the ideal justification for it: race.[16] Beyond the local level, newspapers published written reports detailing the circumstances of incidents of lynching, photographers recorded the events in a visual form, and postcards were sold and mailed.[17] Arrows and crosses were drawn on postcards, showing where exactly in the crowd the sender stood and watched. "I was there," "I saw it."[18] How can one justify watching and participating in murder without invoking the *ideological justification* of this act? Based on the "truth" of racial ideas, racial lynching ceases to be murder; it becomes justified, frequently as an act in defense of civilization (Bederman 1995: 47–53). And in the process, racial ideas themselves are solidified and justified as true, while the *repetition* of the act produces a sense of normalcy for both the practice and the ideas. Postcards showed the faces of men, women, and children in the crowd: they are seen smiling and laughing as if they were at a street fair, on a joyous afternoon.[19] And hence, not only is it justified to lynch a black man without trial, it is also an occasion to rejoice. The people in the crowd are neither outlaws nor mentally disturbed; they are just regular white families, engaged in a normal practice.

[16] For instance, on the back of a postcard of the lynching of Lige Daniels in 1920: "This was made in the court yard in Center, Texas. He is a 16 year old Black boy. He killed Earl's grandma. She was Florence's mother. Give this to Bud. From Aunt Myrtle."

[17] Numerous photos of lynchings were taken; many were displayed in the exhibition "Without Sanctuary" and the subsequent book published by Twin Palms Publishers (Allen 2000). Many photographs were sold, often as postcards. For instance, studio photographer Lawrence Beitler took a picture of the lynching of Thomas Shipp and Abram Smith in Marion, Indiana, in 1930; he printed "thousands of copies, which sold for fifty cents a piece" (Allen 2000).

[18] On the back of a postcard depicting the charred corpse of Jesse Washington in Robinson (lynched in Texas in 1916) is written the following information: "This is the barbecue we had last night. My picture is to the left with a cross over it. Your son Joe."

[19] For instance, the picture of the lynching of Thomas Shipp and Abram Smith in Marion, Indiana, in 1930, on which are smiling women and men, the postcard of the lynching of Lige Daniels in Center, Texas, in 1920, on which are young boys and men, or the postcard of the lynching of Rubin Stacy in Fort Lauderdale, Florida, in 1935, on which are men, women, and four young girls.

Lynching is a good example of the way a social practice helps to establish racial ideas as true, as justified, and, ultimately, as natural. First, the idea upon which the act is based, and to which it refers, gains reality from being enacted, from being put into tangible action. Second, the repetition of the act, especially when it is disseminated throughout society, normalizes both the act and the idea linked to it. Lynching is an extreme case, but other less dramatic illustrations of the role of racial practice in legitimizing and normalizing racial ideas are numerous (the practice of racial profiling in the American criminal justice system is only one example). It is difficult to maintain the belief that race does not exist when one lives in a society in which race is enacted and acted upon on a daily basis. Not only does this mechanism of normalization exist at the collective and institutional levels, it is also found at the level of individual experience – a level at which race is most susceptible to become naturalized, and is most resilient: "at the level of experience and common sense identities are generally expressed . . . precisely because they *feel* natural and essential" (Ang 2000: 2).

Insofar as race (or rather racial identity) is *claimed* by individuals and groups, *experience* enters sociological inquiry at the level of social relationships. Some scholars claim experience enables the understanding of race: hence the claim that "white scholars" cannot truly understand the (racial) experiences of "people of color." Others use the existence of "racial experiences" as evidence that racial categories are analytically pertinent. Still others use the term "collective experience," implying that there is a form of experience that is shared by all the members of a given racial group.[20] Although these three ways of "claiming experience" are different, they converge on the view that "experience" defines "social life" in a significant manner.

Several problems are raised by the use of the term "experience" in scholarly accounts of race, both definitional and methodological (indeed, what is experience and how does one gain access to it?). It might prove fruitful, therefore, to articulate racial experience through the concept of racial practice. The concept of practice itself has a complex history, which can be traced to both the Marxist tradition and phenomenology. However, in recent decades the concept of practice has come to play an important role in the study of culture. Practice theory places emphasis not on holistic visions or worldviews held by a group but rather on the repertoire of symbolic practices that are undertaken by

---

[20] The term "black" or "African-American experience" is widely used, in particular in African-American and Africana studies; numerous examples include book titles, course titles, etc.

groups.[21] Thus, in terms of the concept of culture, practices are viewed as culture insofar as they express something symbolic about a group. Consequently, practice theorists attend to rituals and performances – i.e., actions and behaviors – that can be observed in the study of the culture of groups. This perspective can be used to specify the relationship in the racial ensemble between racial ideas and racial practices. It is a common occurrence for particular practices to be identified with specific racial groups: music, food, clothing, and behaviors are claimed by or attributed to races by both scholars and laypersons. For example, jazz music is held to be black music and conversely, individuals who play jazz are described as doing something that is black. On a conceptual level, such views attribute race to practices. In other words, the practices and performances themselves are held to be racial and are often associated with *experience* (i.e., jazz music is part of the black experience). We argue, on the contrary, that practices that are attributed to, or claimed by, racial groups cannot be inherently defined by race; they are dependent on racial ideas. Nonetheless, once these practices are undertaken with regularity, if they become customary, they are understood (i.e., experienced) as racial practices, both inside and outside the group. These actions are then described as part of a racial experience. In other words, racial practice grounds racial ideas in experience, yet it does not produce these ideas; racial practice attaches ideas to social action and behavior.

Conclusion

We have articulated a conceptual framework, the racial ensemble, which is adequate to an object that is simultaneously real and unreal, and the relations internal to the ensemble that comprise the belief in race. It should be clear that rather than seeking to demolish race as an object, to show its impossibility from the standpoint of any logical fit between the concept race and an empirical referent, we have sought to describe race as a possible object of belief that entails definite logical relations between the idea of race and various objects that are drawn into its orbit. Rather than being determined – or lacking determination – by an empirical object, the idea of race exerts a gravitational force upon the objects in the racial ensemble and, at the same time, the idea of race is held in a specific relationship to these objects, a relationship

---

[21] See, for example, the different discussions of practice theory in anthropology (Ortner 1984) and sociology (Swidler 1986; Schatzki *et al.* 2001).

which confirms the reality of the ideas. The knowledge problem that is produced by an object that is at one and the same time true and untrue, real and unreal, possible and impossible, is therefore not transcended in our account, but rather is described so that the tools of social analysis that are usually applied to the study of race can be used more efficiently and, perhaps, with fewer internal contradictions. In other words, the stakes in the debate over the reality of race can shift from settling the question of whether it is true or false – and the implications of either answer, which we have shown are unsatisfactory – to the question of the conditions of possibility for the existence of such a vexatious object. The question of race is not a matter of the truth or falsity of racial ideas, but rather one of belief in racial ideas, and, from this perspective, both the unreal and real aspects of race can be analyzed not in opposition but in consonance. The conceptual frame proposed in the racial ensemble therefore avoids certain inadequate analytical moves on the plane of knowledge: the move to deny race and to reduce it to something else (such as social class), the shift of the object of analysis from race to racism (which thereby postpones the thorny epistemological question of what race is as an object until some point in the future when racism is vanquished), the turn to an equally vexatious concept of ethnicity (which is employed without the dose of empirical skepticism found in Weber's ideal-type), and the substitution of the concept of diaspora (which continues to employ race in the form of what we have described as the social perception of the phenotype). However, among the four objects in the racial ensemble which are put forward most frequently as a justification for the claim of the reality of race is the practice of racism: as the argument goes, as long as racism persists, the concept of race is indispensable. Race is declared to be a false, and yet a necessary, idea: racism makes race a reality that is not illusory but true. We have already described the fundamental logical contradiction in this standpoint at the level of knowledge, a problem that can be avoided only by placing the belief in race (i.e., racial ideas) as the central object in an ensemble of racial objects (one of which is racist practice). But there remains a problem in reality: how then to conceptualize the persistence not of the practice of racism but of racial ideas themselves (upon which racist practices depend)? We have briefly touched this issue by showing how racial ideas benefit from their possible recognition in nature (with the phenotype) as well as from their being enacted in social practice: in both cases, racial ideas solidify and are susceptible to either naturalization or normalization. Nonetheless, that is not all there is to the persistence of race. To address it, a shift in perspective is required, from the epistemological frame of the preceding chapters to the frame of meaning;

from an analytical accounting of the object in all its complexity to an understanding of the modalities of meaningful attachment to the object. Thus we turn our attention from the knowledge of race to the memory of, and the desire for, race.

8 The politics of memory and race

> All history shows how easily political action can give rise to the belief in blood relationship.
>
> (Weber 1978: 393)

Having analyzed the relations between racial ideas and the secondary objects within the racial ensemble, we can now to turn to the question of the attachment to racial ideas. If the belief in racial ideas persists over time, then some account must be made of the processes that reproduce this belief. We shall address two such processes, one related to the politics of memory and the other manifested in the form of desire (in the following chapter). As discussed earlier (Chapter 1), a strong claim in favor of the perpetuity of the idea of race takes the form of an ethico-political argument: racism and its *experiential consequences* cannot be fought against without the idea of race, and both political movements and the social scientific research that informs anti-discrimination policies depend on the continued recognition of race. Accordingly, the idea of race remains indispensable as long as racism exists. This transformation of race from an object of epistemological questioning into an object that contributes to the political interests and goals of subordinate (thought-to-be) racial groups can be seen as a process of attachment to racial ideas. The political use of social memory in support of the idea of race has been a significant vehicle for the perpetuation of belief; attachment to racial ideas occurs through memory work, that is, conceptual efforts – either explicit or implicit – that remember experiences from the past as racial experiences. Efforts to utilize the past in this way not only can be understood as the creation of historical narratives, they are also efforts that make the past relevant for thought about racial groups *in the present*. In other words, the memory of race brings *past, and now dead, experience* into *living thought*. Moreover, the mobilization of social memory figures into the politics of group making, which involves defining who is inside and outside a racial group, the assertion of racial solidarity in the face of subordination and domination, and the act of distinguishing between authentic and inauthentic ways of racial *being* and racial *thinking*.

We understand the politics of memory as those discursive efforts to bind together individuals – often separated in time and space – in a virtual political community based on the memory of experience. Typically, such memory divides into two orientations to the past: the memory of subjection (i.e., racism, discrimination, domination) and the memory of a shared identity over time; these two orientations to the past are actually tightly connected processes. The politicization of memory raises and responds to several questions involving race. Who should belong to the (thought-to-be) racial group? What are authentic social manifestations of race? Who may properly define the meaning of race?

Memory, experience, and political community

In his classic work on the sociology of memory, Maurice Halbwachs posits the existence of social frameworks of memory and asserts "it is to the degree that our individual thought places itself in these frameworks and participates in this memory that it is capable of an act of recollection" (1992: 38). These frameworks are seen as tools that enable recollection; and they are dependent on the "predominant thoughts of society" (1992: 40) in a given epoch. Halbwachs therefore emphasizes the role of the present in the elaboration of a collective memory, which is seen as a reconstruction of the past made on the basis of the present:

In reality the past does not recur as such . . . everything seems to indicate that the past is not preserved but is reconstructed on the basis of the present . . . Collective frameworks are . . . precisely the instruments used by the collective memory to reconstruct an image of the past which is in accord, in each epoch, with the predominant thoughts of society. (Halbwachs 1992: 39–40)

Social memory in which the "past is reconstructed on the basis of the present" operates at both the individual and social level. As Halbwachs points out, in the course of an individual's life, memories of earlier periods are not exact replicas of what occurred then but rather are influenced by contemporary conditions, so much so that "they have lost the form and the appearance they once had" (Halbwachs 1992: 47).[1]

---

[1] Halbwachs (1992: 46) offers the following illustrative example of the re-reading in adulthood of books one enjoyed in childhood. Rather than allowing one to "relive the memory of childhood" in a more exact form that memory allows, the new reading has the opposite, disruptive effect: "But what happens frequently is that we actually seem to be reading a new book, or at least an altered version. The book seems to lack pages, developments, or details that were there when we first read it; at the same time, additions seem to have been made because our interest is now attracted to and our reflections focused on a number of aspects of the action and the characters which, we well know, we

A similar claim is made by Freud (1899, 1910), who argues that childhood memories are reconstructions that depend not only on the actual event that happened at a given time in the past but also on its continuous interpretation and reinterpretation in the light of the present; "It is perhaps altogether questionable whether we have any conscious memories *from* childhood: perhaps we have only memories *of* childhood" (Freud 1899: 21). Indeed, both Halbwachs and Freud argue against the common view of memory, which holds that remembrance is a linear conservation up to the present of something that happened in the past; in other words, both emphasize the fact that, although memories refer to events that occurred in the past, individuals remember these events from the standpoint and social frames of the present.[2]

While Freud does in fact mention the level of society and the question of history (1910: 61),[3] it is of course to Halbwachs that we owe an analysis of memory at the social level. For Halbwachs, the same two-way movement between the past and the present exists in the case of what he calls "collective memory," that is, the memory of groups. One aspect of collective memory has to do with the importance of the group for the organization of memory, what Halbwachs understands as social frameworks of memory. Halbwachs, whose work addresses the central question of the relationship between individual and collective representations, argues that memory is first and foremost a social phenomenon rather than an individual one. Although memory appears to be a matter of individual psychology, "it is in society that people formally acquire their memories. It is also in society that they recall, recognize, and localize their memories" (Halbwachs 1992: 18). Consequently, individual memories are associated with group life: "One may say that the individual remembers by placing himself in the perspective of the group, but one may also affirm that the memory of the group realizes and

---

were incapable of noticing then. These stories moreover seem less extraordinary to us, more formulaic and less lively."

[2] There is, of course, the peculiar case of "invented memories," which Freud discusses in his essays on screen memories (1899) and on Leonardo da Vinci (1910).

[3] Freud distinguishes between an "unhistorical" age and a "new age" in which "the writing of history, which had begun as a continuous record of current events, now looked back into the past . . . and so created a history of the primeval period. Inevitably this primeval history was more an expression of present opinions and wishes than a depiction of the past, for many things had been eliminated from popular memory and others had been distorted. Some traces of the past were misleadingly interpreted in accordance with current ideas. Moreover, the motive behind the writing of history was not objective curiosity, but a desire to influence contemporaries, to stimulate and uplift them, or to hold a mirror up to them" (1910: 61). Hence the past is a creation, an expression of the present, and an interpretation; the past is created and interpreted with the present as its motive.

manifests itself in individual memories" (Halbwachs 1992: 40). From this perspective we can say that we are never alone in our thoughts, which are always attached to the groups to which we belong; this perspective can be considered the cornerstone of Halbwachs's analysis of collective memory.[4]

What Halbwachs calls "the social frameworks of memory" are a collection of elements that induce and organize individual memories: spatial and temporal markers, historical, geographical, biographical, political notions, common experiences and familiar worldviews; any recollection is in relationship with the whole material and moral life of the societies.[5] Hence the frameworks are social, because they relate to the "outside," to others' memories as well as to the life of the group. It is important to understand that the frameworks of memory do not *replace* individual memories but rather *frame* them. Frameworks are systems of social logic and conventions of chronology and of topography.

People living in society use words that they find intelligible: this is the precondition for collective thought. But each word (that is understood) is accompanied by recollections. There are no recollections to which words cannot be made to correspond. We speak of our recollections before calling them to mind. It is language, and the whole system of social conventions attached to it, that allows us at every moment to reconstruct our past. (Halbwachs 1980: 173)

However, Halbwachs's theory is not deterministic in the sense that the collective frames automatically determine individual memory. He also acknowledges the individual process of remembering, an active work that is carried out in interaction with society. Additionally, because each individual belongs to different groups, individual memory is formed at the intersection between these groups, in a complex articulation between what is unique to the individual and what is shared with others. In *The Collective Memory*, Halbwachs defines individual memory as "a point of view on collective memory" and notes that this point of view "changes

---

[4] "Mais nos souvenirs demeurent collectifs, et ils nous sont rappelés par les autres, alors même qu'il s'agit d'événements auxquels nous seul avons été mêlé, et d'objets que nous seuls avons vus. C'est qu'en réalité nous ne sommes jamais seuls. Il n'est pas nécessaire que d'autres hommes soient là, qui se distinguent matériellement de nous: car nous portons toujours avec nous et en nous une quantité de personnes qui ne se confondent pas" (Halbwachs 1997: 52).

[5] "Tout souvenir, si personnel soit-il, même ceux des événements dont nous avons été seuls témoins, même ceux de pensées et de sentiments inexprimés, est en rapport avec tout un ensemble de notions que beaucoup d'autres que nous possèdent, avec des personnes, des groupes, des lieux, des dates, des mots et formes du langage, avec des raisonnements aussi et des idées, *c'est à dire avec toute la vie matérielle et morale des sociétés dont nous faisons ou dont nous avons fait partie*" (Halbwachs 1994: 38, emphasis added).

depending on the place that one occupies, and this place itself changes depending on the relations that one has with other groups" (1997: 94–95; our translation). Each individual uses the common tool (the frameworks) in his own way, which depends on the groups to which he belongs or has belonged, and on the order of belonging. Therefore, there is an interpenetration of individual and collective memory: individual memory builds on collective memory. However, collective memory is not simply the sum of individual memories. The frameworks of memory assume a normative function: they organize memory. They are a system of signification, a system of meaning into which individual memories are dynamically ascribed. The social frameworks of memory can be construed as *a common tool that individuals use to remember*. But because they are a system of meaning, they also are subject to change: what matters for the group at one point in time might not matter at some other point; hence some frameworks will be set aside, ignored, and ultimately forgotten.

In *The Social Frameworks* (Halbwachs 1994), Halbwachs demonstrates the plurality of collective memories: familial, religious, etc. Each group has its own collective memory, and all these coexist within society just like all groups coexist within society. This plurality of collective memories is theoretically infinite. It also arises in time and space: a plurality in society is also accompanied by a temporal plurality. Because the group changes, so too does its memory. Halbwachs argues that modernity, and specifically the division of labor, gives way to a multiplication of collective memories that concern fewer and fewer individuals. As spheres become differentiated, memory is fragmented. The multiplicity of memory is both diachronic and synchronic; and memory is fundamentally dynamic: the group lets go of what does not matter from its point of view and conserves what matters.[6] In short, collective memory coincides with the boundaries of the group and is constructed through the processes of retaining and forgetting, as well as inventing, the past in light of a group's interests *in the present*.

---

[6] Indeed, how can society hold together if memories are being multiplied and fragmented? *The Social Frameworks of Memory* leaves us with the impossibility of resolving the negative quality of this plurality: multiple memories, and a crisis in collective representation. As Jacques Namer argues, this problem is solved by Halbwachs in *The Collective Memory*. The multiplicity of collective memories becomes a positive phenomenon as opposed to factual history, and it does so by switching from *memories of events* (in *The Social Frameworks*) to *memories of meaning and values* (in *The Collective Memory*). The notion that supports Halbwachs's switching to social memory is the notion of *currents of memory*. Individual memory becomes the actualization of social memory, therefore a point of meeting between different collective memories or currents of memory. See Namer's postface in Halbwachs (1997).

What are the principal traits that distinguish our present society from the society [from the past] in which we immerse ourselves in thought? First of all, the latter does not impose itself on us and we are free to evoke it whenever we wish. We are free to choose from the past the period into which we wish to immerse ourselves . . . Whereas in our present society we occupy a definite position and are subject to the constraints that go with it, memory gives us the illusion of living in the midst of groups which do not imprison us, which impose themselves on us only so far and so long as we accept them . . . There is incongruity in many respects between the constraints of yesterday and those of today, from which it follows that we can only imagine those of the past incompletely and imperfectly. We can evoke places and times different from those in which we find ourselves because we place both within a framework which encompasses them all. But how can we simultaneously experience various constraints of a social order when these constraints are incompatible? Here it is only one framework that counts – that which is constituted by the commandments of our present society and which necessarily excludes all the others. (Halbwachs 1992: 50)

We can draw out two points from Halbwachs's theory that are relevant for understanding memory and race. First, insofar as history figures into the idea of a racial group that persists, it does so in the form of a social memory of past experiences (as *racial* experiences) that are constructed from the standpoint of the present. Second, memory of the past is less constrained by the social facts of the past than it is by the "commandments" of the present.

In the twentieth century, one "group" to which memories adhere is the nation: historical narrative gains authority under its sign (White 1987). If in modern societies the state embodies a "monopoly of the universal," i.e., a monopoly over the legitimate use of "physical and symbolic violence" by bureaucratic agencies (Bourdieu 1998a: 58), then nationalist discourse (analogous to religious discourse) represents a universal claim over the meaning of, and boundaries between, social groups. The imaginary of the nation has been a powerful, ubiquitous, and perhaps indispensable form of attachment to the idea of race. The aspect of power in nationalist discourse, its claim to define the reality of groups, makes the memory of race a political act. Consequently, the claim that blacks form a "nation," which promotes ethical obligations internally and the assertion of honor externally, is an act of usurpation.[7] To return to Weber's ideal-type of the ethnic group, we find a model of the relationship between blood ties and the discourse of the people as a political community.

---

[7] Weber's (1978: 932–933) description of the usurpation of status honor is applicable to the discourse of black nationalism.

There is a corresponding ambiguity of concepts denoting ethnically determined action, that means, determined by the belief in blood relationship. Such concepts are *Völkerschaft*, *Stamm* (tribe), *Volk* (people) . . . Using such terms, one usually implies either the existence of a contemporary political community, no matter how loosely organized, or memories of an extinct political community, such as they are preserved in epic tales and legends; or the existence of a linguistic or dialect group, or, finally, of a religious group. (Weber 1978: 392–393)

The concept of nation, for Weber, binds the idea of political community to memory: "Hence, the concept seems to refer – if it refers at all to a uniform phenomenon – to a specific kind of pathos which is linked to the idea of a powerful political community of people who share a common language, or religion, or common customs, or political memories; such a state may already exist or it may be desired" (Weber 1978: 398). What matters for the politics of memory is that a plausible narrative account of past experiences, whether positive or negative, enables people living in the present to use the deictic referent "we" (i.e., the first person plural) when describing the experiences of people who lived in the past. What connects the past and present in black nationalist discourse is the memory of race. The criticism of the concept of nation (as an inadequate way to conceptualize race) in the work of Omi and Winant (1994: 47), which they argue is "not free of epiphenomenalism" and "fails to demonstrate the existence of racial minority or colonized 'nations' internal to the US and structurally separated from the majority society," does not recognize the function of the nationalist imaginary: it fosters the persistence of the belief in race at the *level of meaning*. It matters less whether a "black nation" actually exists or whether it "has been mainly a refuge for activists and intellectuals disaffected by the intransigence of the racial order and disillusioned by moderate programs for change" (1994: 47) than whether the construction of this nation's memory attaches racial ideas to narratives of "experience," and that this attachment is *perceived* and *felt* to be significant.

From epistemology to meaning: memory and the belief in race

In this chapter, we propose to understand the reproduction of racial belief at the level of thought, in this case, thought *qua* social memory. What interests us in memory is the way in which it reactivates the past for the purposes of the present. The claim made by political activists, scholars, and students that one has to know his or her history (the history of blacks or African-Americans) in order to participate effectively in contemporary struggles against racism became a *raison d'etre* for disciplines such as Black Studies (later renamed African-American Studies or Africana Studies), Ethnic Studies, and Black (or African-American) History. An individual's "history" is self-evidently conceived collectively, as the history of the racial group to which one identifies or in which one is ascribed. Moreover, the relationship to this history is not distant or dispassionate – i.e., history is not an object of disinterested observation. Rather knowledge of the past enables a subjective identification to occur, which turns "their history" into "our history," and elicits a feeling of a shared experience. The process of claiming a social memory of black experience can be analyzed along the lines developed by Halbwachs: it is shaped by the social constraints of the present on individuals and groups. These constraints, consequently, lead to a selective reconstruction of the past. "The individual calls recollections to mind by relying on the frameworks of social memory. In other words, the various groups that compose society are capable at every moment of reconstructing their past. But . . . they most frequently distort the past in the act of reconstructing it" (Halbwachs 1992: 182). Reclaiming the past, knowing one's history (which is not a singular history, but a collective or shared history), and the emphasis on experience – i.e., the ethical injunctions of Black Studies and African-American history – are the motivational forces for the social memory of *blackness* that selectively remembers the past of the race.

To further develop this argument, we shall initially consider writings by Tommie Shelby, Anthony Appiah, and W. E. B. Du Bois. Both Shelby and Appiah bring a critical perspective to the relationship of memory and the belief in race. Shelby, in his advocacy of a concept of black racial solidarity, argues that a thick concept of collective black identity – such as can be found in black nationalist thought – is not necessary for solidarity. In a different vein, Appiah criticizes Du Bois's effort to establish a concept of race on the basis of history as a means to transcend a scientific (i.e., biological) concept of race. We discuss Du Bois in relation to these two critical perspectives, by interpreting his claims in "The conservation of races" and *The Souls of Black Folk* as examples of memory work whose validity, contra Appiah, is not exhausted by its apparent empirical inadequacy and which, contra Shelby, is necessary for the belief in race – which is the basis of any claim for racial solidarity – to persist.

Memory, race, and meaning

Shelby's study of black political thought is useful for situating the analysis at this level, both for its analytical insights and as an example of the way in which memory fosters an attachment to racial ideas. Shelby mounts a defense of the idea of "blackness as an emancipatory tool" through a philosophical interrogation of "black political thought." He introduces the topic by identifying two forms in which black solidarity enters into political action.

Traditionally, this sense of solidarity has a dual basis, one positive and the other negative. The shared racial identity and cultural heritage of African Americans provide a foundation for black unity, and those in the ethnoracial community of African descent often seek to preserve and celebrate the group's cultural distinctiveness through group loyalty, communal intercourse, ritual, and collective self-organization. On the negative side, the black experience of unjust treatment and discrimination has helped create strong bonds of identification. A common history of oppression and vulnerability to racism has engendered a need for political solidarity and group self-reliance. (Shelby 2005: 1)

Shelby comments that "this dual foundation for black unity . . . is often taken for granted, treated as a matter of common sense." However, this description of the conditions of black solidarity, based on positive and negative conditions, and the taken-for-grantedness of these conditions as the basis for this solidarity, is only the starting point for Shelby. He also acknowledges the challenges to the concept of racial solidarity built on these dual bases in recent years, from critics who dispute the analytical value of "race" and its divisive effects in an era of multiculturalism as well as from critics of identity politics. Shelby's intention is to salvage a principle of black solidarity that is non-essentialist. He argues for an approach termed an "oppression-based conception of black solidarity" which shifts "the focus away from issues of social identity as such and toward the various dimensions of racial injustice. This would be a form of political solidarity that would subordinate questions of who blacks are as a people to questions about the ways in which they have been and continue to be unfairly treated" (Shelby 2005: 4).

In order to carry out this project, Shelby begins with the tradition of black nationalist thought. In his view, black nationalists "advocate such things as black self-determination, racial solidarity and group reliance, various forms of voluntary racial separation, pride in the historical achievements of persons of African descent, a concerted effort to overcome racial self-hate and to instill black self-love, militant collective resistance to white supremacy, the development and preservation of a distinctive black cultural identity, and the recognition of Africa as the true homeland of those who are racially black" (Shelby 2005: 24). Taking the writings of Martin Delany as one of the earliest examples of black nationalist thought, Shelby wonders why Delany used the term nation to describe blacks living in the United States in the mid nineteenth century: "Given the forced migration to the New World brought about by the transatlantic slave trade, the vast majority of blacks in America are not properly described as immigrants or descendants of immigrants either" (Shelby 2005: 25). To avoid the empirical problems (evidenced by Delany) of an application of the term nationalism to persons who do not fit the conventional definition of a nation, Shelby then distinguishes between strong and weak black nationalism. He construes "strong black nationalism" as a "political program of black solidarity and voluntary separation," as a "worthwhile end in itself," and as "constitutive of an enduring component of the collective self-realization of blacks as a people." In contrast, Shelby describes "weak black nationalism" – his preferred formulation for a foundation of racial solidarity – as a "political program of black solidarity and group self-organization" that "functions as a means to create greater freedom and social equality for blacks" (Shelby 2005: 25). The difference between these two "nationalisms" is, therefore, one between a position that constructs the existence of a racial group on the basis of a shared cultural heritage and nation (or region) of origin and a position that constructs the racial group as a strategy to combat racial oppression. Shelby calls this latter position "pragmatic nationalism."

The characterization of two trends within black nationalist political thought is, of course, not articulated in this form by the writers whom Shelby considers. He is not unaware of this and, therefore, his methodological reflections on his reconstructive effort are worth noting.

For the philosopher, the core elements of the black nationalist tradition, like all intellectual traditions, must be reconstructed retrospectively. We look to our nearest contemporary exponents of the doctrine and ask whom they consider to be their most important intellectual forebears. We then look to those designated persons to see whom they refer to as forebears, and so on. We also look to "founding texts," the ones studied by all who claim affinity with the tradition. We include works by figures who everyone agrees are part of the tradition – such as Delany, Garvey, and Malcolm X. We then trace the intertextual dialogue between these figures and their critics. These sources give us something approaching a canon, which we use as a basis for interpreting the most important features of the tradition. (Shelby 2005: 31)

These reflections also hold true for his discussion of black cultural nationalism later in the book, in which he reconstructs this tradition based on a canon of writings by figures such as W. E. B. Du Bois, Alain Locke, Amiri Baraka, Harold Cruse, Haki Madhubuti, Maulana Karenga, and Molefi

Asante. Shelby reprises his criticism of classical nationalism in his consideration of cultural nationalism, arguing that while "blacks should be free to develop and maintain their cultural identities" such a claim does not necessitate that their "cultural identities must be rooted in *black* culture, no matter how black culture is defined" (Shelby 2005: 168). On his account, "Blacks can restore and maintain their dignity in the face of the legacy of white cultural imperialism and the devaluation of black culture(s) without adopting a collective cultural consciousness" (Shelby 2005: 169).

This critical position on cultural nationalism distances Shelby's notion of racial solidarity from the charge of essentialism on the one hand, and the critique of "identity politics" on the other hand. However, racial solidarity depends on some idea of the existence of a racial group and here he responds to the most anti-essentialist position possible, one that holds that race is not real and largely an ideological construct.

The fact that black racial identity has its origins in the ideological fiction of "race" does not undermine the idea of blacks as a people. Other national identities are derived from similar myths . . . The trouble with the position under consideration is not that blacks are not a people but rather that it does not follow that blacks have a *duty* to embrace black culture simply because they are racially black. (Shelby 2005: 175)

This claim, that a fictive notion of the racial group is not problematic, in effect splits the difference between the critique of essentialism and the insistence on the necessity of race. Shelby rejects the normative claim that has been asserted on the basis of the fictive notion of blacks as a people: the *normative obligation* for blacks to *be black* culturally. However, he defends the fiction of a black "people" not as a normative obligation or necessary component of individual identity but rather as a condition of possibility for racial solidarity in the face of various forms of racial injustice. Rather than a concept of normativity grounded in racial identity, Shelby opts for pragmatic racial solidarity and a thin notion of blackness over the thick notion of blackness that political and cultural nationalism(s) entail.

Shelby's alternative to the classical nationalists' idea of a collective racial identity based on culture is what could be described as an instrumental conception of racial solidarity. For example, he argues (against the criticism that his notion of thin blackness is too thin) "a shared belief in the value of a common 'black identity' is not needed to ground 'black' solidarity against racial domination. The basis of blacks' group identification is not their attachment to their thin black identity but rather their shared experience with antiblack racism and their mutual commitment to ending it" (Shelby 2005: 237).[8] While this perspective may underestimate how much adherence to cultural identity is needed for the mobilization of anti-racist political action, we are not primarily concerned with this point of difference; instead, we find another problem in Shelby's understanding of those classic arguments for a thick culture of blackness. The instrumental view of the conditions for racial solidarity misses the function of the assertion of collective identity that is relevant to understand the persistence of racial ideas: the creation of the ties themselves through thought, and in particular the memory of shared experience. Shelby in fact acknowledges this function while misrecognizing its significance. His methodological reflection on the construction of a canon of black nationalist thought and defense of the myths upon which various peoples are founded (whether these are myths of national origins or racial origins) participates in the making of the memory of a black race. For the type of black solidarity Shelby advocates, the function of memory in the creation of the feeling of group bonds is crucial.

With this insight in mind, we can return to W. E. B. Du Bois, one of the canonical figures in Shelby's analysis of ethnoracial nationalism. At least two purposes can be seen in Du Bois's essay "The conservation of races." On the one hand, Du Bois the social scientist is concerned to develop a concept of race that is not reducible to the "gross physical differences of color, hair, and bone." As discussed earlier, the race concept for Du Bois has two dimensions, one biological, the other – which is more important – cultural. On the other hand, Du Bois the politically engaged intellectual seeks not only to articulate a common cultural heritage for the black race *writ large* but also to establish a bond between blacks in the United States, which would enable them to confront successfully the discriminatory practices of racial segregation. Regarding a common black cultural heritage, Du Bois describes what can be called the memory of black experience. Du Bois specifies in the Negro "Academy creed" the special mission of the "Negro people" to make a "contribution to . . . civilization and humanity." This mission requires that "Americans of Negro descent" should "maintain their race identity until this mission of the Negro people is accomplished" (Du Bois 1986a: 825). The "Academy" itself is fictive, the imagined collection of "all these products of the Negro Mind" (Du Bois 1986a: 822). This special obligation on

---

[8] In the language of Anglo-American political theory, Shelby opts for a liberal rather than a communitarian conception of racial solidarity, which is grounded more in voluntary action (i.e., choice) than primordial cultural bonds (i.e., identity). For representative examples from the now voluminous debate between liberal and communitarian political theorists see Rawls (1993) and Taylor (1994).

the part of blacks in America derives from a shared past that Du Bois describes less in the form of a convincing historical narrative (i.e., the lyricism of the narrative is mythopoetic rather than factual) and more in the form of his own memory or recollection of this past. In a passage dealing with the question of whether one should be a Negro or an American first, Du Bois recalls this memory that stretches back into the dark forests of Africa.

We are Americans, not only by birth and by citizenship, but by our political ideals, our language, our religion. Farther than that, our Americanism does not go. At that point, we are Negroes, members of a vast historic race that from the very dawn of creation has slept, but half awakening in the dark forests of its African fatherland. We are the first fruits of this new nation, the harbinger of that black to-morrow which is yet destined to soften the whiteness of the Teutonic to-day. (Du Bois 1986a: 822)

This memory of a common past can be challenged – as it has been by Anthony Appiah – on empirical grounds. To Du Bois's assertion of an historical continuity between American blacks at the turn of the twentieth century and people living in Africa at the dawn of creation, Appiah argues that "whatever holds Du Bois's races conceptually together, then, it cannot be a common history" (Appiah 1992: 32). Nonetheless, Appiah correctly identifies the function of Du Bois's account of a common history as a " 'long memory' " while failing to recognize that "The conservation of races" is more about memory than history: "Du Bois's attempt to make sense of racial identity through time by way of a figurative 'long memory' subserves the same function as John Locke's attempt – in his essay *Concerning Human Understanding* – to make literal memory the core of the soul's identity through time . . . Locke's view was that two souls at different times were, in the philosopher's jargon, 'time slices' of the same individual if the later one had memories of the earlier one" (Appiah 1992: 32). Because Appiah is focused exclusively on the epistemological value of this "literal memory" rather than on the attachment of meaning to historical experience, he finds it less than adequate for logical reasons:

But, as philosophers since Locke have pointed out, we cannot tell whether a memory is evidence of the rememberer's identity, even if what is "remembered" really did happen to an earlier person, unless we know already that the rememberer and the earlier person are one. For it is quite conceivable that someone should think that they recall something that actually happened to somebody else. I have simply applied this same strategy of argument against Du Bois. History may have made us what we are, but the choice of a slice of the past in a period before your birth as your own history is exactly that: a choice. The phrase the "invention of tradition" is a pleonasm. (Appiah 1992: 32)

What Appiah exploits is a logical impossibility of a common history –
and common ancestry – to establish the ties of race that go beyond mere
biology. But is this argument really damaging to Du Bois's claim? The
fact that the slice of the past that figures into Du Bois's "remembering"
is a choice marks it as an example of social memory, precisely the
invention of a tradition, rather than an empirically accurate statement
of historical continuities between identities at two different points in
history. In other words, whereas Du Bois's argument for historical
continuity among members of the black race fails to achieve the
standards of historical truth that can be accepted by philosophy, this
failure does not stand in the way of it being serviceable on a practical
level for the purpose of bringing the past into the memory of the present,
that is, for bringing together what are otherwise temporally incommen-
surable experiences of race. To paraphrase Guyer (1996), Du Bois's
invention of tradition is not incompatible with "traditions of invention"
that go hand in hand with the belief in race.[9]

Positive and negative memory

We have characterized two ideal-typical forms of racial memory, one
that emphasizes subjection and discrimination, and the other that
emphasizes affirmative experiences of resistance, perseverance, and
cultural creativity. In reality both types, negative and positive, appear
together since they are frequently linked in narratives as well as in the
teneur of social relationships: subjection leads to resistance, etc.[10] Yet the
two can be considered as distinct moments in memory work; these
thoroughly negative conditions could as easily produce an avoidance of
race as they could an attachment to race. If the memory of race was
simply the memory of displacement and subjugation, no positive *content*
could be given to race itself. It would simply stand as a social stigma
imposed from without, rather than as an affirmation of a way of being. It
is possible to read the concepts of race and ethnicity along this positive
and negative divide: race is imposed and is entirely negating of the
humanity of subjected racial groups whereas ethnicity is constructed
(i.e., ethnicity comes *from the people*) and affirms the humanity of the ethnic
group. The work of memory falls most significantly on the positive side,
on the side of an ethnoracial imaginary. In Du Bois, the history of race
(in particular the black race) is reflected positively.

---

[9] We thank Ron Kassimir for bringing the felicitous title of Guyer's article to our attention.
[10] For a general description of the techniques of resistance see Scott (1992).

The history of the world is the history, not of individuals, but of groups, not of nations, but of races, and he who ignores or seeks to override the race idea in human history ignores and overrides the central thought of all history. What, then, is a race? It is a vast family of human beings, generally of common blood and language, always of common history, traditions and impulses, who are both voluntarily and involuntarily striving together for the accomplishment of certain more or less vividly conceived ideals of life. (Du Bois 1986a: 817)

The Negroes of America have a special mission not because of their physical difference from the "Teutons"; this mission is brought forward by the historical and cultural continuity among members of the black race. Du Bois finds the "race idea" to be universal and a significant human achievement: "Turning to real history, there can be no doubt, first, as to the widespread, nay, universal, prevalence of the race idea, the race spirit, the race ideal, and as to its efficiency as the vastest and most ingenious invention of human progress" (Du Bois 1986a: 817). For this reason, Du Bois argues against the "individualistic philosophy of the Declaration of Independence and the laisser-faire philosophy of Adam Smith" that stands opposed to the "racial spirit."

It is precisely the possibility of a positive memory of race that is put into doubt by Appiah's (1992: 32) criticism of Du Bois. In Appiah's view, the only thing that can hold together Du Bois's "races" is "his true criterion" (which is "scientific," i.e., biological) and not history (i.e., common descent, language, and "impulses and strivings," etc.). Consequently, he argues that

The real difference in Du Bois's conception, therefore, is not that his definition of race is at odds with the scientific one: it is rather, as the dialectic requires, that he assigns to race a different moral and metaphysical significance from the majority of his white contemporaries. The distinctive claim is that the Negro race has a positive message, a message that is not only different but valuable . . . By studying history, we can discern the outlines of the message of each race. (Appiah 1992: 34)

This is indeed a significant difference from the scientific view of race circa 1897 in Du Bois's claims. What he adds, without (we have argued) entirely abandoning a biological concept of race, is a positive content of racial meaning that reaches beyond gross physical differences and the negative imposition of an increasingly rigid color line in the United States (which dates, in the main, from the 1880s). Although the empirical basis might be suspect, what Du Bois communicates about history can be interpreted in another way. In order to bind blacks in America to the idea of race rather than Americanism, he asserts the importance of history, which holds insights about the contribution blacks have made to American culture in the past (music and literature) and the task of the race in the future (to make a unique and valuable contribution to human civilization). Du Bois reiterates this perspective in *The Souls of Black Folk*, as he seeks to negotiate "two unreconciled strivings" that arise from the "double-consciousness" of the American Negro.

[The American Negro] would not Africanize America, for America has too much to teach the world and Africa. He would not bleach his Negro soul in a flood of white Americanism, for he knows that Negro blood has a message for the world . . . This, then, is the end of his striving: to be a co-worker in the kingdom of culture, to escape both death and isolation, to husband and use his best powers and his latent genius. These powers of body and mind have in the past been strangely wasted, dispersed, or forgotten. The shadow of a mighty Negro past flits through the tale of Ethiopia the Shadowy and of Egypt the Sphinx. (Du Bois 1986b: 365)

This detour through Shelby's work on black nationalism, Du Bois's memory work in race history, and Appiah's critique of Du Bois has raised the central theoretical problematic: to understand how attachment to racial ideas occurs through the work of collective memory. The fictive account that sustains the idea of a "people" which shares a common history is an essential component of the social memory of race, to which black nationalist thought and Du Bois (among others) have made significant contributions. If we broaden Halbwachs's notion of commandments to include the perceived needs of the present, then we can interpret the black nationalist and Du Boisian racialist narratives as creative and selective recollections of a past that includes ancestral and cultural bonds that are perceived from the present. Du Bois's "The conservation of races" is less a faithful historical recapitulation of the socio-historical continuity of the black race, from primeval Africa to the American Negro of late nineteenth-century America, than it is an imagined recollection of a *black past* through the lens of contemporary (circa 1897) American society. Second, Du Bois's *choice* of recalling an *African past* as the core component of his identity, rather than the "Dutch" past of his European ancestors, can be better understood within the frame of memory of the group within which he was ascribed in late nineteenth-century America. As an aspect of social memory, Du Bois's recollection is not constrained by the past societies towards which he turned his thoughts; he is, however, constrained by the "commandments" of the late nineteenth century, which imposed a racial vision on social groups and a stigma on blacks in particular. The black race, as Appiah correctly points out, is revalued in Du Bois's discourse, not through a historically accurate reconstruction but through the imputation of a special mission for the black race and a claim for its special contributions ("Negro genius, of Negro literature and art, of Negro spirit").[11]

To reiterate the implications of this understanding of social memory for the persistence of racial ideas: taking black nationalism as an example, the thought of the black nation is localized in the context of present group relations. The aspect of power in black nationalist discourse which Shelby found suspect, the assertion that blackness entails loyalty to a collective black identity (manifested primarily in cultural practices), makes the memory of race a political act. The claim that blacks form a nation, which promotes ethical obligations internally and the assertion of honor externally, is not constrained by empirical facts but rather is based on a belief in race.

African-American history

Du Bois's belief in the strivings inherent to the black race in particular (and all races in general) and awareness of the forgetting of past achievements prefigures the memory work of historians in African-American history, scholars in the afrocentric intellectual movement, and black feminist thought. Because the range of contributions to African-American historiography is too vast to explore, for the purpose of understanding the function of memory in relation to the belief in racial ideas, we will limit our discussion to a recent book that is exemplary in its reflexivity. Nell Irvin Painter's *Creating Black Americans* constructs the memory of a black past in America, which is created from the concerns of the present. Painter argues that "history exists in two time frames: the past and the present . . . in order to make sense of what took place, you need to select what is important from all the other, trivial things that happened in the past." The process of selection "takes place in the present," and historians perform this task. "Making sense of the past is the work of historians, who create *historical narrative*. Historical narrative constructs a coherent story that makes sense to us now" (Painter 2006: ix). Painter acknowledges that the "present" from which the historical narrative of black people in America is written – and

---

[11] "We are that people whose subtle sense of song has given America its only American music, its only American fairy tales, its only touch of pathos and humor amid its mad money-making plutocracy" (Du Bois 1986a: 822).

concomitantly the historical narrative itself – "changes over time." She dates the historical interest in blacks to the Civil Rights era of the 1960s, because prior to that time "relatively few readers of history wanted to know what African Americans were doing and thinking" (Painter 2006: ix). Writing from the present of 2006, she argues that as the present shifts so do the questions which historical narrative must address.[12]

What makes her narrative unique, however, is her intent to "share the story with non-historians, notably black visual artists," who "like most people who are not historians, engage more emotionally with the African-American past" (Painter 2006: x). These artists, who "create artwork from their own personal experiences and from their understanding of the culture in which they live," represent "black historical *agency*, which makes black people historical actors, not passive victims of history" (Painter 2006: x). In this way these artists help to create black Americans.

Thus visual artists play a significant role in the continuing creation of black Americans. The work of black artists contradicts the conventional images of black people and puts black people's conception of themselves at the core of African-American history. Whereas US culture has depicted black people as ugly and worthless, black artists dwell on the beauty and value of black people. Art, by definition, says, "this is beautiful, this is valuable." (Painter 2006: x)

Like "The conservation of races," Painter asserts a positive vision of a race that is otherwise depicted negatively. Black artists are understood to play a special role as image-makers. The imagery produced by black artists is particularly advantageous for this task, according to Painter, because artists are emotionally attached to their subject matter and create from their experiences.

However, while the book purports to tell a story about black Americans since 1619, Painter acknowledges that many of the art works discussed and represented in her narrative were created after 1920 because "very little work by black artists existed" before this time. Consequently, some of the images depict figures or events that were not experienced by the artist. For example, in a chapter entitled "Those Who Were Enslaved, ca. 1770–1859," Painter includes Charles White's "Wanted poster series" from 1970, which "shows twentieth-century black people as

---

[12] "As new issues emerge, new questions surface, and the past yields new answers. For this reason, an African-American history written a generation ago no longer gives today's readers all the answers they seek. Not only have things happened in intervening years, but also we ask different questions of the past" (Painter 2006: ix–x).

nineteenth-century fugitive slaves" (Painter 2006: 97). Painter interprets the dates which appear on the poster, 1619 and 19??, as the artist's belief that nothing had changed for black Americans since the first Africans arrived on the North American continent. In this example, a double-level construction of the meaning of the past, from the standpoint of two "presents," is created. The first level of meaning is constructed by the artist, who creates a visual continuity between enslaved blacks in 1619 and free blacks in the twentieth century as one continuous chain of experience; the second level of meaning is created by Painter, who uses White's art to construct a written narrative that binds the experience of living black Americans to the memory of those who are no longer alive. The work of historical narrative, she argues, involves meaning that takes shape in knowledge and commemoration.

The theme of meaning relates to the changing production of historical narrative in two ways: first, knowledge as a *process*, and, second, historical commemoration . . . Writers, artists and musicians produced a steady stream of work presenting their versions of historical meaning. Historical commemoration – the process of creating holidays, monuments, and museums – began in the nineteenth century. *Creating Black Americans* takes note of the commemoration as part of a process of creating a coherent black American identity that also includes scholarship, art, and commentary. (Painter 2006: xiii)

It is worth noting that in this conception of historical knowledge and memory, coherence in black American identity does not inhere in the *history* of black Americans. It is created – according to the unique perspective found in Painter's book – by artists, scholars, and critics. Interspersed between a recitation of familiar facts of the African Diaspora and hardships faced by Africans in the New World are the representations of this experience by black artists; representations created, as mentioned above, in the twentieth century. This pairing of *dead facts* with visual representation has the function, as Halbwachs might suggest, of bringing these facts into living memory: the "emotional engagement" of the artists (as perceived by Painter) is advantageous for this task as a supplement to the dispassionate gaze of the professional historian.

When describing contemporary life in America, Painter indicates that a new diversity has emerged in the post-Civil Rights era, with a growing divide between poor and middle-class blacks, and between political orientations (black conservatives and black democrats). Culture also registers a divide in coherent presentations of the black experience. According to Painter "quarrels over Afrocentism and African-American studies took place among people engaged in higher education," while, "at the other end of the cultural spectrum, young people in the streets were creating new cultural forms called hip-hop" (Painter 2006: 333). She presents this latter street-centered cultural production as providing both coherence and division: "Rap music and hip-hop culture create a coherent image of black people as centered in poor, urban neighbor-hoods . . . In hip-hop culture, the middle-class, wealthy, and educated black people who are becoming more numerous either disappear or pose a threat to authentic African Americans" (Painter 2006: 339). Indeed, in the epilogue to the book, Painter's "Snapshot of African Americans in the Early Twenty-First Century" presents a statistical description of "a growing divide between those doing well and those doing poorly," and the demographic diversity of black Americans that has resulted from an influx of immigrants from Africa and is measurable by the fact that "millions of African Americans proclaim themselves to be of more than one race" (Painter 2006: 345, 346). Yet the book closes with an emphasis on the themes of creation and commemoration, which go beyond the "familiar" burdens of race: "This book reflects a range of creations, to show that at every point in history, African Americans have protested in justice and commemorated their heroes and history" (Painter 2006: 359). This conclusion, while based on a story grounded in specific events (slavery, reconstruction, segregation, and civil rights struggles) and represented in visual form, is analogous to the assertions of a common history evoked by Du Bois in a decidedly more lyrical and theological form. While the language of common strivings is absent in Painter's writing, the project remains similar: to remember the history of the race, its struggles and, more importantly, its creative life. The projects of Du Bois and Painter both reflect the political needs of their particular historical situation: at the turn of both the twentieth and twenty-first centuries a race-based sense of group identity was (and is) being called into question (respectively) by the prospect of American-ization and the growth of class divisions within the black "community."

Gendered memories: the margin as home

Alongside this current in African-American studies – as represented by Painter – that seeks to commemorate what is understood to be the black experience, the intersection of gender and race has figured into the social memory constructed by feminist writers. An example of this type of memory work is illustrated in the claims for identity politics made by bell hooks. The political engagement which hooks seeks in the present corresponds to the constraints on the frame of memory imposed by the partial triumph of the principle of racial integration in the post-Civil

Rights Movement era. In particular, hooks acknowledges the various cleavages among African-Americans based on gender, class, and cultural distinctions, and her discussion of cultural differences forms the basis of an experiential concept of identity politics. The red thread running through her work is the common denominator of oppression, which is the criterion for classifying political struggles. Defining oppression as the "absence of choices," hooks denies the universalistic claim of "global sisterhood" of the early (in her view) white women's movement, in order to open up space for feminist theorizing shaped by the specific experiences of black women (hooks 1984: 5). She argues that "there is much evidence substantiating the reality that race and class identity creates differences in quality of life, social status, and lifestyle that take precedence over the common experience women share – differences which are rarely transcended" (hooks 1984: 4). Likewise, hooks's arguments concerning the liberatory potential of a politics based on racial identity directs attention to the cultural effects of the transformed class hierarchy among American blacks since the 1960s. In order to overcome these cleavages within the black community, she endeavors to locate sources of resistance to racism within a community of the oppressed living at the margins of American society.

According to hooks, the opportunities opened by the racial integrationist strategies which aimed to achieve racial equality have merely provided an alternative means to perpetuate the domination of the majority of blacks. Racial integration and assimilation became the preferred means by which some black Americans have become complicit in the maintenance of white supremacy.

At this historical moment, when a few black people no longer experience the racial apartheid and brutal racism that still determine the lot of many black people, it is easier for the few to ally themselves politically with the dominant racist white group. Assimilation is the strategy that has provided social legitimation for this shift in allegiance. It is a strategy deeply rooted in the ideology of white supremacy and its advocates urge black people to negate blackness, to imitate racist white people so as to better absorb their values, their way of life. Ironically, many changes in social policy and social attitudes that were once seen as ways to end racial domination have served to reinforce and perpetuate white supremacy. This is especially true of social policy that has encouraged and promoted racial integration. (hooks 1989: 113–114)

hooks posits a direct connection between integration, capitalism, and the demise of an ethical culture among African-Americans. The experience of a common black culture and the pervasiveness of a consumerist ethos among blacks are held to be contradictory. She argues "we have been reluctant, as a people, to say that capitalism poses a direct threat to the survival of an ethical belief system in Black life."[13] This belief system is the source of collective action and racial identity. By breaking down the barriers to material success, integration encourages economically privileged blacks to reject an affirmative relationship to black culture. On this account, a "tragic irony" of black life is that "individuals succeed in acquiring material privilege often by sacrificing their positive connection to black culture and black experience" (hooks 1992: 19). Drawing on the theme of Paule Marshall's novel *Praisesong for the Widow*, in which the temptations of material success destroy the family life of the protagonist, hooks proposes a "love of blackness" as a means to self-recovery: "To recover herself, Avey [the protagonist] has to relearn the past, understand her culture and history, affirm her ancestors, and assume responsibility for helping other black folks to decolonize their minds" (hooks 1992: 19). Thus, the success of racial integration in raising the economic standing of one class of African-Americans is responsible for the devaluation of a traditional black culture that now needs to be recuperated because, as hooks maintains, this culture is the source of a positive, loving relationship to blackness.

For hooks, then, it is precisely racial integration that stands in the way of a liberatory black politics. However, hooks does not turn to a nationalist version of identity politics as a counterhegemonic, anti-racist symbolic system; rather, she locates the roots of counterhegemony in what she repeatedly refers to as the "margin."[14] Marginality is defined as "a site of transformation where liberatory black subjectivity can fully emerge." She distinguishes between "the marginality which is imposed by oppressive structure and that marginality one chooses as site of resistance, as location of radical openness and possibility" (hooks 1990: 22). Hence, hooks constructs the margin as a place of positive memory. The margin is not simply a metaphor, but a concrete location from which liberatory black politics can be theorized; as a "position and place of resistance," it is "crucial for oppressed, exploited, colonized people." hooks is concerned to point out that the margin is not a "mythic notion," but rather it "comes from lived experience" (hooks 1990: 150). On these

---

[13] Dialogue of bell hooks in bell hooks and Cornel West (1991: 95).

[14] Indeed, hooks is critical of the nationalist and pan-Africanist movement of the 1960s for a vision that "was not particularly distinctive or revolutionary." Because these movements were premised on a patriarchal vision of black liberation, "equating [it] with black men gaining access to male privilege that would enable them to assert power over black women," hooks finds that the potential for radical struggle was undermined. "Certainly the core of Black Muslim liberatory efforts also centered around gaining access to material privileges (though from the standpoint of black self-determination and control), the kind of nation-building which would place black men in positions of authority and power" (hooks 1990: 16).

terms, she claims not to "romantically re-inscribe the notion of that space of marginality where the oppressed live apart from their oppressors as 'pure.' " The margin has been both the site of oppression as well as resistance, including the patriarchal oppression of black women by black men.

Indeed, hooks recognizes that the margin is stratified by social class. All blacks do not share the same experience of marginality: "This experience of space and location is not the same for black folks who have always been privileged, or for black folks who desire only to move from underclass status to points of privilege; not the same for those of us from poor backgrounds who have had to continually engage in actual political struggle both within and outside of black communities to assert an aesthetic and critical presence" (1990: 148). Thus, not all experiences of the margin are necessarily radical or liberatory. hooks claims that the "oppositional black culture that emerged in the context of apartheid and segregation has been one of the few locations" in which "loving blackness" is made possible. Again, strategies of integration and assimilation play a decisive role in the erosion of the oppositional character of this space. She asserts "racial integration in a social context where white supremacist systems are intact undermines marginal spaces of resistance by promoting the assumption that social equality can be attained without changes in the culture's attitudes about blackness and black people" (hooks 1992: 10).

In her advocacy of a "politics of radical black subjectivity," hooks calls for the conceptualization of blacks as "subjects" from the standpoint of the "marginal space of difference." The memory of this marginal space is, however, culturally specific. hooks often invokes a vision of the rural, black folk culture of her own experience.

To be in the margin is to be part of the whole but outside the main body. As black Americans living in a small Kentucky town, the railroad tracks were a daily reminder of our marginality . . . We could enter that world [across the tracks] but we could not live there. We had always to return to the margin, to cross the tracks, to shacks and abandoned houses on the edge of town. (hooks 1984: preface, n.p.)

The fact that one could not "live there" because "laws ensured our return" is the ground of black solidarity. A radical black subjectivity is premised on the positive evaluation of the experience of blackness that was molded under the conditions of involuntary confinement at the margins of white society. Besides autobiographical references, hooks often invokes a historical memory of, and contemporary solidarity with, the oppression of black women, such as the "plight of black women domestic servants in South Africa, black women laboring in white homes." While generally affirming the more rural context of black experience, hooks is more ambivalent about the urban black experience. Although the culture of the urban black "underclass," exemplified by rap and hip hop music, is described as a "form of 'testimony'" that "enabled underclass black [male] youth to develop a critical voice" (hooks 1990: 27), hooks also points out that "much rap music is riddled with sexism and misogyny" (hooks 1992: 35). Thus, it is black folk culture, as the cultural experience and memory of the most oppressed, which provides the specific content for the space of the margin.

An important space within the margin is home (or "homeplace" in hooks's terminology) as a site of resistance. According to hooks, "historically, African-American people believed that the construction of a homeplace, however fragile and tenuous (the slave hut, the wooden shack), had a radical political dimension." As the product of the struggles primarily waged by black women to maintain a haven in a heartless racist world, hooks identifies the "domestic space" as a "crucial site for organizing, for forming political solidarity . . . its structure was defined less by whether or not black women or men were conforming to sexist behavior norms and more by our struggle to uplift ourselves as a people, our struggle to resist racist domination and oppression" (hooks 1990: 47). Homeplace stands as a foundation from which blacks "can regain lost perspective, give life new meaning," a space where "we can return for renewal and self-recovery, where we can heal our wounds and become whole" (hooks 1990: 49).

Memory and the reality of race

The three genres of memory work we have considered here, ranging from the romantic vision of Du Bois, the experience in African-American history narrated through an aesthetic of blackness, and the standpoint of black feminist discourse, illustrate the force of racial ideas upon the meaning of experience. Belief in race is made real through practice, in this case through the construction of the memory of a shared experience that extends back in time. These examples illustrate the epigraph at the head of this chapter: "All history shows how easily political action can give rise to the belief in blood relationship" (Weber 1978: 393). The interest in mounting a political opposition to conditions of inequality associated with racism coincides with efforts to demarcate a history of the racial group, to give it coherence and continuity in the face of dispersion and fragmentation. Geography (place of origin) and blood (lineage), two of the more effective means by which racial groups have been made, intersect in the collective memory of race. From origins in Africa (the Old World) and a biological inheritance based on the one-drop rule (an invention of the New World), the memory of the black "racial group" is constructed in such a way as to transcend the empirical multiplication of experiences identified as racial experiences, and the anachronism of the one-drop rule is supplanted by positive bonds of resistance and perseverance. As Hervieu-Léger notes with respect to religious memory, "At the source of all religious belief . . . there is belief in the continuity of the lineage of believers. This continuity transcends history" (Hervieu-Léger 2000: 125). Insofar as racial belief functions in an analogous manner, it is not paradoxical to say that the memory of race is a historical construction that is, simultaneously, a denial of history (and this is precisely the point of Appiah's objection to Du Bois). Although there are many ways of being black, the recognition of which raises empirical problems for an overarching concept of race, one *is* black in spite of all differences and group affiliations. What matters most is the memory and commemoration of a *racial* past that connects individuals living in the present with the "experiences" of their racial ancestors.

At the same time, a normative dimension is introduced into collective memory. Once again, Hervieu-Léger brings the matter into sharp focus: the "normative dimension to memory is not of itself specific to religious memory. It characterizes any collective memory which forms and endures through the process of selective forgetting, sifting and retrospective inventing" (Hervieu-Léger 2000: 124). Painter describes the normative stakes in contemporary creation and commemoration as follows:

After the end of legalized segregation, the notion of authentic blackness became a preoccupation of the hip-hop generation. The need to define what constituted authentic – as opposed to inauthentic – blackness related to the increasingly visible diversity among people considering themselves African American. (Painter 2006: 321)

To the extent that the normative question of the authentic and the inauthentic was raised in the past, perhaps it was not felt with the urgency suggested by Painter for contemporary blacks. Yet this judgment on authenticity, which delineates the boundaries of the groups, appears whenever black nationalist discourse is present, in the disputes between Du Bois and Booker T. Washington and between Martin Luther King Jr. and Malcolm X, and the changing conceptions of the meaning of "black creole" (Domínguez 1986). The combination of political action (the struggle against conditions associated with racism) and the intensity of feeling mobilized by collective memory (identification with a lineage that transcends history and the normative judgment of the authenticity of behaviors) create the conditions for what Freud describes as the "narcissism of minor differences" (Freud 1930: 72), affirming the conviction that race has a reality and, ultimately, confirming the belief in race.

9   Desire

> Psychoanalysis has already shown that speech is not merely the medium
> which manifests – or dissembles – desire; it is also the object of desire.
>
> (Foucault 1972: 216)

We have reached a stage in our discussion of race at which the analysis
might typically break off. Initially, we considered styles of thought on
race, which were found wanting insofar as each one – in different ways
and for different reasons – proved inadequate to the task of conceptualizing this vexatious object. Yet when observed from a different angle,
these styles of thought all pursue a rational reconstruction of the existence of race, its conditions of emergence, persistence, and potential
denouement. We have also sought a rational reconstruction of race as an
object of inquiry, but with a critical difference. Our reconstructive
analysis has redefined the object as belief in racial ideas, as a set of logical
relations binding together the components of the racial ensemble and
reinforcing the belief in race (i.e., racial ideas); and, furthermore, we
have highlighted how the reproduction of the racial ensemble is carried
out in *conscious* ways. In our discussion of the politics of memory, we
have shown how the belief in race is made real through the remembrance
of a racial past that is organized in relation to social groups and concerns
of the present. This would ordinarily be enough to satisfy the require-
ments of research in social theory: the re-description of the theoretical
object for the purpose of resolving hitherto existing problems. However,
in the case of race, our intuition is that one additional avenue of inquiry
remains to be explored, which has to do with a type of attachment that is
neither explicable on a purely logical basis nor dependent on conscious
activity. In other words, what remains to be placed within our theoretical
framework is the question of what motivates the attachment to race.

One answer to this question can be found in the sociology of race
relations: an attachment to race exists because there is an *interest* in race
that is collective, and that is produced by external, social conditions.
As Bonilla-Silva argues, "Insofar as the races receive different social

190

rewards at all levels, they develop dissimilar objective interests . . . In other words, although the races' interests can be detected from their practices, they are not subjective and individual but collective and shaped by the field of real practical alternatives, which is itself rooted in the power struggles between the races" (Bonilla-Silva 1997: 470). The answer that follows from this claim is that objective interests bind people together as races. Moreover, this binding together of groups as races can be construed along the lines of a rational and conscious process of calculating benefits and costs that are entailed by the changing fortunes of power struggles between racial groups. The attachment to race can, therefore, be described as being motivated by a rational reaction to the social conditions that confront different races in a racialized social order.

The use of the term *rational* in relation to the motivational sources of the attachment to race requires explanation. This term is applied not in the broad sense of an opposition to the pejorative meaning of *irrational*, but rather in the more technical sense of rational action (i.e., instrumental or purposive rationality) that has been conceptualized by Weber: such action is "*instrumentally* rational (*zweckrational*), that is, determined by expectations as to the behavior of objects in the environment and of other human beings; these expectations are used as 'conditions' or 'means' for the attainment of the actor's own rationally pursued and calculated ends" (Weber 1978: 24). Weber distinguishes instrumental rationality from value rational (i.e., "determined by a conscious belief in the value for its own sake" [Weber 1978: 25–26]) and traditional (i.e., customary or habitual) forms of social action. He treats these *pure types* of action equally from an empirical standpoint. However, Weber privileges rational action for methodological reasons.

For the purposes of a typological scientific analysis it is convenient to treat all irrational, affectually determined elements of behavior as factors of deviation from a conceptually pure type of rational action . . . The construction of a purely rational course of action in such cases serves the sociologist as a type (ideal type) which has the merit of clear understandability and lack of ambiguity. By comparison with this it is possible to understand the way in which actual action is influenced by irrational forces of all sorts, such as affects and errors, in that they account for the deviation from the line of conduct which would be expected on the hypothesis that the action were purely rational. (Weber 1978: 6)

We can interpret the explanation of objective interests that orient individuals to race in Bonilla-Silva's account along these lines as an explanation of the instrumental rational action that underpins the formation of racial groups. The analysis of race achieves "clear understandability and lack of ambiguity" if behavior is analyzed as rational action. Weber is careful to point out that action has various other influences, which cannot be excluded by methodological *fiat*. Bonilla-Silva's intent, in contrast, is to ground the analysis of racism on strictly rational forms of action and reaction, and, therefore, opposes the study of racism as a type of irrational prejudice (Bonilla-Silva 1997: 486). Weber, however, suggests such an insistently rationalistic approach to social action is only warranted for methodological reasons.

> Only in this respect and for these reasons of methodological convenience is the method of sociology "rationalistic." It is naturally not legitimate to interpret this procedure as involving a rationalistic bias of sociology, but only as a methodological device. It certainly does not involve a belief in the actual predominance of rational elements in human life, for on the question of how far this predominance does or does not exist, nothing whatever has been said. That there is, however, a danger of rationalistic interpretations where they are out of place cannot be denied. (Weber 1978: 6–7)

This warning against misplaced "rationalistic interpretations" is well suited to an understanding of the attachment to race as social action. Not only objective, instrumental-rational reasons but also subjective reasons connect individuals and groups to racial beliefs.

Hence, while we do not disagree with the idea that the motivation driving individuals to identify with racial ideas can be interpreted as an instrumental-rational type of social action, we also sense that it does not arise solely from conscious reactions to external conditions and events. In this chapter, we pursue the question of the pertinacious attachment to race as a matter of affect and fantasy. Consequently, our analysis departs from a strictly *instrumental-rational* framework. We explore this attachment, from the standpoint of a *psychoanalytic* framework, as an aspect of sexuality, of sexual object choice, or, to use everyday language, as an aspect of desire: a desire for race. The attachment to racial ideas, in this view, may have more to do with pleasure than with the rational calculation of the utility of these ideas. We are led to take up this angle of analysis by the intuition that without reaching the level of an unconscious desire for race, we cannot achieve a fully adequate explanation of the continuing attachment to ideas and categories that are *unreal*. In order to do so, we borrow a concept from outside the sociological field, the concept of *libido* that was central to the early formation of psychoanalysis as a field of inquiry and practice.[1] This concept will enable us to

---

[1] According to Laplanche and Pontalis (1973: 239), the concept libido has no single meaning in Freud's work. The word itself derives from Latin: "The Latin word *libido* means wish or desire." Laplanche and Pontalis offer the following definition: "Energy postulated by Freud as underlying the transformation of the sexual instinct with respect

articulate several characteristics of the desire for race: the wishes, pleasures, and fantasies associated with the belief in race and racial categories, as well as its uncanny quality as a real/unreal thing.

A social fact with an unconscious dimension?

There is very little questioning, within sociological analysis, of the conscious character of social practices; or rather, it is usually taken for granted that people are aware of what they are doing and saying.[2] When it does arise, the question is most often reserved for the issue of structure, and yet, particularly from a Weberian standpoint, there is something that deserves to be explored not only at the structural level, but also at the level of both individual actions and thoughts: if the object of sociological analysis is meaningfully oriented action, does the unconscious character of this orientation matter?

The borrowing of the concept libido (desire) from psychoanalysis to account for the unconscious dimension of meaningful action, however, presents an immediate problem: it is incommensurate with the language of *interests* that remains ubiquitous in sociology. Interests are set in opposition to passions (which are irrational and potentially dangerous) and prejudices (understood as biased, and possibly irrational preconceptions).[3] In particular, passions are found wanting for being too arbitrary to have predictive value in explanations of social action. One social theorist who has made use of the concept of libido is Pierre Bourdieu, who, nonetheless, reiterates the necessity of the concept of rational interests: "One cannot do sociology without accepting what classical philosophers called the 'principle of sufficient reason' and without assuming, among other things, that social agents don't do just anything, that they are not foolish, that they do not act without reason" (Bourdieu 1998b: 75). This position stands not against passions, but rather against the possibility that social action could be "disinterested"

to its object (displacement of cathexes), with respect to its aim (e.g., sublimation), and with respect to the source of sexual excitation (diversity of the erotogenic zones)."

[2] A good example of this assumption can be found in manuals of ethnography, and research methods in general; the issue of the unconscious is seldom raised, and it is assumed that one only needs to look at people, hear what they say, and see what they do to know what is happening. It is also assumed that what people do and say reflects what they consciously think.

[3] Here we intend to distance ourselves from these twin negative perspectives. We do not see the desire for race as connoting something irrational or dangerous (as the previous chapter on memory indicates). Moreover, we do not associate the desire for race with what is understood in the social psychological studies as prejudice: insofar as racial prejudice is premised on the belief in race, it is a secondary mental process. Our interest lies in the attachment to the idea of race rather than prejudice.

(i.e., motivated by disinterestedness); hence, his argument for sufficient reason is opposed to the notion that social agents engage in "gratuitous acts" (Bourdieu 1998b: 76). However, in making the case for socio-logical skepticism towards disinterestedness, he seeks to replace the notion of interest with "more rigorous notions such as *illusio, investment,* or even *libido*" (Bourdieu 1998b: 76). What does Bourdieu mean by libido in a sociological context? He offers two brief sentences of explanation:

One of the tasks of sociology is to determine how the social world constitutes the biological libido, an undifferentiated impulse, as a specific social libido. There are in effect as many kinds of libido as there are fields: the work of socialization of the libido is precisely what transforms impulses into specific interests, socially constituted interests, which only exist in relation to a social space in which certain things are important and others don't matter and for socialized agents who are constituted in such a way as to make distinctions corresponding to the objective differences in that space. (Bourdieu 1998b: 78–79)

From this we can draw out his core claim: the undifferentiated biological impulses are transposed into social libido, that is, "socially constituted interests," which are made manifest in relation to specific areas of social life. The relationship of the social libido and social space is described by Bourdieu as the *illusio*, in which social "agents" are "well-adjusted to the game" and are therefore "possessed by the game" (Bourdieu 1998b: 79). This feel or sense of the game allows agents to master the game, to make the proper investments. Bourdieu then distinguishes this concept with the notion of interested action found in utilitarian social thought.

First, [utilitarians] pretend agents are moved by conscious reasons, as if they consciously posed the objectives of their action and acted in such a way as to obtain the maximum efficacy with the least cost. The second, anthropological hypothesis: they reduce everything that can motivate agents to economic inter-est, to monetary profit. They assume, in a word, that the principle of action is well-thought-out economic interest and its objective is material profit, posed consciously through rational calculation. (Bourdieu 1998b: 79)

To avoid this economistic understanding of interests, Bourdieu proposes his concept of habitus: "To the reduction of conscious calculation, I oppose the relationship of ontological complicity between the habitus and the field. Between agents and the social world there is a relationship of infraconscious, infralinguistic complicity" (Bourdieu 1998b: 79). The idea of "ontological complicity" implies that people are motivated by social interests, which are unconscious, and yet rational. The habitus concept connotes the idea that social perception is unconsciously adjusted to reality. "Social agents who have a feel for the game, who have embodied a host of practical schemes of perception and appreciation functioning as instruments of reality construction . . . do not need to pose the objectives of their practices as ends" (Bourdieu 1998b: 80).

The essential elements of Bourdieu's concept of interest can be summarized as follows. Interests are not given to immediate cognition but rather remain unconscious or silent in social action. However, as implicit "practical schemes," they are adjusted to, and anticipate, reality. Such an understanding of the motivational conditions for social action serves Bourdieu's overarching account of social reproduction. However, the concept of a *racial habitus* as a non-utilitarian conceptualization of the interest underlying social action that is oriented to a racial reality is, for our purposes, inadequate for the following reason: it does not fit the peculiarities of race as an object. The unconscious desire for race cannot be conceived as being adjusted to reality (i.e., adjusted to the rules of the social game played out in different areas of the social space) even though racial ideas coincide with features of reality (i.e., physical differences, perception of the phenotype, and practices): the nature of the object, the belief in race, is – in psychoanalytic terms – in tension with the *reality principle*. It is grounded in a wish or fantasy about reality. What is required is a theory of the different dimensions of desire for an object that is both real and unreal, rather than a theory of a biological libido that is transformed into a social libido, i.e., interests. We therefore turn to psychoanalysis proper for essential elements of a theory of attachment (or "object-cathexis") to racial ideas and categories. Concepts drawn from a psychoanalytic framework enable an articulation of the *subjective* side of race that does not render the attachment to race as an entirely rational, cognitive, or political act.

Returning to our initial question of the reality of race, the issue of attachment to race is more directly specified. Given the difficulties that arise in conceptualizing the relationship between the thought of race and the reality of race, how can an account be given of an affective attachment to something that is unreal? The relationship between thought and reality is a fundamental concern in Freud's writings, which offer insights in four areas. First, Freud provides a typological account of the relationship between conscious and unconscious mental life, in which the unconscious is a ubiquitous condition of thought. Second, his analysis of a form of thought that gains omnipotence over reality offers a model for understanding how racial thoughts take precedence over the reality. Third, the psychoanalytic frame can help to unpack the feeling of reality in relation to racial categories. The paradox in the racial ensemble – that racial ideas feel real (i.e., as experience rather than thought) – can be explicated by the psychoanalytic notion that thought can be pleasurable (i.e., is a type of sexuality). Finally, this framework can help make sense of the simultaneous association of race as a social fact with, on the one hand, danger, threat, and disgust and with, on the other hand, desire.

The unconscious, fantasy, and reality

Unconscious thoughts shape not only perception but also the boundaries between thought and a reality that exists beyond thought: in dreams and screen memories, the unconscious takes precedence over reality. What is allowed into consciousness during dreams and in the recollection of experiences in memory are those images that the unconscious allows to seep into conscious thought. Such a view is consonant with Freud's topographical representation of the levels of the unconscious in *The Ego and the Id*. Freud points out that conscious life is fleeting; it is but a small portion of the mental life of the individual (Freud 1923: 3–4). The ego is a thin, perceptive surface of our mental apparatus, which is connected directly to the unconscious (the id) and perceives stimuli from external reality. The id (i.e., the unconscious) plays a driving role. Freud uses the metaphor of a horse and rider to represent the relationship of the ego (consciousness) and the id (the unconscious). The ego is like a rider of a horse (the unconscious) that has superior strength and is "obliged to guide it where it wants to go"; similarly, "the ego is in the habit of transforming the id's will into action as if it were its own" (Freud 1923: 15). On this account, there is only the appearance that conscious mental activity seeks its *own* ends; instead, consciousness is pushed in directions determined by unconscious wishes and the repression of these wishes.

This typology of ego and id is built upon earlier works that deal with mental phenomena that are not fully part of conscious life. In *The Interpretation of Dreams* (1900), Freud defines dreams as the fulfillment of unconscious wishes: "*When the work of interpretation has been completed, we perceive that a dream is the fulfillment of a wish*" (Freud 1900: 154). However, these wishes are frequently distorted by a force that inhibits the full realization of the wish. In order to make sense of the dream, the psychoanalyst engages the *analysand* in a process of interpretation that has as its goal a layer of meaning – the latent content or "dream thoughts" – that is not immediately accessible in the manifest content of the dream. Freud asserts that his theory "is not based on a consideration of the manifest content of dreams but refers to the thoughts which are shown by the work of interpretation to lie behind dreams. We must make a contrast between the *manifest* and the *latent* content of dreams" (Freud 1900: 168). This attention to the latent content allows Freud to argue that anxiety dreams are also dreams in which a fulfillment of a wish occurs. But the expression of the wish involves two purposes, one of which attempts to force back the other: "But in cases where the wish-fulfillment is unrecognizable, where it has been disguised, there must have existed some inclination to put up a defence against the wish; and owing to this defence the wish was unable to express itself except in a distorted shape" (Freud 1900: 175). Sixteen years later, in *The Introductory Lectures on Psychoanalysis* (1916), Freud argues that parapraxes (which include slips of the tongue, misreading, mishearing, forgetting, mislaying, losing, and the like) are a compromise between two psychical forces: "But parapraxes are the outcome of a compromise: they constituted a half-success and a half-failure. For each of the two intentions; the intention which is being challenged is neither completely suppressed nor, apart from special cases, carried through quite unscathed" (Freud 1916: 66).

As mentioned earlier, Freud treats fantasy as a significant component of mental life, not only in dreams but also in memories. Concerning what he calls screen memories, Freud argues that gaps in our memory of events we have experienced are not forgotten but rather omitted (i.e., repressed). Memories are subject to the same psychic mechanisms as are dreams.

> We then conceive of the idea that two psychical forces are involved in producing these memories. One of them takes the importance of the experience as a motive for wanting it remembered, but the other – the force of resistance – opposes this preferential choice. The two contending forces do not cancel each other out, nor does the one motive overpower the other, with or without loss to itself. Instead, a compromise is reached, rather like the resultant in a parallelogram of forces. The upshot of this compromise is that it is not the experience itself that supplies the memory image – in this respect the resistance carries the day – but another psychical element, which is closely associated with the one that proved objectionable. (Freud 1899: 6–7).

Memories, like dreams, are fragmented and distorted thoughts in which reality (events of prior days or actual experiences) is represented in displaced and condensed images.[4] Reality comes into consciousness – that

---

[4] Compare Freud's description of screen memories and the mechanism of the *dream-work*: "Hence, the result of the conflict is that, instead of the memory image that was justified by the original experience, we are presented with another, which is to some extent associatively *displaced* from it" (Freud 1899: 7). "One and one only of these logical relations is very highly favoured by the mechanism of dream-formation: namely, the relation of similarity, consonance or approximation – the relation of 'just as' . . . Parallels or instances of 'just as' inherent in the material of the dream-thoughts constitute the first

is, into dreams and memories – not in a logical, conceptual form but rather in tropes: metaphor, synecdoche, and metonym. This is the consequence of the compromises between the two psychical forces: on the one hand, wishes, fantasy, desire, and, on the other hand, the mechanism of repression.

What is the significance of these arguments about dreams, memories, desire, and the unconscious for race? The psychoanalytic framework attends to conditions of the perception of, and attachment to, reality. We emphasize this aspect of psychoanalysis because race, as we have argued, is largely a phenomenon of ideas and of belief. An analogy can be drawn between racial ideas and the structure of thought characteristic of dreams, parapraxes, and screen memories. For both racial ideas and the mental processes described by Freud, the reality outside the mind is superseded by *thoughts*. Similar to dreams and memories, racial ideas make use of bits of reality (physical differences, perceptions of phenotype, and practices), but, at the same time, they never lose their independence from reality. Finally, and most controversially, it is also plausible to carry the analogy to the level of the unconscious. It might be pertinent to argue that dreams, memories, and racial ideas are all produced by unconscious processes: neither the dreamer nor the individual who believes in race is conscious of the mental operations that give rise to the manifest dream or the sense that race is a thing in reality. Moreover, what is expressed in dreams and in the belief in race is a wish or desire. However, rather than pursuing the concept of repression to describe the desire for race, this desire can be understood as a form of pleasure that is taken in race in thought as well as in practice. In other words, race, which is an idea, feels real because of an unconscious wish for it to be real.

Racial ideas as omnipotence of thought

It should not be forgotten that Freud's analytical framework of mental phenomena and processes is constructed from cases and examples of psychical disturbance, especially disturbance manifested in the psychoneuroses (i.e., hysteria). He specified the workings of normal forms of psychological life from his study of its abnormal forms. As a result, when Freud sought to explain totemism and the incest taboo, he considered a

foundation for the construction of a dream; and no inconsiderable part of the dream-work consists in creating fresh parallels where those which are already present cannot find their way into the dream owing to the censorship imposed by resistance" (Freud 1900: 354, 355).

form of thought that was abnormal in hysterics (i.e., infantile) and normal in so-called "primitive peoples": animism. Based on ethnographic materials reflecting the state of anthropological knowledge of his time, Freud describes animism as "the highly remarkable view of nature and the universe" which fills "the world with innumerable spiritual beings both benevolent and malignant; and these spirits and demons [are regarded] as the causes of natural phenomena . . . not only animals and plants but all the inanimate objects in the world are animated by them" (Freud 1912: 95). He is primarily interested in animism as a "system of thought" (he includes it with religion and science as the "three great pictures of the universe"): "It does not merely give an explanation of a particular phenomenon, but allows us to grasp the whole universe as a single unity from a single point of view" (Freud 1912: 97). Freud speculates on the functional origin of animistic thought.

It is not to be supposed that men were inspired to create their first system of the universe by pure speculative curiosity. The practical need for controlling the world around them must have played its part. So we are not surprised to learn that, hand in hand with the animistic system, there went a body of instructions upon how to obtain mastery over men, beasts and things – or rather, over their spirits. These instructions go by the names of "sorcery" and "magic". (Freud 1912: 97–98)

Magical acts, such as those used to produce rain or fertility, function through the imitation of clouds and storms or a "dramatic representation of human intercourse." Freud asserts that the "operative factor" in various examples of magic is "the *similarity* between the act performed and the result expected" (Freud 1912: 101). Other cases of magic involve contiguity or "association" (e.g., taking possession of something belonging to an enemy that one wishes to harm). According to James Frazer, from whom Freud draws many examples, the essence of magic involves "mistaking an ideal connection for a real one." Freud finds this explanation inadequate, arguing "it does not explain its true essence, namely the misunderstanding which leads it to replace the laws of nature by psychological ones" (Freud 1912: 104). Comparing the psychical state of children and "primitives," the use of play and representation "is the easily understandable result of the paramount virtue they ascribe to their wishes, or the will that is associated with those wishes and of the methods by which those wishes operate" (Freud 1912: 105). However, Freud argues that as time passes the "psychological accent shifts" from these "motives" to the "measures" taken (i.e., the magical act). It then "appears as though it is the magical act itself which, owing to its similarity with the desired result, alone determines the occurrence of their result" (Freud 1912: 105). The apparent efficacy of such animistic thinking relies on mental and physical acts that are not subject to the need for objective verification. The question of objective evidence only arises when "the psychical phenomenon of doubt has begun to emerge as an expression of a tendency to repression" (Freud 1912: 105–106).[5]

In order to return to the motives or wishes in animism, Freud describes the nature of animistic thought as an "over-valuation of all mental processes." This entails "an attitude towards the world, that is, which in view of our knowledge of the relation between reality and thought, cannot fail to strike *us* as an over-valuation of the latter. Relations which hold between ideas of things are assumed to hold equally between the things themselves" (Freud 1912: 106). Freud finds an analogous over-valuation of thought in the symptoms of obsessional neuroses. "It is in obsessional neuroses that the survival of the omnipotence of thoughts is most clearly visible and that the consequences of this primitive mode of thinking come closest to consciousness . . . what determines the formation of symptoms is the reality not of experience but of thought" (Freud 1912: 108). "Neurotics," Freud writes, "live in a world apart."

What hysterics repeat in their attacks and fix by means of their symptoms are experiences which have occurred in that form only in their imagination – though it is true that in the last resort those imagined experiences go back to actual events or are based upon them. To attribute the neurotic sense of guilt to real misdeeds would show an equal misunderstanding. (Freud 1912: 108)

Just as in the case of animism, neurotics' "thought" takes precedence over experience: "the omnipotence of thoughts, the overvaluation of mental processes as compared with reality, is seen to have unrestricted play in the emotional life of neurotic patients and in everything that derives from it" (Freud 1912: 109).

Freud draws an analogy between the thought of "primitives" and that of neurotic patients in order to shed light on the former based on what was known about neuroses (by Freud and others) from psychoanalytic practice, thereby extending the historical scope of psychoanalysis. What is significant, for our purpose, is not the association of the mental life of neurotics with animistic thought, but rather the relationship found

---

[5] Freud draws the connection between ideas and belief. After doubt is introduced, "men will be ready to admit that conjuring up spirits has no result unless it is accompanied by faith, and that the magical power of prayer fails if there is no piety at work behind it" (Freud 1912: 106).

between, on the one hand, the mental processes associated with both animism and neuroses and, on the other hand, external reality. In both cases, thought is over-valued in relation to reality. The exercise of control over ideas is substituted for a control over physical reality for the "primitive" and control over psychical reality (i.e., unconscious compulsions) for the neurotic person; ritualistic behavior such as the imitation of rain or the repetition of acts aimed at the removal of contamination (in obsessional neurosis) presents, from a scientific (i.e., psychoanalytic) point of view, the fantasy of control, but it *is* reality in the *system of thought* of animism and neurosis. As Freud writes of animism, "the first picture which man formed of the world – animism – was a psychological one . . . We are thus prepared to find that primitive man transposed the structural conditions of his own mind into the external world" (1912: 114). The omnipotence of thought in the case of animism bears a striking resemblance to the relationship of racial ideas to reality. What we have presented as the racial ensemble operates unconsciously, on a psychical level. Racial ideas make use of reality (of experience and of perceptions), yet reality is secondary to the ideas: the belief in race not only makes race real *as thought*, it also has the capacity to account for the relationship between things *in reality*. This capacity is illustrated by the striking effect that the social perception of the phenotype has in creating distinct racial groups, on describing minute and yet significant differences between these groups, on the construction of the memory of the group, etc.

However, there is more. In the psychoanalytic framework, pleasure is achieved by extinguishing mental and physical stimuli that are perceived as "unpleasure" (for example, hunger is an unpleasant stimulus which is satiated by the ingestion of nourishment). In the case of primitive animism, the stimulus is external, produced by the environment (i.e., the problem of material scarcity that constantly threatened the social order of the group and the very existence of the group). In the case of the neurotic patient, the stimulus is internal, produced by the "environment" of the unconscious (i.e., the persistent conflict between two forces: desire and repression). Pleasure, then, is associated with the fantasy of control over the spirits of things and in holding back an overwhelming feeling of guilt. Freud describes the peculiar "sexuality" of neurotics, who are unable to tolerate the "frustrations of sexual life": "The neurotic creates substitute satisfactions for himself *in his symptoms*, and these either cause him suffering in themselves or become sources of suffering for him by raising difficulties in his relations with his environment and the society he belongs to" (Freud 1930: 64). In other words, the neurotic symptoms, which take the form of fantasies and obsessional behaviors, *are* the sexuality of the neurotic patient; they are the distorted form that desire takes as a compromise (in this case, exceedingly repressive) between the forces of desire and repression.[6] Similarly, the desire for racial ideas can be understood, on this account, to be a form of pleasure for individuals who believe in these ideas because of their capacity to bring *order* into differences perceived in nature and in social practices *at the level of thought* itself. To be sure, the perception of race or the invocation of race in repetitive rituals as diverse as lynching, and the recollections of social memory, need not be understood as neurotic. Nonetheless, insofar as unconscious mental life is tied to sexuality (in the broad sense of desire and pleasure rather than a narrow concept of genital sexuality), racial thought partakes in pleasure in an unrecognized form. The "passions and the interests" should not be divided, the latter stripped away from the former in order to produce an account of unambiguous motives of action. Thus, we insist that equal weight should be given to the reverse of Bourdieu's claim cited above, that "One of the tasks of sociology is to determine how the social world constitutes the biological libido, an undifferentiated impulse, as a specific social libido" (Bourdieu 1998b: 78). To be sure, the "social" channels libidinal impulses in safe directions; nevertheless, the social libido retains archaic libidinal impulses that remain beyond the reach of the social. In the case of a racial libido, social practices reinforce the sense of the reality of racial ideas, but this alone cannot account for the attachment to the ideas in the first place. The sublimated (i.e., displaced) form of sexual pleasure in racial thought remains internally constituted (by unconscious mental processes) in a way that is analogous to animistic thought.

[6] In *The Interpretation of Dreams*, Freud argues that wishes often appear in dreams in a distorted form. Hence an "anxiety dream" that leaves the dreamer with an uneasy feeling upon waking could be interpreted as a wish that has been displaced into an unrecognizable form: "we are justified in linking the unpleasurable character of these dreams with the fact of dream-distortion. And we are justified in concluding that these dreams are distorted and the wish-fulfillment contained in them disguised to the point of being unrecognizable precisely owing to the repugnance felt for the topic of the dream or for the wish derived from it and to an intention to repress them. The distortion in the dream is thus shown in fact to be an act of censorship" (Freud 1900: 193). In his case study of the hysteric "Dora," published five years after *The Interpretation of Dreams*, Freud describes the distortion or displacement of sexual excitation in his patient: "This perception [of her embrace by a male friend of her father] was revolting to her; it was dismissed from her memory, repressed, and replaced by the innocent sensation of pressure upon her thorax, which in turn derived an excessive intensity from its repressed source. Once more, therefore, we find a displacement from the lower part of the body to the upper. On the other hand, the obsession which she exhibited in her behavior was formed as though it were derived from the undistorted recollection of the scene" (Freud 1905a: 23).

Pleasure, the body, and racial belief

The relationship between desire and race arises also because the body is central to racial thought. The *signified body* becomes the template upon which racial thought manifests its creative powers. However, the *physical body* is not created by ideas but rather through sexual reproduction. Hence, thinking about race is inevitably linked to sexuality. The multiplication of ideas about race coincides with the multiplication of bodies bearing what are perceived to be – and believed to be – signs of race. Neither racial ideas nor racially perceived bodies can exist meaningfully without each other. However, because race is not *in the body* but imposed from without, the relationships between physical bodies bring pleasure to bear not only on the bodies themselves but also on the racial ideas that contribute to the social perception of the body. Perception *qua* looking is itself a type of pleasure: it is probably not an accident that racial discourse has been occupied with visual descriptions of racialized bodies (in a comparative fashion), and sometimes evaluates judgments that appreciate or denigrate them.[7]

One study of the impact of affect in race relations demonstrates the significance of pleasure and the body: Eric Lott's interpretive analysis of blackface minstrelsy. Minstrelsy was the most popular commercial entertainment in the United States in the nineteenth century. Minstrel performances, which took place primarily in larger cities in the north-eastern United States and drew a predominantly working-class audience, featured white entertainers who put burnt cork on their faces to take on the appearance of blacks. Musical numbers with licentious themes, dramatic interludes, and olios were staples of the minstrel stage.[8] Minstrelsy is mostly known for the ridicule of blacks and, therefore, it has been viewed primarily as a racist, anti-black cultural product. Lott, however, noticed that despite the derisory attitude towards blacks displayed in minstrel shows, minstrel performers often sought a faithful imitation of what were taken to be black cultural practices

---

[7] See Freud's remarks on scopophilia, the pleasure in looking, and its relationship to touching (1905c: 22–23).

[8] Minstrel acts typically included four or five male performers "made up with facial blacking of greasepaint or burnt cork and adorned in outrageously oversized and/or ragged 'Negro' costumes. Armed with an array of instruments, usually banjo, fiddle, bone castanets, and tambourine, the performers would stage a tripartite show. The first part offered up a random selection of songs interspersed with what passed for black wit and japery; the second part (or 'olio') featured a group of novelty performances (comic dialogues, malapropistic 'stump speeches,' cross-dressed 'wench' performances, and the like; and the third part was a narrative skit, usually set in the South, containing dancing, music, and burlesque" (Lott 1995: 5–6).

(frequently observed in northern working-class areas) that were pro-
jected into a representation of plantation life in the ante-bellum
American South. Moreover, audiences were drawn to minstrel acts and
enjoyed entertainments offered by men appearing to be black. Lott
captures this aspect of minstrelsy by framing the attraction of blackface
minstrel performances as a matter of affect: "What the minstrel show did
was to capture an antebellum structure of racial feeling . . . [It] was less
the incarnation of an age-old racism than an emergent social semantic
figure highly responsive to the emotional demands and troubled fantasies of its audiences" (Lott 1995: 6). As the title of Lott's book (*Love and
Theft*) indicates, Lott views minstrelsy as an ambivalent cultural
performance, in which attraction, derision, appreciation, and appropri-
ation helped to shape the "racial feeling" of its performers and its
audience. The "investment" in black men (and their bodies), the willing
imitation of black dancers on the part of middle-class white performers,
and the emotional and political bond that developed between immigrant, working-class audiences and *their* culture (of which minstrely was
a highly visible example),[9] is not, in Lott's view, characterizable as
simply racist.

The body is central to understanding minstrelsy. According to Lott,
the "'black' body's dangerous power was remarked by nearly all
observers of the minstrel phenomenon; it was probably mainly responsible for minstrelsy's already growing reputation for 'vulgarity'" (Lott
1995: 116). A crucial problem, consequently, was how to ensure that
"one of the very first constitutive discourses on the body in American
culture" remained within safe boundaries.

Certainly minstrelsy's commercial production of the black male body was a
fundamental source of its threat and its fascination for white men . . . The
problem this cultural form faces was how to ensure that what it invoked was
safely rerouted, not through white *meanings* – for even the anarchic, threatening
associations of black male sexuality were created by white cultural meanings –
but through a kind of disappearing act in which blackface made "blackness"
flicker on and off so as simultaneously to produce and disintegrate the body.
(Lott 1995: 117)

Bawdy lyrics and song sheets depicting, metaphorically, outsized male
genitalia were, for Lott, indicative of both white male fear of miscegenation and homoerotic desire: "since the black male seems the real object
of scrutiny here, it is difficult (perhaps even pointless) to distinguish

---

[9] The cultural divide between bourgeois theatre and working-class entertainment came
into high relief during the Astor Place riot of 1849. See Lott (1995: 66–67).

those fears from homosexual fantasies, or at the very least envy, of black men" (Lott 1995: 121).[10] However, the predominant feeling among the white audience, in Lott's interpretation, was racial pleasure, which was structured by anxiety and fear (of black bodies and of black labor) on one side, and desire (for the sexual and physical power represented by the black male body) on the other. As a result it figured in the formation and vitalization of the working class in the mid nineteenth century.

Racial feeling was intrinsic to minstrel joking . . . While it is true that audiences in the mid-1840s appear to have been drawn principally to the scabrous fun, it is also true that a special kind of racial pleasure proved so irresistible to minstrel-show audiences. That racist pleasure has proven so resistant to analysis is per-haps only symptomatic of the scandal of pleasure itself, which is notoriously difficult to domesticate and very often goes against the grain of responsible social practice. (Lott 1995: 142)

Lott's purpose is to demonstrate how minstrelsy, as an "ethnographic miniature," contributed to the formation of a white working class: he subsequently revises the one-sided evaluation of minstrelsy as an example of racism *par excellence* into a more nuanced judgment. Min-strelsy was implicated in a capitalist system that was buttressed by the unfree labor of blacks in the south and the nominally free labor of white immigrants in the northeast. However, by treating minstrelsy as a system of meanings that involved love, Lott brings to the forefront the positive identification with black laborers by the immigrant workers, an identi-fication that took the form of an object-cathexis.

Lott focuses on the body as a site for the making of a white working-class identity through racial performance and consumption; he does not bring racial ideas into the frame of analysis. Is it possible that pleasure in racial thoughts also contributed to the attraction and enjoyment of blackface minstrelsy? To the extent that racial ideas influence the perception of physical differences as racial differences, it is plausible to argue that thoughts are conducive to the enjoyment of blackface. But another question can be asked about racial belief itself, which is prior to perception: what sort of enjoyment might be derived from believing in race? Freud shows one pathway towards an answer to this question. In *Civilization and Its Discontents*, Freud responds to criticism that in *The Future of an Illusion* (1927) he had misconstrued the "true source of religious sentiments." His friend Romain Rolland offered Freud a

---

[10] Lott points out the significance of the exaggeration of bodily zones: "Fat lips, gaping mouths, sucks on the sugarcane; big heels, huge noses, enormous bustles: here is a child's-eye view of sexuality, a 'pornotopia'" (Lott 1995: 145).

keyword for the understanding of these sentiments. "This, he says, consists in a peculiar feeling, which he himself is never without, which he finds confirmed by many others, and which he may suppose is present in millions of people. It is a feeling which he would like to call a sensation of 'eternity,' a feeling as something limitless, unbounded – as it were, 'oceanic'" (Freud 1930: 10–11). Freud interprets this "oceanic feeling" as an "indissoluble bond, of being one with the external world as a whole" (Freud 1930: 12), thereby turning this conception of belief into a relationship between the ego (both its mental and physical aspects) and the world. He argues that ordinarily the boundaries between the ego and the external world are clearly demarcated; in sociological terms, the ego is increasingly differentiated from other people and other things in its environment. It follows that the oceanic feeling suspends this distinction between ego and world, and Freud considers normal and pathological cases of this condition. In the case of love (a normal psychological state), "the boundary between ego and object threatens to melt away." In another case (which is pathological), a person "ascribes to the external world things that clearly originate in his own ego and that ought to be acknowledged by it" (Freud 1930: 13). This latter case, which accords with animistic thought, is pertinent insofar as the projection of the ego's own feelings and ideas into the world fits an analogous model for the relationship between racial ideas and reality (with the caveat that the origin of racial ideas is social rather than individual). Such a mental de-differentiation of ego and world sets the condition for the feelings of oceanic oneness with the world.

However, the merger *in thought* of ego and world is not necessarily pathological in the sense that it relegates the ego to a relationship with reality that impairs normal functioning. In the course of a child's psychological development, an original merged state of the ego with the mother (in Freud's model) is eventually broken during the course of the child's psychosexual development (see Freud 1905c). The "pleasure-ego" is forced to acknowledge an external world; eventually, the ego "detaches itself from the external world" that subsequently becomes a source of unpleasure (Freud 1930: 15). Nevertheless, the original "ego-feeling" persists in persons with a normal psychological constitution. "If we may assume that there are many people in whose mental life this primary ego-feeling has persisted to a greater or less degree, it would exist in them side by side with the narrower and more sharply demarcated ego-feeling of maturity, like a kind of counterpart to it. In that case, the ideational contents appropriate to it would be precisely those of limitlessness and a bond with the universe – the same ideas with which my friend elucidated the 'oceanic' feelings" (Freud 1930: 15). One manner in which the unpleasure that arises because of the mature differentiation of the ego and the world (namely, the external world produces stimuli that are not easily controlled by the ego) is overcome is through a return of the primary ego-feeling; the original psychosexual disposition of the infantile stage survives into the stage of maturity.

What matters for understanding the pleasure associated with believing in race is that Freud treats this feeling of oneness with the world, which is archaic in terms of the individual's psychical maturation, as the unconscious, psychological structure of religion, or believing. The projection of thought into the world, the assimilation of the world of ideas to the world of things may bring about an oceanic feeling for individuals, whose attachment to racial ideas – which attach individuals to a racial group – offers protection from the unpleasant stimuli that emanate from a recalcitrant world. Through the operation of binding ideas to the world, the individual reawakens the feelings of the pleasure-ego in its most archaic state. The ideas that are the objects of belief are felt as an object of reality because the oceanic feeling has been experienced before during the first years of life.

Racial ideas and the uncanny

We have described race as a *vexatious* object that partakes of ideality and reality. It is also an *ambivalent* object. At the same time that racial ideas and pleasure are intertwined, it is equally the case that racial ideas have aroused hatred, fear, and particularly, disgust. In the United States, anti-miscegenation laws, which were only found to be unconstitutional in 1967 (*Loving* v. *Virginia*, 388 U.S. 1 [1967]), registered a sense of repugnance towards the intermixing of "blood." This repugnance was not restricted to the racial science of the nineteenth century, which was concerned to find out (or to demonstrate) that racial hybrids were inferior to pure racial types (Smedley 1999; Nobles 2000). The association of subordinate racial groups, as well as immigrants from Southern and Eastern Europe, with insufficient hygiene and mental degeneracy was openly debated during the debate over immigration policies in the 1910s and 1920s, which culminated in the restrictive Johnson-Reed Act of 1924 (King 2000).

An instrumental-rational, *conscious* motivation, related to the maintenance of the existing status and class hierarchies in the southern United States, can be found to underlie this sensibility. To the extent that freedom during the period of legal slavery and property rights in the post-Civil War era depended on an individual's paternity, anti-miscegenation laws prevented the status of freedom and property rights from being handed down from a white father to his mixed race (i.e., black) offspring (Higginbotham 1978). As documented by anthropologist Virginia Domínguez (1986), the state of Louisiana in particular undertook significant measures to police the borders between groups based on blood ties. Taking this approach, an interest-centered argument can be made that the repugnance and disgust articulated around inter-racial sexual couplings conceal a more fundamental politics of social status and social class. In other words, what explains efforts to restrict these couplings is the material interests of whites, whose class domination over blacks would have been jeopardized both materially and symbolically if the status of "white" – in terms of property rights – could pass to individuals who were held to be black (marriage partners or children) according to commonsense views of racial identity; i.e., "white" property would have passed into "black hands."

Yet something remains unaccounted for in the interest-centered explanation: what explains these negative feelings towards individuals who are categorized by ideas that have no reality outside belief? If emotional responses that are related to racial ideas could elicit sexual attraction (e.g., blackface minstrelsy), they could also elicit feelings of repulsion. The *conscious* expression of repulsion can be seen in representations of the "black" body in American popular culture during the nineteenth and twentieth centuries, which frequently accented and exaggerated perceived phenotypical differences in the texture of hair, fullness of lips, and physical build. Such grotesque images contrasted strongly with representations of the ideal-typical white physique in movies and magazines.[11] These phenomena can be investigated not merely as irrational, racist excesses, or as epiphenomenal to objective racial interests (such as restricting black civil and political rights), but rather as instances of unconscious attachment to racial ideas despite an apparently antithetical view expressed in racial caricatures.

In one of his studies of the aesthetic domain, Freud turned to an analysis of what he termed the "uncanny," which he associated with a particular genre of literature (and literary effects). He defined the uncanny as belonging "to the realm of the frightening, of what evokes fear and dread" (Freud 1919: 123). He initiates his inquiry with a lengthy discussion of the German word *unheimlich* (which Freud notes is translated as uncanny or eerie in English, "but etymologically corresponds to 'unhomely'"). Based on this etymological beginning, he

---

[11] See the examples of exaggerated images of a black phenotype found in popular advertising and minstrel performances that are collected in Marlon Riggs's documentary *Ethnic Notions* (1987).

proposes that the uncanny "is that species of the frightening that goes back to what was once well known and had long been familiar" (Freud 1919: 124). Freud examines this proposal through a consideration of examples of the uncanny (of persons, things, impressions, processes, and situations), many of which are drawn from literary works. But he also finds that the uncanny, the evocation of fear of something that is already known, emerges in relation to infantile wishes. He offers the examples of children's play with dolls: "in their games, [they] make no sharp distinction between the animate and the inanimate, and that they are especially fond of treating their dolls as if they were alive" (Freud 1919: 141). Ordinarily, the possibility that something inanimate could become animated, such as a corpse, would produce a feeling of dread. However, Freud argues that "children are not afraid of their dolls coming to life – they may even want them to. Here, then, the sense of the uncanny would derive not from an infantile fear, but from an infantile wish, or simply from an infantile belief" (Freud 1919: 141). This apparent contradiction of a fear and a wish fits well with the psychoanalytic framework: the coexistence of a fear of, and attraction to, some thing or persons indicates the presence of two conflicting, unconscious mental processes.

If psychoanalytic theory is right in asserting that every affect arising from an emotional impulse – of whatever kind – is converted into fear by being repressed, it follows that among those things that are felt to be frightening there must be one group in which it can be shown that the frightening element is something that has been repressed and now returns. . . If this really is the secret nature of the uncanny, we can understand why German usage allows the familiar (*das Heimlich*, the "homely") to switch to its opposite, the uncanny (*das Unheimliche*, the "unhomely"), for this uncanny element is actually nothing new or strange, but something that was long familiar to the psyche and was estranged from it only through being repressed. (Freud 1919: 147, 148)

An example of this psychical configuration of the uncanny is provided by animism and the omnipotence of thought. The animistic view of the universe endows the physical world with "human spirits" by, among of other means, "the attribution of carefully graded magical powers (*mana*) to alien persons and things, and by all the inventions with which the unbounded narcissism of that period of development sought to defend itself against the unmistakable sanctions of reality" (Freud 1919: 146). Consequently, if this animistic state eventually comes to be repressed, such as in the stage of childhood development in which the child's narcissistic relation to her own body, people, and things in her surrounding environment is challenged, "this phase did not pass without leaving behind in us residual traces that can still make themselves felt, and ... everything we now find 'uncanny' meets the criterion that is linked with these remnants of animistic mental activity and prompts them to express themselves" (Freud 1919: 147). In a more direct elaboration of this claim later in the essay, Freud states: "the uncanny element we know from experience arises either when repressed childhood complexes are revived by some impression, or when primitive beliefs that had been *surmounted* appear to be once again confirmed" (Freud 1919: 155).

From this discussion of the uncanny, two elements are relevant to understanding the sense of disgust that has been evoked by racial ideas. First, racial ideas remain part of an animistic system of thought that persists even in the face of a scientific system of thought that shows these ideas lack an objective basis. The power of racial ideas is akin to that of magical acts of animistic thinking. As a case of the omnipotence of thought, racial ideas transcend reality; they have the power to create a sense of reality (i.e., of the reality of race) and to subject reality to themselves by bringing to social life – i.e., into the field of meaning – inanimate physical characteristics which racial ideas endow with magical powers that both attract and repel, and which create desire and anxiety, veneration and fear. For example, when imbued with the idea of race, an invisible phenotypical difference of blood acquires the capacity to "blacken" whiteness (in the case of miscegenation). To be suspect of being touched by race (in the parlance of Louisiana, the "touch of the tarbrush" [Domínguez 1986: 133]) was a particular danger for French Creoles in the post-Civil War period; racial ideas conveyed the risk of impurity to family lineages. Insofar as racial ideas are primarily applied to non-whites, they function as a totem that is both venerated – in the form of being granted legitimacy in common and social scientific thought – and feared – in the form of social contact.

Second, Freud explored the "emotional ambivalence" displayed toward taboo objects in *Totem and Taboo*, and his analysis is pertinent to the negative attachment to racial ideas. Arguing that "the source of taboo is attributed to a peculiar magical power which is inherent in persons and spirits and can be conveyed by them through the medium of inanimate objects" (Freud 1912: 26–27), Freud observes the double significance of the totem person, animal, or plant that cannot be touched or consumed. "The meaning of 'taboo,' as we see it, diverges in two contrary directions. To us, it means, on the one hand, 'sacred,' 'consecrated,' and on the other 'uncanny,' 'dangerous,' 'forbidden,' 'unclean'" (Freud 1912: 24). Not only do such taboos elicit this ambivalence, but also the breaking of the taboo has the effect of making the transgressor contagious (i.e., taboo).

Behind all these prohibitions there seems to be something of a theory that they are necessary because certain persons and things are charged with a dangerous power, which can be transferred through contact with them, almost like an infection . . . The strangest fact seems to be that anyone who has transgressed one of these prohibitions himself acquires the characteristics of being prohibited – as though the whole of the dangerous charge had been transferred over to him. (Freud 1912: 28–29)

Contact with racial ideas by way of groups perceived through phenotypical differences or racial practices places an individual at risk of contamination. Miscegenation presents a heightened danger that goes beyond the individuals involved; it brings the contagion of race (e.g., blackness) into the bloodstream. When, for example, a registrar of vital statistics in Louisiana "race-flagged" birth certificates on the suspicion of racial misclassification (i.e., that individuals had been misclassified as "white"), entire family lines that were understood to be "white" suddenly became "black" through a bureaucratic measure.[12] Although this case is atypical, it represents the power of racial ideas: individuals' experiences were redefined by racial ideas, their reality superseded by the category itself.[13]

An understanding of the uncanny quality of racial ideas – their group-making and group-destroying potential – crystallizes the negative attachment to an unreal phenomenon. Such negative attachment is typified by feelings of fear and disgust of individuals and practices that are perceived to be racially *other*. This antipathy expressed towards perceived racial differences is not explicable solely as the result of excess conflict of interests between racial groups that exist on a conscious level. That both affective states, desire and disgust, can exist at the same time in relation to the same object is explained from a psychoanalytic perspective as ambivalence.[14] The desire for a thing, racial ideas, does not disappear in the face of the danger these ideas represent.

[12] See the discussion of Naomi Drake, who supervised the racial reclassification of individuals while holding the position of supervisor at the Louisiana Bureau of Vital Statistics, and the case of Susie Phipps, who petitioned a court in Louisiana to recognize her claim to the legal status of a white person in Domínguez (1986).

[13] Freud explains the vigilance in maintaining taboos in a way that illuminates the negative feelings elicited by racial ideas: "It is equally clear why it is that the violation of certain taboo prohibitions constitutes a social danger which must be punished or atoned for by *all* members of the community if they are not all to suffer injury. If we replace unconscious desires by conscious impulses we shall see that the danger is a real one. It lies in the risk of imitation, which would quickly lead to the dissolution of the community" (Freud 1912: 43). See Durkheim (1984) for a sociological account of expiatory punishment under conditions of mechanical solidarity that echoes Freud's psychological account of social prohibitions.

[14] "The principal characteristic of the psychological constellation which becomes fixed in this way is what might be described as the subject's *ambivalent* attitude towards a single

Desire and race

By pursuing the link between racial thought and reality into the realm of the unconscious, and by posing the question of attachment to racial ideas in relation to pleasure, our inquiry has likely transgressed the acceptable limits of the study of race. Yet we have taken this course not as a merely provocative end point to a book that employs what are otherwise conventional means to achieve critical knowledge of a common sociological object. On the contrary, the notion that desire shapes the social perception of race has guided our argument from the first sentence. Posing race as a matter of belief entails an interrogation of the different ways in which belief has been understood. More than any other science, psychoanalysis has insistently demanded that desire should be brought into the knowledge of mental life, thought, and belief. The question of why individuals *want* race, why they connect to a thing that is not real, is as significant for our claims as the questions of what individuals *do* with race and what race *does* to individuals. The privileged position that has been occupied by the latter questions has helped to prevent the former question, and all it implies, from being raised.

Nonetheless, psychoanalysis has a unique contribution to make to the study of race precisely because it treats fantasy and pleasure as an essential dimension of the psychology of individuals. Both dimensions figure in the structure of motivation for human behavior. Sociology, as was discussed above, tends to have a rationalistic bias when it comes to understanding why individuals and groups seek after things such as money, status, or power. However, by bringing a psychoanalytic approach to bear on the persistence of racial thinking – thinking that is undeterred by empirical skepticism about race itself – we have explored the unconscious yet systematic dimension of desire that is cathected to thought itself. Such an approach, as we have shown, does not evade the difficult question of why racial thinking persists; in fact, it may offer an amendment to Howard Winant's claim that race "is no more likely to disappear than other forms of human inequality and difference" (Winant 1994: xii–xiii). If race does not disappear, it is likely to be because of

object, or rather towards one act in connection with that object. He is constantly wishing to perform this act (the touching), [and looks on it as his supreme enjoyment, but he must not perform it] and detests it as well. The conflict between these two currents cannot be promptly settled because – there is no other way of putting it – they are localized in the subject's mind in such a manner that they cannot come up against each other. The prohibition is noisily conscious, while the persistent desire to touch is unconscious and the subject knows nothing of it" (Freud 1912: 38).

desire as much as objective interests: if, despite its acknowledged unreal character, race perdures, it will not only be because of social coercion, habituation, normalization, or because of the peculiar solidity and pervasiveness of the complex system of meaning and practice formed by the racial ensemble; it will also be because individuals find pleasure in their belief.

Conclusion

Reflections on theory and method

> Indeed, it is a fundamental postulate of sociology that a human institution cannot rest upon error or falsehood. If it did, it could not endure. If it had not been grounded in the nature of things, in those very things it would have met resistance that it could not have overcome . . . But we must know how to reach beneath the symbol to grasp the reality it represents and that gives the symbol its true meaning.
>
> (Durkheim 1995: 2)

We conclude our analysis by returning to the launching point of this inquiry: the question of the reality of race. We have maintained a singular focus on the articulation of the reality of what is essentially an idea. We have sought to demonstrate that the reality of race is not determined by an original moment of culture contact, experience, or practice, but rather by the peculiar force of the belief in the idea of race. Long ago, Émile Durkheim put forward the claim that religion, like all human institutions, "begins nowhere."[1] We hold the same view of race: it begins nowhere insofar as no historical moment or context of emergence can explain the efficacy and persistence of the idea itself.[2] However, the idea of race is made real in multiple sites and ways. Belief in race is reinforced by the pursuit of origins, by the anamnesis of the past, the statistical and theoretical affirmation of the existence of racial groups, and modes of unconscious attachment. From lynching to the memory of the history of people marked by an idea, from the racial sciences of the nineteenth century (which sought the biological truth of race) to the social sciences of race in the twentieth century (which seek the social and political truth of racism) – these varying and even contradictory practices have

---

[1] "There is no radical instant when religion began to exist, and the point is not to find a roundabout way of conveying ourselves there in thought. Like every other human institution, religion begins nowhere" (Durkheim 1995: 7).

[2] Consequently, we have not pursued the historical approach found in Gossett (1997) and Isaac (2004), although a history of the idea of race and its social uses is not only enlightening but also necessary.

214

contributed (and continue to contribute) to the *sense of reality* of the idea of race. Hence we have sought to demonstrate that the reality of race, an object that is simultaneously real and unreal (i.e., ideal), must be conceptualized in all of its complexity; rather than emphasizing its material presence at the price of ignoring its ideality, both the real and the ideal must be thought together as constituting a whole made up of relations among elements (ideas, the phenotype, perceptions of the phenotype, and practices). Our most significant claim, that the unreal side of the object – the belief in racial ideas – is indispensable for an adequate understanding of race, separates our analyses from the ideal-typical forms of social thought on race discussed in the first part of the book. This claim is precisely what enables us to revisit the relationship of the idea of race to nature, a relationship that is almost universally denied in contemporary studies of race, without risking a return to biological essentialism. By stressing the influence of racial ideas on the social perception of the phenotype (the physical differences found among individuals), the presence of biology that remains latent in the social concept of race is thereby directly addressed and, finally, put into proper perspective.

Although we have stressed the inadequacy of various approaches to the study of race, it does not mean that they are without merit. Indeed, their strength (and subsequent weakness) lies in the fact that they capture partial aspects of the racial ensemble. American sociologists of race who emphasize social practices locate the reality of race in racism, that is, in social structure, race relations, or political movements pursuing racial *interests*. But these analyses characteristically leave unaddressed the relationship of the idea of race, physical differences, and the social perception of these differences, which are the condition for the existence of racial groups and racism. In contrast, because of its explicit theory of knowledge, the Marxist account of race concerns itself with the relation of ideas to reality and correctly emphasizes the *unreality* of race. Marxists rightly detect the *independence* of the idea of race from reality but overstate this independence when it is described as ideology or as reification – according to the view that thought and material life must interpenetrate dialectically – and give primacy to the materiality of social class relations. We have shown that although racial ideas are independent (i.e., they lack a material basis in the biological constitution of human beings), they are not reified; they entertain a relationship with material conditions (the physical differences and social practices), but this relationship is not one of dependence but rather of coincidence and efficiency. Social anthropologists rightly emphasize practices and processes as functional elements of the formation of groups. However, the insistence that social relations are the primary unit of analysis and the relegation of "culture" to the "stuff" that maintains boundaries between groups might lead to an understatement of the role of ideas and beliefs in the making of racial groups. The practical dimension of racial groups is dependent upon the belief in race itself, which has more than an arbitrary relationship to race relations. Moreover, the social memory of race also reinforces the primacy of racial ideas by constituting what is remembered of the past from the perspective of the belief in race in the present. The various social anthropologists who work more or less loosely from the Barthian hypothesis all offer enlightening accounts of the way in which race is used, as an idea, in the construction of identity boundaries between groups and in everyday social interactions; but the concept of ethnicity produces not a disappearance, but a vagueness of a nonetheless present notion of race. Finally, vagueness also lingers in the analysis found in cultural studies, which provides many fertile openings but no precise, well-bound conceptual tool, and suffers from dispersion.

Our intent, therefore, is not to supplant or replace these styles of thought *in toto*: discrimination, economic inequality, group boundaries, and the hybrid social identities that are characteristic of diaspora remain distinctive phenomena the understanding of which has been facilitated by race relations theory, class theory, social anthropology, and cultural studies. However, to the extent that race is understood to intersect with these and other phenomena, a rethinking of the concept of race as relations between racial ideas and other elements in the racial ensemble is necessary to avoid two pitfalls: the reproduction of folk notions of race under the guise of a social scientific concept (i.e., the covert affirmation of an essentialist concept of race) or the displacement of race itself.

The way we have constructed our analysis of race, which emphasizes the notion of belief, and the concept of the racial ensemble we have deployed to make sense of the relation of the belief in racial ideas to both "nature" and the social, is indebted to "classical" social thought. Thinkers such as Durkheim, Mauss, Weber, Halbwachs, and Freud are recurrent touchstones in our analysis. What we find congenial in these thinkers is their concern with the definition of objects; they provide exemplary models for conceptualizing the reality and unreality of race. An attentive reader might have been troubled from the start by this apparently eclectic group of thinkers from which we have drawn concepts and also *an attitude towards social things*. On the surface, it would appear that a lack of compatibility between Durkheim and Weber, or between Freud and Halbwachs, would doom any project that attempts to bring them together. Hence we could be criticized for combining orientations that should, for the sake of theoretical integrity, be kept apart. However, behind such a critique lies an assumption that social theory must be synthetic; that each conceptual piece must fit together seamlessly in a tessellated pattern. And, indeed, it would not be wrong to hold this position as a relevant evaluative standard for theory *qua* theory, of theory that primarily seeks to work through – and work out of – conceptual problems specific to a system of thought. Our study is not, however, a theoretical work aimed at the sorting out of conceptual problems related to a system. Rather, our theorizing is aimed at an object, albeit a peculiar object: an idea that has saturated reality. The use of diverse theories that originate in diverse theoretical traditions has been carried out with the intent to account for this object. In other words, we have not endeavored to produce a new racial theory or discourse *of* race. On the contrary, we have sought to construct a theory *on* race.[3] Because of the nature of the object, we found it necessary to conduct our analysis along the lines of a theoretical bricoleur.[4] We have used heterogeneous theories that bear "no relation to the current project" in a situation in which theories that are normally deployed to analyze race do not suffice. Theories used in the study of religious rites and beliefs, collective memory, and the unconscious foundation of mental life were not fashioned for the analysis of race. We have refashioned them for this purpose, using conceptual elements that illuminate features of race that, when treated in isolation, fail to be adequate to the multi-sidedness of the object.

We have also characterized our approach to race as both a sociology of knowledge and a sociology of meaning. A justification of our approach is warranted. Clifford Geertz has argued that the "sociology of knowledge

---

[3] Theodor Adorno's formulation of the relation of subject and object remains invaluable in an era that valorizes subjective experience: "What is known through consciousness must be something: mediation aims at the mediated. But the subject, the epitome of mediation, is the How – never the What, as opposed to the object – that is postulated by any comprehensible idea of its concept. Potentially, even if not actually, objectivity can be conceived without a subject; not so subjectivity without an object" (Adorno 1982: 502).

[4] Lévi-Strauss, in his well-known description, argues that the bricoleur, unlike the engineer, "does not subordinate each of [his diverse tasks] to the availability of raw materials and tools conceived and procured for the purpose of the project. His universe of instruments is closed and the rules of his game are always to make do with 'whatever is at hand', that is to say with a set of tools and materials which is always finite and is also heterogeneous because what it contains bears no relation to the current project, or indeed to any particular project, but is the contingent result of all the occasions there have been to renew or enrich the stock or to maintain it with the remains of previous constructions or destructions . . . The elements which the 'bricoleur' collects and uses are 'pre-constrained' like the constitutive units of myth, the possible combinations of which are restricted by the fact that they are drawn from the language where they already possess a sense which sets a limit on their freedom of manoeuvre" (Lévi-Strauss 1966: 17, 19).

ought to be called the sociology of meaning, for what is socially determined is not the nature of conception but the vehicles of conception" (1973: 212). We disagree with this claim, for there is no empirical reason why the problem of knowledge should be subsumed under the question of meaning. With respect to the analysis of race, a concern for both the "nature of conception" (knowledge) and the "vehicles of conception" (meaning) is unavoidable. Initially, we have made an epistemological break with existing forms of knowledge, meaning, and experiences of race in order to clarify the conditions of possibility for *knowing the object*. It is not enough to ask how this object "race" is understood; one must first explain how it is constituted *in thought*. Afterwards, we return to the sociology of meaning, not as an adjunct to clarifying "experience," but rather as an account of the *meaningful ways* in which "race" – an object that is fundamentally constituted *by thought and belief* – is kept alive, is made real, and is *experienced* as a *real* thing and as an object of desire. Among the four styles of thought discussed in the first part of the book, the sociology of race has, in the contemporary era, characteristically circumvented the question of the reality of race as a problem of knowledge in favor of the study of racism (i.e., the effects of discrimination) or the politics of race (i.e., the ways in which race figures in social conflict). Consequently, the necessity of this initial epistemological break is most pressing in the case of the sociology of race in America, whose knowledge of race mirrors the racial common sense of American society. The plurivocal nature of the conception of race in American sociology – social at the manifest level; biological at the latent level – raises the problem of the adequacy of this category of social knowledge.

There are different pathways into this reflection. Within the tradition of French social thought, one can find the postulation of the existence of an unconscious zone constitutive of the social, part of a three-tiered construct. On the first level of social life are found conscious actions and thoughts, things that can easily be seen and which can be considered as the primary material for sociological analysis (or, at least, for sociological observation, whether it uses qualitative or quantitative methods). At the second level of social life is found social structure (and/or social relationships), which is not visible through immediate observation. A specific method (namely, the sociological method) must be applied in order to gain access to the second level; in the French tradition of social thought, this method is best described by Durkheim in *The Rules of Sociological Method*. Finally, a third level of social life, this one unconscious, is found in language, and the grammar that structures it. This is the level that structural analysis seeks to observe and reveal (e.g., in Lévi-Strauss's *Structural Anthropology* [1963]).

Durkheim's methodological prescriptions open onto the first and second levels of social life. The postulate here is that there is something that cannot be seen as long as one remains embedded in social practices. Method is defined and elaborated by Durkheim precisely because social facts do not offer themselves immediately to analysis; it provides the sociologist with a specific position (or "attitude") that, in turn, enables her to see, and further, analyze, something that is not seen. One of the strongest of Durkheim's *Rules* pertains to the need for the sociologist to detach from "lay ideas," which obscure the object of analysis, even if they often also provide a kernel of truth.[5] It is not that lay ideas are necessarily false; what matters is that they act as a veil between the sociologist and the object. And so the detachment of the sociologist from lay ideas is characterized, above all, by an exit from the sphere of common sense (e.g., experience).

One implication of this conception of the social – which, we have seen, is necessarily linked with the definition of a sociological method – has been central to our project: the necessity of detaching the definition of race from the politics of race. We have argued, for instance, that the emphasis on practice (or experience) in some *sociological* theories of race could be analyzed as obeying political and social exigencies that practice or experience place upon us *as long as we are embedded in it.* In other words, following Durkheim, we argued that the sociological analysis of race must free itself from lay ideas, and hence from practice. At the conceptual level especially, knowledge must not be submitted to the limitations placed upon it by practice, including discursive practices.[6] In particular, in the case of race, it means that a clear boundary has to be drawn between "what people do or say" and the definition of the object "race" from a theoretical standpoint. Once this step has been taken, the conceptual apparatus thereby formed can be used to look back at social reality (e.g., at social practices and discourses, social relationships and structure) without the risk of the reproduction of commonsense ideas of

[5] See in particular (but not only) page 53 in *The Rules* (1982): "We are the victims of an illusion which leads us to believe we have ourselves produced what has been imposed upon us externally." For Durkheim, free will is therefore an illusion, for the simple reason that much of what we, as individuals, think and do is influenced – if not produced – by social facts or the social relationships we entertain with others. An interesting parallel can be traced here with Karl Mannheim's sociology of knowledge, which supports the idea that thought is necessarily situated within limits placed upon it by the social context. In both cases, a specific positionality of the thinker can provide the ability to go beyond situational limits – the sociological method for Durkheim, the "floating" status of the intellectual for Mannheim.

[6] This, we argue, is the goal of the sociological method. Whether this goal is fully reachable or not is not certain, of course, as one hundred years of methodological and epistemological debate testify.

race. Without this step, no satisfying conceptualization of race can occur.

But there is another implication of Durkheim's method. If there is something in social life that is not "seen" while in practice, it also means that there is something that is not fully *known*, at least not in a conscious way. There is the hypothesis that no individual can be fully aware of the conditions of his participation in social life. Notwithstanding the issue of the "whole," for which functionalism has been widely criticized, it remains that indeed no one leads their life by being exhaustively aware of the conditions of their participation in social life. In other words, there is an unconscious level in the social sphere, which the individual, embedded in practice, does not consciously know, or only knows partially. Scholars as different as Foucault, Mannheim, and Bourdieu have demonstrated that thoughts and actions depend upon the possibilities and, therefore, the limits of discursive systems or currents of thought. Racial discourses and practices also have a coercive effect upon individuals and groups, which might be largely unconscious.[7] Once racial ideas are normalized in relation to racial practices, it becomes very difficult to escape them. It is at this point that an epistemological break with the commonsense notion of race that remains latent in American sociology becomes a methodological necessity.

Besides this *attitude toward the object*, which is the hallmark of Durkheimian social theory, we have explicitly drawn on the framework Marcel Mauss used in his study of the relation of seasonal change, social time, and social morphology to account for the relations between ideas (which are not *real*) and the *reality* to which they are ineluctably tied in both racial common sense and scholarship that attempts to construct an entirely social concept of race. Racial ideas stand as one form of social knowledge about "nature." They classify specific features of physical differences as markers of racial differences. So whereas *race does not exist in nature, nature does exist in racial ideas*. What matters, then, is how this relationship of nature to racial ideas should be understood. A typical formulation of this relationship is found in the work of Omi and Winant: "the concept of race invokes biologically based human characteristics (so-called 'phenotypes')"; however, "selection of these particular human features for purposes of racial signification is always and necessarily a social and historical process." This formulation allows for a rejection of any "biological basis for distinguishing among human groups along the

---

[7] The case of anti-racist struggle is instructive, because it shows the difficulty in escaping a dominant discursive system; indeed, anti-racism remains located within a racial discourse. See for instance Gilroy (2000) and Hall (1992).

lines of race" (1994: 55). Peter Wade, whom we discuss briefly in the introduction to this book, agrees with this view, but takes a further step by arguing that the phenotype is not only not found in nature – that is to say, it is not "a neutral, objective biological fact" – but its construction also varies "in different contexts" (2002: 5). Wade summarizes his view as follows:

Racial ideas do make reference to human biology, nature and phenotype, but these ideas do not always straightforwardly invoke fixity or permanence. This means that what may appear to be a discourse of fixity may actually allow a measure of malleability and change, but it also means that a discourse of malleability can acquire meanings of permanence. (2002: 14)

Our disagreement with Wade is subtle, yet decisive, for we argue that something exists *on the other side of the perception of the phenotype* to which racial ideas refer: physical differences. The historical argument, that "some aspects of phenotype are worked into *racial* signifiers and they are the aspects that were originally seen to be ways of distinguishing between Europeans and those they encountered in their colonial explorations" (Wade 2002: 14), is a necessary but not a sufficient condition to account for racial ideas. Hence the importance of Mauss for our argument that physical differences, like the changes in environmental conditions (i.e., seasonal variations), are *represented* as *natural phenomena*, but they are objectively independent of representation. The relationship that requires analysis then is not only the one between *racial constructions of nature* (which we have termed the social perception of the phenotype) and racial ideas, but also the relationship between physical differences – objective conditions whose existence does not depend *on thought,* that is, *on constructions* – and racial ideas. Mirroring Mauss, we have argued that this relationship is one of *coincidence* rather than *causality*: racial ideas do not produce physical difference. Hence, the perception of the phenotype stands fully on the side of culture – as social perception derived from the belief in racial ideas – rather than nature. For this reason we asserted earlier (in the introduction) that race is not based on phenotype, but rather on social representations that are attached to physical differences. The recognition of physical differences comes prior to the recognition of phenotypical difference as a socially relevant means to understand physical differences.

The relationship between racial ideas and "nature" can be conceived differently within a Durkheimian perspective. For example, regarding the social organization found in "totemic" societies, Radcliffe-Brown asserts that collective representations are not "a projection of society into external nature," but rather should be seen as a process "by which, in the fashioning of culture, external nature, so called, comes to be incorporated in the social order as an essential part of it" (1952: 131). However, even taking this view, which Radcliffe-Brown introduces as an improvement on the account of totemism found in *The Elementary Forms of Religious Life* (Durkheim 1995), it would not be plausible to hold that a specific species of bird that is taken up as a totemic object is a construction of social representations. As with species of birds, physical differences are independent of social construction, although, like birds, they become meaningful within a system of collective representations (such as race). If these physical differences are reduced to thought, are seen only as social constructions, then the social theory of race would simply *reproduce the logic of racial ideas without accounting for this logic*. Thus, with the help of the racial ensemble, we have shown the theoretical necessity of the recognition that physical differences are not racial. This is because there are two objects: physical differences and racial differences. The first object, physical differences, is natural; the second object, racial differences, is social. These objects are bound together by the belief in racial ideas. Although we do not pursue a specifically structuralist approach, our conception of the relationship between physical and racial differences is analogous to Lévi-Strauss's analysis of the relation between nature and culture in "totemism." He argues that binary relations found in "totemic" thought (for example, such as the relation of the opposition between "birds of the above" and "birds of the below" with the opposition of "twins" and "ordinary humans" among the Nuer) are "a series of logical connections uniting mental relations" (1963: 80). In this case, the logical operations of the mind take place on something that is external to it (twins and birds): "Twins 'are birds,' not because they are confused with them or because they look like them, but because twins, in relation to other men, are as 'persons of the above' to 'persons of below,' and, in relation to birds, as 'birds of below' are to 'birds of the above'" (1963: 80–81). The existence of birds and twins is not predicated on Nuer thought; however, their relation to each other is predicated on thought.

This emphasis on *relations* between objects in our analysis of the link between racial ideas and nature is the hallmark of Durkheimian sociology. Social facts, as collective representations, are related to each other as well as to the reality to which they refer (as the epigraph to this chapter indicates). We develop the concept of the racial ensemble, which articulates the relationship between ideas, nature, social perceptions, and social practices, for the purpose of accounting for these multiple relations. The racial ensemble is analytically advantageous because it brings together elements that can only be adequately understood in relation to each other. Social perceptions, representations, and racial practices (e.g., racism) must be brought back into relation with the belief in racial ideas that are themselves related to physical differences.

Once conceptual problems related to theorizing the "object" have been addressed, the question of meaning can be brought back in. Whereas Durkheim and Mauss help to articulate the relationship between collective representations (i.e., racial ideas) and nature in a non-deterministic, non-essentialist way, a relationship which has been repressed in contemporary social inquiry, the theoretical orientations of Weber, Halbwachs, and Freud help to articulate the conditions of believing, and the reproduction of believing, in racial ideas. It is not a mere coincidence that we have explicitly employed theoretical resources from the sociology of religion to make sense of an object that is both real and unreal. Not only does the sociology of religion offer insights into the belief in race, it is also a framework that allows us to go beyond the Marxist treatment of racial ideas as ideology. The analogy we have drawn between religion (namely, the act of believing in things, such as God, the Devil, Angels, Heaven, and Hell, which, from a rationalist perspective, have no material manifestation) and racial ideas (which lack an essential material basis) serves two purposes. First, if scientific thought about race (that it has no permanent biological grounding) does not attenuate the belief in race (just as modern science does not supplant religion as an effective system of thought), then it would be better to frame the ana-lytical problem presented by race as a matter of belief rather than as a matter of rational, scientific thought.[8] In other words, the tendency to conceive of race as a *failed* scientific idea makes what philosophers have

---

[8] To be sure, the distinction between religious and scientific thought is not absolute. Durkheim's remarks at the end of *The Elementary Forms of Religious Life* on scientific concepts as collective representations are pertinent: "Inversely, even when constructed in accordance with all the rules of science, concepts are far from taking their authority from their objective value alone. To be believed, it is not enough that they be true. If they are not in harmony with other beliefs and other opinions – in short, with the whole set of collective representations – they will be denied; minds will be closed to them; as a result, they will be and yet not be. If bearing the seal of science is usually enough today to gain a sort of privileged credibility, that is because we have faith in science. But that faith is not essentially different from religious faith. The value we attribute to science depends, in the last analysis, upon the idea we collectively have of its nature and role in life, which is to say that it expresses a state of opinion. The reason is that everything in social life rests on opinion, including science itself. To be sure, we can make opinion an object of study, and create a science of it; that is what sociology principally consists in. Still the science of opinion does not create opinion, but can only clarify it and make it more conscious of itself. In this way, it is true, science can lead opinion to change, but science remains the product of opinion even at the moment it seems to rule opinion; for as I have shown, science draws the strength it takes to act upon opinion from opinion itself" (1995: 439–440).

termed a *category mistake*. To treat race as an object whose *truth* can be ascertained according to the criteria of rational scientific thought is to fundamentally misconstrue it, which is precisely the error of the racial science of the nineteenth century. What must be analyzed is not the *truth of race*, but the *belief in racial ideas* (which, to be sure, has been "supported" by science but which does not require this support to be viable in society): how it operates and how it is reproduced.

This belief gives to racial ideas a force that explains why they do not wither in the face of the claims of science; this force also endows racial ideas with the capacity to over-ride the material reality of class relations that are purported by Marxist theory to be the real basis of the ideas. Groups are socially constructed on the basis of the force of belief. But racial ideas do more than classify a set of, from the Marxist standpoint, "illusory" relations – and this is the second purpose for the analogy drawn between religion and racial ideas. They also influence the attribution of meaning to groups of individuals so classified and the social relations (both vertical and horizontal) that are erected on this basis. Hence, the sociology of meaning that lies at the heart of Weberian sociology is indispensable for an understanding of the force of the belief in racial ideas. The chapter on ethnic groups in *Economy and Society* remains an under-utilized resource for the analysis of meaning attribution in the creation of racial groups. Racial ideas become meaningful when they are taken up in social action; in other words, when they are recognized among individuals in their orientation to each other. The participation of racial ideas in the formation of groups depends on this subjective recognition, which is enhanced, Weber argues, through an imagined association with a "tradition" and with a "political community" (Weber 1978).

We turned to the concept of collective memory developed by Maurice Halbwachs to account for the process in which racial ideas are made real in the remembrance of a racial tradition and the imagery of a racial political community. Taking as an example African-American social and political thought, Halbwachs's notion of frameworks of social memory illuminates the way in which recollections of the past give a sense of *racial* reality to experiences, which are seen to connect unrelated individuals across generations under the rubric of a racial identity. The past becomes usable from the standpoint of the social groups existing in the present; history, which is conceived by Halbwachs as "dead memory," is resuscitated through frameworks of social memory, which we argue is one of the functions of African-American historical studies and the discourses of black nationalism and pan-Africanism. As such, the past remains, from the standpoint of social memory, revenant for any living generation that seeks to trace the lineage of a racial group. The memory of race attaches persons in the present to persons from the past through the mediation of racial ideas.

Finally, we have pursued the subjective perception of race, formed under the influence of racial ideas, to the level of the unconscious. This move is necessitated because of the noticeable amount of affect that circulates around the idea of race, in the expression of attraction and repulsion towards racial "others," and the positive identification with racial categories. Based on the methodological assumption that individuals and groups are more possessed by racial ideas than possessing them, we have defined this unconscious attachment to racial ideas as a desire for race. Freud's writings proved salient for this purpose, because they frequently analyze the individual's cathexis to ideas. In his work on group psychology, in which he argued that "libidinal ties are what characterize a group" (1921: 33), Freud noted that love for the leader could be replaced by a leading idea: "The leader or the leading idea might also, so to speak, be negative; in just the same unifying way, and might call up the same kind of emotional ties as positive attachment" (1921: 32). We have not sought to develop a thoroughly libidinal theory of race. However, a focus on the unconscious dimension of social life is a fundamental premise of the sociological method; it could be argued that there is an unconscious knowledge of society embedded in practice itself.[9] Our hypothesis is that some, if not most, of men's actions and thoughts either do not mean what they seem to mean, or are performed without the performer being fully aware of what they mean.

Racial discourses and practices also have a coercive effect upon individuals and groups, which is largely unconscious. Once racial ideas are normalized, and accompanied by varied racial practices that are also normalized, it becomes very difficult to escape them. It is at this very point that the racial ensemble becomes necessary for an understanding of race: none of its elements can work on its own, but together, through a system of mutual relationships of confirmation, they produce an efficient system of belief that is able not only to emerge, but also to endure through time. The racial ensemble follows the rules of efficiency; none of the elements it contains, indeed, is necessary, nor certainly sufficient, for establishing "race" as a solid, long-lasting, and widely penetrating idea; it is the articulation between practice and ideas, fuelled by a recognition in nature, that builds the solidity of the system; and the way in which this system functions is neither intentional (it does not depend on the intentional action of individuals and groups) nor conscious. Indeed, the

---

[9] This point has been put forward by Loïc Wacquant (2003), who argues that the body is both the medium and the vector for social structure.

notion of an unconscious dimension of attachment to race explains the persistence (and even solidification) of belief in the absence of scientific evidence, and even against scientific evidence. The desire for race, which we have elucidated with psychoanalytic concepts, entails something that cannot be explained *only* by a social interest in race that is generated by the functioning of the racial ensemble.

One of the concerns motivating this study is the problem of essentialism, and our intuition that essentialism has not been avoided despite the best efforts within the sociology of race, Marxist social science, social anthropology, and cultural studies to transcend essentialist conceptions of race. In the styles of thought analyzed in the first part of the book, the binary of essentialism and anti-essentialism is held in place by a specific demand: that categories should be "true" to the nature of things. Consequently, in their refusal to find race in the nature *of nature*, these styles of thought have displaced the concept of race itself, which, unfortunately, does not do away with essentialism directly. The racial ensemble is intended to address this problem directly, in particular the distinction between physical differences (the phenotype) and the social perception of the phenotype.

However, there remains the problem of the *essentialism of the concept* (which is one of the main targets of British cultural studies). In other words, concepts function as binary oppositions; they aggregate *data* in a dichotomous fashion.[10] Thus, additional theoretical work is required at the level of the concept of race itself. It would entail a break with binary oppositions *within* the concept of race, which mirror commonsense understandings. If it were possible to maintain (in thought) a discontinuity between racialized bodies and culturally constructed races, then a variety of racial categories (of whatever kind) can attach to any *body* and the number of racial meanings would logically be unlimited by anything other than the limits of language and the imagination (e.g., Tiger Woods's self-designation as "cablinasian" or "caucasian-black-indian-asian"). In this respect, the phenomenon of *passing* (which is, perhaps, specific to the American context) is an as yet under-theorized, but potentially crucial, *object* for breaking with this essentialism of binary constructions within the race concept.[11]

In recognition of this second form of essentialism, this time on the conceptual level, the problem of the use of racial categories (derived from

[10] Methodological problems that arise from the use of dichotomous variables in social science research are analyzed in Ragin (2000).

[11] Biographical accounts, such as a recent book by Bliss Broyard (2007), offer rich materials for thinking through the problem of concept essentialism.

racial ideas) in empirical research can be accurately described. The risk arising from the position that "racial categories are legitimate subjects of empirical sociological investigation" is not only, as the American Sociological Association (2002) argues, "the danger of contributing to the popular conception of race as biological." The danger lies also in turning the popular conception of binary racial categories (which is indistinguishable from the ASA's conception) into a natural vision – and feature – of the *social* world; this is the methodological risk of such notions as "racialized social systems." The cessation of the collection of racial data (which is coded according to binary racial categories) by sociologists would not preclude the study of "race." It would rightly lead sociologists to study, on the one hand, the work of racial ideas in binding together physical differences, social perceptions, and practices and, on the other hand, the reproduction of attachment to these ideas as a form of belief. As we have argued, the commitment to racial ideas bears the marks of religious belief in modernity: "the expression of believing, the memory of continuity, and the legitimizing reference to an authorized version of such memory, that is to say to a tradition ... From this standpoint, what is specific to religious activity is that it is wholly directed to the production, management, and distribution of the particular form of believing which draws its legitimacy from reference to a tradition" (Hervieu-Léger 2000: 97, 101). The social science of race has been implicated in this system of believing. Among the various sites where the "memory of continuity" and the "legitimized reference to an authorized version of such memory" is articulated is the social science of race. In other words, the cumulative discourse of race relations scholarship constitutes one aspect of the tradition that is the wellspring, and legitimizing source, of the belief in racial ideas.[12] Thus, far from "preserv[ing] the status quo" (American Sociological Association 2002 [Executive Summary]), the refusal to acknowledge popular binary conceptions of race as social scientific categories would mark an epistemological break with popular belief that is the racial common sense of society.[13]

[12] The practical effects of the ASA's position on race come close to those which result from the operations of the magician, who "does nothing, or almost nothing, but makes everyone believe that he is doing everything, and all the more so since he puts to work collective forces and ideas to help the individual imagination in its belief. The art of the magician involves suggesting means, enlarging on the virtues of objects, anticipating effects, and by these methods fully satisfying the desires and expectations which have been fostered by entire generations in common" (Mauss and Hubert 2001: 175).

[13] "Refusing to acknowledge the fact of racial classification, feelings, and actions, and refusing to measure their consequences will not eliminate racial inequalities. At best, it will preserve the status quo" (American Sociological Association 2002 [Executive Summary]). This claim exemplifies the tendency (discussed in Chapter 1) to evaluate

There is another risk relating to the *politics* of knowledge that comes
with empirical research on race. On Foucault's account, nineteenth-
century sexology and its techniques of self-confession and physical
examination forced each individual to have a specific sex (normal,
abnormal, female, male, heterosexual, homosexual). In particular, the
homosexual

became a personage, a past, a case history, and a childhood, in addition to being
a type of life, a life form, and a morphology, with an indiscreet anatomy and
possibly a mysterious physiology. Nothing that went into his total composition
was unaffected by his sexuality. It was everywhere present in him: at the root of
all his actions because it was their insidious and indefinitely active principle;
written immodestly on his face and body because it was a secret that always gave
itself away. It was consubstantial with him, less as a habitual sin than as a
singular nature. (Foucault 1990: 43)

An analogous trend can be seen in the racial disciplines. Since the nineteenth century, a variety of racial disciplines have emerged and evolved –
or, as in the case of phrenology and the theory of polygenism, disappeared.
Like the homosexual, the "dark races" were also investigated in the settler
societies of the New World; at the very moment when liberation from
perpetual servitude became a realizable dream, these races were subjected
to the scientific discourse of race. While its exact dimensions remained
elusive to the scientific method, race came to define the personhood of
individuals, whose most varied personalities were reduced down to this
elementary truth. Concomitantly, the "white race," or at least one segment
of it, was given several tasks, to win the war of the races, and to defend
civilization against encroaching savagery and extend it around the world.[14]
Biology as destiny was also the "white man's burden." Much like nineteenth-century sexology, the racial disciplines of the twentieth century
(including sociology), and their techniques (self-confession, demography,
and ethnographic observation), have coded each individual with a "race"
(a singular one), about which a *social truth* is sought. Hence, social categories of race have become destiny.

This risk, which can be understood as involving the vicissitudes of
power, is endemic to social science. The present study was not intended
to address the *politics* of race. Nevertheless, our re-conceptualization of

---

an epistemological choice according to its purported political consequences. Social
theory should resist the temptation to make a scientific virtue of an alleged practical
necessity.

[14] See, for example, the discussion of the efforts of G. Stanley Hall and Theodore
Roosevelt to advance the civilizing project of the West (and the white race) in
Bederman (1995: 77–120, 170–215).

race, from the narrow question of its objective truth to the processes of belief and attachment, is one small way to de-align the social science of race from the *productive power* of disciplinary projects.

> In reality, the disciplines have their own discourse. They engender, for the reasons of which we spoke earlier, apparatuses of knowledge (*savoir*) and a multiplicity of new domains of understanding. They are extraordinarily inventive participants in the order of these knowledge-producing apparatuses. Disciplines are the bearers of a discourse, but this cannot be the discourse of right. The discourse of discipline has nothing in common with that of law, rule, or sovereign will. The disciplines may well be the carriers of a discourse that speaks of a rule, but this is not the juridical rule deriving from sovereignty, but a natural rule, a norm. The code they come to define is not that of law but that of normalization. (Foucault 1980: 106–107)

Properly understood, the politics of the *discourse of race* does not only entail the alternatives of the acknowledgement or denial of the existence of racism; it involves the *normalization* of the truth of race. We have not aimed at uncovering a new non-sovereign "right," as prescribed by Foucault, which would contest disciplinary power directly. However, we have demonstrated several of the conceptual limits of the disciplinary discourse of race on its own grounds. If there is no *truth* of sex, there is also no *truth* of race; the rending of the veil of the *scientia sexualis* and the (social) science of race reveals the authority of belief.

Ultimately, race persists because the belief in it persists. This conclusion will not satisfy the rationalist critics and proponents of "race," for whom race is either an illusion or a social structural necessity, or those who seek to eradicate race from the public sphere. If uncertainty is warranted regarding the possibility that society will give up the "illusion" of race, it is not because of the world-historical imbrication of race and Western civilization, but rather because racial ideas have found an efficient relationship with "worldly" things. This efficient relationship is assisted by the act of *believing* in racial ideas, which instills confidence in the answers "race" gives to the existential questions that are raised in social life. Racial ideas locate individuals in social time and space, make sense of experiences of suffering and success, and even carry what Walter Benjamin (1969: 254) called a "weak messianic power" that binds together the past with the present. The past and future of race will be better understood through the sociological analysis of the religious and the psychical underpinnings of the belief in, and desire for, this vexatious and ambivalent social object.

Bibliography

Adorno, Theodor W. 1982. "Subject and object." Pp. 497–511 in *The Essential Frankfurt School Reader*, edited by Andrew Arato and Eike Gebhardt. New York: Continuum.

Allen, James, Hilton Als, John Lewis, *et al.* eds. 2000. *Without Sanctuary: Lynching Photography in America*. Santa Fe, NM: Twin Palm Publishers.

Althusser, Louis. 2001. "Ideology and ideological state apparatuses." Pp. 85–126 in *"Lenin and Philosophy" and Other Essays*. New York. The Monthly Review Press.

American Anthropological Association. 1998. *American Anthropological Association Statement on "Race."* Retrieved on www.aaanet.org/stmts/racepp.htm on January 5, 2007.

American Sociological Association. 2002. *The Importance of Collecting Data and Doing Social Scientific Research on Race*. Retrieved on http://www2.asanet.org/media/asa_race_statement.pdf on November 17, 2007.

Ang, Ien. 2000. "Identity blues." Pp. 1–13 in *Without Guarantees: In Honour of Stuart Hall*, edited by P. Gilroy, L. Grossberg, and A. McRobbie. London: Verso.

Anthias, Floya. 1998. "Evaluating 'diaspora': beyond ethnicity?" *Sociology*: 32 (3), 557–580.

Appiah, Anthony Kwame. 1992. "Illusions of race." Pp. 28–46 in *In My Father's House: Africa in the Philosophy of Culture*. Oxford: Oxford University Press.

Asante, Molefi Kete. 2001. Review of Paul Gilroy's *Against Race*. *Journal of Black Studies*: 31 (6), 847–851.

Barth, Fredrik. 1969. "Introduction." Pp. 9–38 in *Ethnic Groups and Boundaries: The Social Organization of Culture Difference*, edited by F. Barth. Prospect Heights, IL: Waveland Press.

Bederman, Gail. 1995. *Manliness and Civilization: A Cultural History of Gender and Race in the United States, 1880–1917*. Chicago: University of Chicago Press.

Benedict, Ruth. 2006 [1934]. *Patterns of Culture*. Boston: Mariner Books.

Benjamin, Walter. 1969. "Theses on the philosophy of history." Pp. 253–264 in *Illuminations*, edited by Hannah Arendt. New York: Schocken Books.

Bonilla-Silva, Eduardo. 1997. "Rethinking racism: toward a structural interpretation." *American Sociological Review*: 62 (3), 465–480.

1999. "The essential social fact of race." *American Sociological Review*: 64 (6), 899–906.

2003. *Racism without Racists: Color-Blind Racism and the Persistence of Racial Inequality in the United States*. Lanham, MD: Rowman and Littlefield.

Bourdieu, Pierre. 1998a. "Rethinking the state: genesis and structure of the bureaucratic field." Pp. 35–63 in *Practical Reason: On the Theory of Action*. Stanford: Stanford University Press.

    1998b. "Is a disinterested act possible?". Pp. 75–91 in *Practical Reason: On the Theory of Action*. Stanford: Stanford University Press.

Boyce Davies, Carole. 2002. "'Against race' or the politics of self-ethnography." *Jenda, A Journal of Culture and African Women Studies*: 2 (1), 1–9.

Broyard, Bliss. 2007. *One Drop: My Father's Hidden Life – A Story of Race and Family Secrets*. New York: Little, Brown and Company.

Butler, Judith. 1999. *Gender Trouble: Feminism and the Subversion of Identity*. New York and London: Routledge.

Cohen, Abner. 1969. *Custom and Politics in Urban Africa*. London: Routledge.

    1974. *Two-Dimensional Man: An Essay on the Anthropology of Power and Symbolism in Complex Society*. Berkeley: University of California Press.

    1981. *The Politics of Elite Culture: Explorations in the Dramaturgy of Power in a Modern African Society*. Berkeley: University of California Press.

Cohen, Anthony. 1985. *The Symbolic Construction of Community*. London: Routledge.

Coogan, Michael D., ed. 2001. *The New Oxford Annotated Bible*, third edition. Oxford: Oxford University Press.

Cox, Oliver Cromwell. 2000. *Race: A Study in Social Dynamics*. New York: Monthly Review Press.

Davis, F. James. 1991. *Who is Black? One Nation's Definition*. University Park, PA: Pennsylvania State University Press.

Dawkins, Richard. 2006. *The God Delusion*. New York: Houghton Mifflin.

Dennett, Daniel C. 2007. *Breaking the Spell: Religion as a Natural Phenomenon*. New York: Penguin.

Derrida, Jacques. 1974. *Of Grammatology*. Baltimore: Johns Hopkins University Press.

    1978. "Force and signification." Pp. 3–30 in *Writing and Difference*. Chicago: University of Chicago Press.

Descartes, René. 1979. *Meditations on First Philosophy*. Indianapolis: Hackett Publishing Company.

    1999. *Discourse on Method and Related Writings*. London: Penguin Books.

Descola, Philippe. 1996a. *In the Society of Nature: A Native Ecology in Amazonia*. Cambridge: Cambridge University Press. [*La nature domestique: symbolisme et praxisme dans l'écologie des Achuars*, Paris: Éditions de la Maison des Sciences de l'Homme, 1986]

    1996b. *The Spears of Twilight: Life and Death in the Amazon Jungle*. New York: The New Press. [*Les lances du crépuscule*, Paris: Plon, 1993]

    2005. *Par-delà nature et culture*. Paris: Gallimard.

Dolby, Karen. 2000. "The shifting ground of race: the role of taste in youth's production of identities." *Race, Ethnicity and Education*: 3 (1), 7–24.

Domínguez, Virginia. 1986. *White by Definition: Social Classification in Creole Louisiana*. New Brunswick: Rutgers University Press.

Douglas, Mary. 1966. *Purity and Danger: An Analysis of the Concepts of Pollution and Taboo*. London: Routledge.

1980. *Evans-Pritchard*. New York: Viking Press.

Du Bois, W. E. B. 1986a. "The conservation of races." Pp. 815–826 in *W. E. B. Du Bois: Writings*. New York: Library of America.

1986b. *The Souls of Black Folk*. Pp. 357–548 in *W. E. B. Du Bois: Writings*. New York: Library of America.

Durkheim, Émile. 1898. "De la définition des phénomènes religieux." *Année Sociologique*: 2, 1–28.

1974 [1898]. "Individual and collective representations." Pp. 1–34 in *Sociology and Philosophy*. New York: Free Press.

1984 [1893]. *The Division of Labor in Society*. New York: Free Press.

1995 [1912]. *The Elementary Forms of Religious Life*. New York: Free Press.

1998. *Lettres à Marcel Mauss*. Paris: Presses universitaires de France.

2004 [1895]. *Les règles de la méthode sociologique*. Paris: Presses universitaires de France. [*The Rules of Sociological Method*, New York: Free Press, 1982]

Ellis, Brian D. 2002. *The Philosophy of Nature: A Guide to the New Essentialism*. Ithaca, NY: McGill-Queen's University Press.

Eriksen, Thomas. 1992. *Us and Them in Modern Societies: Ethnicity and Nationalism in Mauritius, Trinidad and Beyond*. Oslo: Scandinavian University Press.

1993. *Ethnicity and Nationalism: Anthropological Perspectives*. London: Pluto.

1998. *Common Denominators: Ethnicity, Nationalism and the Politics of Compromise in Mauritius*. Oxford: Berg.

Ethnic Notions. 1987. Produced and directed by Marlon Riggs. California Newsreel.

Evans-Pritchard, Edward E. 1937. *Witchcraft, Oracles and Magic among the Azande*. Oxford: Clarendon Press.

1939. "Nuer time-reckoning." *Africa*: 12 (2), 189–216.

1940. *The Nuer: A Description of the Modes of Livelihood and Political Institutions of a Nilotic People*. Oxford: Clarendon Press.

1950. "Social anthropology: past and present (The Marett Lecture, 1950)." *Man*: 50, 118–124.

1956. *Social Anthropology*. London: Cohen & West.

Forster, E. M. 1993 [1907]. *The Longest Journey*. New York: Vintage.

Foucault, Michel. 1972. *The Archaeology of Knowledge*. New York: Pantheon Books.

1980. "Two lectures." Pp. 78–108 in *Power/Knowledge: Selected Interviews and Other Writings 1972–1977*, edited by Colin Gordon. New York: Pantheon Books.

1990. *The History of Sexuality: An Introduction*, volume I. New York: Vintage Books.

Freud, Sigmund. 1899. "Screen memories." Pp. 1–22 in *The Uncanny*. New York: Penguin, 2003.

1900. *The Interpretation of Dreams*. New York: Avon Books, 1965.

1905a. "Fragment of an analysis of a case of hysteria". Pp. 1–112 in *Dora: An Analysis of a Case of Hysteria*. New York: Touchstone, 1997.

1905b. "My views on the part played by sexuality in the aetiology of the neuroses." Pp. 1–9 in *Sexuality and the Psychology of Love*. New York: Touchstone, 1997.

1905c. *Three Essays on the Theory of Sexuality*. New York: Basic Books, 1962.

1910. "Leonardo da Vinci and a memory of his childhood." Pp. 43–120 in *The Uncanny*. New York: Penguin, 2003.

1912. *Totem and Taboo*. New York: W. W. Norton, 1950.

1916. *Introductory Lectures on Psychoanalysis*. New York: W. W. Norton, 1966.

1919. "The uncanny." Pp. 123–162 in *The Uncanny*. New York, Penguin, 2003.

1921. *Group Psychology and the Analysis of the Ego*. New York: W. W. Norton, 1959.

1923. *The Ego and the Id*. New York: W. W. Norton, 1960.

1927. *The Future of an Illusion*. New York: W. W. Norton, 1961.

1930. *Civilization and Its Discontents*. New York: W. W. Norton, 1961.

1956. *Introduction à la psychanalyse*. Paris: Payot. [*Introductory Lectures on Psychoanalysis*, New York: W. W. Norton, 1989]

Freud, Sigmund and Josef Breuer. 1895. *Studies in Hysteria*. London: Penguin Books, 2004.

Fuss, Diana. 1990. *Essentially Speaking: Gender, Nature and Difference*. London: Routledge.

Gadamer, Hans-Georg. 1989. *Truth and Method*. New York: Continuum.

Gedalof, Irene. 2000. *Against Purity: Rethinking Identity with Indian and Western Feminisms*. London: Routledge.

Geertz, Clifford. 1973. *The Interpretation of Cultures*. New York: Basic Books.

Gilroy, Paul. 1987. *There Ain't No Black in the Union Jack: The Cultural Politics of Race and Nation*. Chicago: University of Chicago Press.

1991a. "It ain't where you're from, it's where you're at: the dialectics of diasporic identification." *Third Text*: 13, 3–16.

1991b. "Sounds authentic: Black music, ethnicity, and the challenge of the changing same." *Black Music Research Journal*: 11 (2), 111–136.

1992. *The Black Atlantic: Modernity and Double Consciousness*. London: Verso.

1998. "Race ends here." *Ethnic and Racial Studies*: 21 (5), 838–847.

2000. *Against Race: Imagining Political Culture beyond the Color Line*. Cambridge, MA: Harvard University Press.

Goody, Jack. 1995. *The Expansive Moment: Anthropology in Britain and Africa, 1918–1970*. Cambridge: Cambridge University Press.

Gossett, Thomas. 1997. *Race: The History of an Idea in America*. New York: Oxford University Press.

Guyer, Jane I. 1996. "Traditions of invention in Equatorial Africa." *African Studies Review*: 39 (3), 1–28.

Habermas, Jürgen. 1984 [1981]. *The Theory of Communicative Action*. Boston: Beacon Press.

Halbwachs, Maurice. 1992. *On Collective Memory*. Chicago: University of Chicago Press. [partial translation of *Les cadres sociaux de la mémoire*, Paris: F. Alcan, 1925]

1994 [1925]. *Les cadres sociaux de la mémoire*. Paris: Albin Michel.

1997 [1950]. *La mémoire collective*. Paris: Albin Michel. [*The Collective Memory*, New York: Harper, 1980]

Hall, Stuart. 1980a. "Cultural studies and the centre: some problematics and problems." Pp. 15–47 in *Culture, Media, Language*, edited by S. Hall, D. Hobson, and A. Lowe. London: Hutchinson.

———. 1980b. "Encoding/decoding." Pp. 128–138 in *Culture, Media, Language*, edited by S. Hall, D. Hobson, and A. Lowe. London: Hutchinson.

———. 1985. "Gramsci's relevance for the study of race and ethnicity." Pp. 411–440 in *Stuart Hall: Critical Dialogues in Cultural Studies*, edited by D. Morley and K. Chen. London: Routledge, 1996.

———. 1989. "New ethnicities." Pp. 441–449 in *Stuart Hall: Critical Dialogues in Cultural Studies*, edited by D. Morley and K. Chen. London: Routledge, 1996.

———. 1992. "What is this 'black' in black popular culture?" Pp. 465–475 in *Stuart Hall: Critical Dialogues in Cultural Studies*, edited by D. Morley and K. Chen. London: Routledge, 1996.

———. 1995. "Negotiating Caribbean identities." *New Left Review*: 209, 3–14.

———. 1997. "Subjects in history: making diasporic identities." Pp. 289–299 in *The House that Race Built*, edited by W. Lubiano. New York: Pantheon.

———. 1999. "Thinking the diaspora: home-thoughts from abroad." *Small Axe*: 6, 1–18.

———. 2002. "Race, articulation, and societies structured in dominance." Pp. 36–68 in *Race Critical Theories: Text and Context*, edited by P. Essed and D. Goldberg. London: Blackwell.

Hall, Stuart, *et al.* 2000 [1996]. *Modernity: An Introduction to Modern Societies*. London: Blackwell.

Hart, Keith. 2003. "British social anthropology's nationalist project." *Anthropology Today*: 19 (6), 1–2.

Haslam, Nick O. 1998. "Natural kinds, human kinds, and essentialism." *Social Research*: 65 (2), 291–314.

Hebdige, Dick. 1987. *Cut'n'Mix: Culture, Identity and Caribbean Music*. London: Routledge.

Hervieu-Léger, Danièle. 2000. *Religion as a Chain of Memory*. New Brunswick: Rutgers University Press. [*La religion pour mémoire*, Paris: Éditions du Cerf, 1993]

Higginbotham, A. Leon, Jr. 1978. *In the Matter of Color: The Colonial Period*. New York: Oxford University Press.

Hirschfeld, Lawrence A. 1998. *Race in the Making: Cognition, Culture, and the Child's Construction of Human Kinds*. Cambridge, MA: The MIT Press.

Hirschman, Albert O. 1977. *The Passions and the Interests: Political Arguments for Capitalism before Its Triumph*. Princeton: Princeton University Press.

hooks, bell. 1984. *Feminist Theory: From Margin to Center*. Boston: South End Press.

———. 1989. *Talking Back: Thinking Feminist, Thinking Black*. Boston: South End Press.

———. 1990. *Yearning: Race, Gender, and Cultural Politics*. Boston: South End Press.

———. 1992. *Black Looks: Race and Representation*. Boston: South End Press.

hooks, bell and Cornel West. 1991. *Breaking Bread: Insurgent Black Intellectual Life*. Boston: South End Press.

Hubert, Henri. 1999 [1905]. *Essay on Time: A Brief Study of the Representation of Time in Religion and Magic*. Oxford: Durkheim Press.

Isaac, Benjamin. 2004. *The Invention of Racism in Antiquity*. Princeton: Princeton University Press.

Jameson, Karen. 2005. "Culture and cognition: what is universal about the representation of color experience?" *Journal of Cognition & Culture*: 5 (3–4), 293–348.

Jenkins, Richard. 1996. *Social Identity*. London: Routledge.

1997. *Rethinking Ethnicity: Arguments and Explorations*. London: Sage.

Kallen, Horace M. 1924. *Culture and Democracy in the United States: Studies in the Group Psychology of the American Peoples*. New York: Boni and Liveright.

Kantorowicz, Ernst H. 1997. *The King's Two Bodies: A Study in Mediaeval Political Theology*. Princeton: Princeton University Press.

King, Desmond. 2000. *Making Americans: Immigration, Race, and the Origins of the Diverse Democracy*. Cambridge, MA: Harvard University Press.

Kripke, Saul. 1980. *Naming and Necessity*. Oxford: Blackwell.

Kuper, Adam. 1975 [1973]. *Anthropology and Anthropologists: The Modern British School*. Harmondsworth: Peregrine.

Laplanche, Jean and Jean-Bertrand Pontalis. 1973. *The Language of Psychoanalysis*. New York: W.W. Norton. [*Le vocabulaire de la psychanalyse*, Paris: Presses Universitaires de France, 1967]

Leach, Edmund. 1954. *Political Systems of Highland Burma: A Study of Kachin Social Structure*. London: London School of Economics.

1966. *Rethinking Anthropology*. Oxford: Berg.

1970. *Claude Lévi-Strauss*. New York: Viking Press.

2001 [1965]. "Claude Lévi-Strauss: anthropologist and philosopher." Pp. 97–112 in *The Essential Edmund Leach*, Volume I: Anthropology and Society, edited by N. Hugh-Jones and James Laidlaw. New Haven: Yale University Press.

Lévi-Strauss, Claude. 1962. *Le Totémisme Aujourd'hui*. Paris: Presses Universitaires de France. [*Totemism*, Boston: Beacon Press, 1963]

1963. *Structural Anthropology*. New York: Basic Books. [*Anthropologie structurale*, Paris: Plon, 1958]

1966. *The Savage Mind*. Chicago: University of Chicago Press.

1987 [1950]. *Introduction to the Work of Marcel Mauss*. New York: Routledge and Kegan Paul.

Lewis, Oscar. 1961. *The Children of Sanchez*. New York: Random House.

1966a. "The culture of poverty." *Scientific American*: 215, 19–25.

1966b. *La Vida: A Puerto Rican Family in the Culture of Poverty – San Juan and New York*. New York: Random House.

Lewontin, Richard. 1993. *Biology as Ideology: The Doctrine of DNA*. New York: Harper Perennial.

1995. *Human Diversity*. New York: Scientific American Library.

Lofgren, Charles A. 1987. *The Plessy Case: A Legal-Historical Interpretation*. Oxford: Oxford University Press.

Lott, Eric. 1995. *Love and Theft: Blackface Minstrelsy and the American Working Class*. New York: Oxford University Press.

Loveman, Mara. 1999. "Is 'race' essential? A comment on Bonilla-Silva." *American Sociological Review*: 64 (6), 891–898.

Malinowski, Bronislaw. 1922. *Argonauts of the Western Pacific: An Account of Native Enterprise and Adventure in the Archipelagoes of Melanesian New Guinea*. London: Routledge and Kegan Paul.

    1926–1927. "Lunar and seasonal calendar in the Trobriands." *Journal of the Anthropological Institute of Great Britain and Ireland*: 56–57, 203–215.

    1944. *A Scientific Theory of Culture and Other Essays*. Chapel Hill: University of North Carolina Press.

Mann, Thomas. 1999 [1948]. *Doctor Faustus*. New York: Vintage.

Mannheim, Karl. 1971. *From Karl Mannheim*. Oxford: Oxford University Press.

    1985. *Ideology and Utopia: An Introduction to the Sociology of Knowledge*. San Diego: Harcourt Brace.

    1986. *Conservatism*. London: Routledge.

Marx, Karl. 1978. *The Marx-Engels Reader*, second edition, edited by Robert C. Tucker. New York: W. W. Norton.

Mauss, Marcel. 2002 [1967]. *Manuel d'ethnographie*. Paris: Payot.

Mauss, Marcel and Henri Beuchat. 1979 [1906]. *Seasonal Variations of the Eskimo: A Study in Social Morphology*. London: Routledge & Kegan Paul. ["Essai sur les variations saisonnières des sociétés eskimo: étude de morphologie sociale," *L'Année sociologique*: 9 (1904–1905), 39–132]

Mauss, Marcel and Henri Hubert. 2001 [1905]. *A General Theory of Magic*. London and New York: Routledge.

McDonald, Sharon. 2001. "British social anthropology." Pp. 60–79 in *Handbook of Ethnography*, edited by P. Atkinson *et al*. London: Sage.

Mercer, Kobena. 2000. "A sociography of diaspora." Pp. 233–244 in *Without Guarantees: In Honour of Stuart Hall*, edited by P. Gilroy, L. Grossberg, and A. McRobbie. London: Verso.

Michaels, Walter Benn. 1995. *Our America: Nativism, Modernism, and Pluralism*. Durham, NC: Duke University Press.

Miles, Robert. 1984. "Marxism versus the sociology of 'race relations'?" *Ethnic and Racial Studies*: 7 (2), 217–237.

    1987. "Recent Marxist theories of nationalism and the issue of racism." *British Journal of Sociology*: 38 (1), 24–43.

    1988. "Beyond the 'race' concept: the reproduction of racism in England." Pp. 7–31 in *The Cultural Construction of Race*, edited by M. de Lepervanche and G. Bottomley. Sydney: Sydney Association for Studies in Society and Culture.

    2000. "A propos the idea of 'race'... again." Pp. 125–143 in *Theories of Race and Racism: A Reader*, edited by L. Back and J. Solomos. London and New York: Routledge.

Miles, Robert and Malcolm Brown. 2003. *Racism*. New York: Routledge.

Moscovici, Serge. 2001. *Social Representations: Essays in Social Psychology*. New York: New York University Press.

Nobles, Melissa. 2000. *Shades of Citizenship: Race and the Census in Modern Politics*. Stanford: Stanford University Press.

Omi, Michael and Howard Winant. 1986. *Racial Formation in the United States: From the 1960s to the 1990s* (second edition 1994). New York: Routledge.

Ortner, Sherry. 1984. "Theory in anthropology since the sixties." *Comparative Studies in Society and History*: 26 (1), 126–160.

Painter, Nell Irvin. 2006. *Creating Black Americans: African-American History and Its Meanings, 1619 to the Present*. New York and Oxford: Oxford University Press.

Park, Robert E. 1931. "Mentality of racial hybrids." *American Journal of Sociology*: 36 (4), 534–551.

1950. *Race and Culture*. Glencoe, IL: Free Press.

Patterson, Orlando. 1998. *Rituals of Blood: Consequences of Slavery in Two American Centuries*. Washington, DC: Civitas/Counterpoint.

Putnam, Hilary. 1975. *Philosophical Papers*, Volume II: *Mind, Language and Reality*. Cambridge: Cambridge University Press.

Radcliffe-Brown, A. R. 1932. *The Andaman Islanders*. Cambridge: Cambridge University Press.

1952. "The sociological theory of totemism." Pp. 117–132 in *Structure and Function in Primitive Society*. New York: Free Press.

1958 [1923]. "The methods of ethnology and social anthropology." Pp. 3–38 in *Method in Social Anthropology: Selected Essays by A. R. Radcliffe-Brown*. Chicago: University of Chicago Press.

Ragin, Charles C. 2000. *Fuzzy-Set Social Science*. Chicago: University of Chicago Press.

Rawls, John. 1993. *Political Liberalism*. New York: Columbia University Press.

Rex, John. 1986. *Race and Ethnicity*. Milton Keynes: Open University Press.

Ricœur, Paul. 1970. *Freud and Philosophy: An Essay on Interpretation*. New Haven: Yale University Press.

1986. *Lectures on Ideology and Utopia*. New York: Columbia University Press.

2005. *The Course of Recognition*. Cambridge, MA: Harvard University Press.

Saladin d'Anglure, Bernard. 2006. *Etre et renaître Inuit: homme, femme ou chamane*. Paris: NRF.

Schatzki, T., K. Knorr Cetina and E. von Savigny (eds.). 2001. *The Practice Turn in Contemporary Theory*. London: Routledge.

Scott, James C. 1992. *Domination and the Arts of Resistance: Hidden Transcripts*. New Haven: Yale University Press.

Shelby, Tommie. 2005. *We Who Are Dark: The Philosophical Foundations of Black Solidarity*. Cambridge, MA: Harvard University Press.

Smedley, Audrey. 1999. *Race in North America: Origin and Evolution of a Worldview*. Boulder, CO: Westview Press.

Spelman, Elizabeth V. 1990. *Inessential Woman*. Boston: Beacon Press.

Stocking, George W. 1984a. "Dr. Durkheim and Mr. Brown: comparative sociology at Cambridge in 1910." Pp. 106–130 in *Functionalism Historicized: Essays on British Social Anthropology*, edited by G. Stocking. Madison: University of Wisconsin Press.

1984b. "Radcliffe-Brown and British social anthropology." Pp. 130–191 in *Functionalism Historicized: Essays on British Social Anthropology*, edited by G. Stocking. Madison: University of Wisconsin Press.

1998. *After Tylor: British Social Anthropology, 1888–1951*. Madison: University of Wisconsin Press.

Swidler, Ann. 1986. "Culture in action: symbols and strategies." *American Sociological Review*: 51 (2), 273–286.

Taylor, Charles. 1994. "The politics of recognition." Pp. 25–74 in *Multiculturalism: Examining the Politics of Recognition*, edited by A. Gutman. Princeton: Princeton University Press.

Tuan, Mia. 1999. *Forever Foreigners or Honorary Whites? The Asian Ethnic Experience Today*. Piscataway, NJ: Rutgers University Press.

Wacquant, Loïc. 2003. *Body and Soul: Notebooks of an Apprentice Boxer*. Oxford: Oxford University Press.

Wade, Peter. 1993a. "Race, nature and culture." *Man*: 28 (1), 17–34.

1993b. *Blackness and Race Mixture: The Dynamics of Racial Identity in Colombia*. Baltimore: Johns Hopkins University Press.

1995. "The cultural politics of blackness in Colombia." *American Ethnologist*: 22 (2), 342–358.

1997. *Race and Ethnicity in Latin America*. London: Pluto.

1999. "Working culture: making cultural identities in Cali, Colombia." *Current Anthropology*: 40 (4), 449–471.

2002. *Race, Nature and Culture: An Anthropological Perspective*. London: Pluto.

2004. "Race and human nature." *Anthropological Theory*: 4 (2), 157–172.

Wallman, Sandra. 1986. "Ethnicity and the boundary process in context. Pp. 226–245 in *Theories of Race and Ethnic Relations*, edited by John Rex and David Mason. Cambridge: Cambridge University Press.

Weber, Max. 1949. "'Objectivity' in social science and social policy." Pp. 49–112 in *The Methodology of the Social Sciences*. New York: Free Press.

1958. "Religious rejections of the world and their directions." Pp. 323–359 in *From Max Weber: Essays in Sociology*. New York: Oxford University Press.

1978. *Economy and Society: An Outline of Interpretive Sociology*. Berkeley: University of California Press.

1993. *The Sociology of Religion*. New York: Beacon Press.

2002. *The Protestant Ethic and the Spirit of Capitalism*. London: Penguin.

White, Hayden. 1987. "The value of narrativity in the representation of reality." Pp. 1–25 in *The Content of the Form: Narrative Discourse and Historical Representation*. Baltimore: Johns Hopkins University Press.

Wilson, William J. 1973. *Power, Racism, and Privilege: Race Relations in Theoretical and Sociohistorical Perspectives*. Chicago: University of Chicago Press.

1980. *The Declining Significance of Race: Blacks and Changing American Institutions*, second edition. Chicago: University of Chicago Press.

Winant, Howard. 1994. *Racial Conditions: Politics, Theory, Comparisons*. Minneapolis and London: University of Minnesota Press.

2002. *The World is a Ghetto: Race and Democracy since World War II*. New York: Basic Books.

Winterson, Jeanette. 1992. *Written on the Body*. New York: Vintage International.

Wuthnow, Robert. 1989. *Communities of Discourse: Ideology and Social Structure in the Reformation, the Enlightenment and European Socialism.* Cambridge, MA: Harvard University Press.

Yelvington, Kevin. 1995. *Producing Power: Ethnicity, Gender and Class in a Caribbean Workplace.* Philadelphia: Temple University Press.

Zangwill, Israel. 1914. *The Melting Pot: A Drama in Four Acts.* New York: Macmillan.

Index